TEACHER D

Series Edito

THE MICROPOLITICS OF EDUCATIONAL LEADERSHIP

THE MICROPOLITICS OF EDUCATIONAL LEADERSHIP:
From Control to Empowerment

Joseph Blase and Gary L. Anderson

Teachers College
Columbia University
New York and London

Published in the United States of America by
Teachers College Press, Columbia University,
1234 Amsterdam Ave., New York, N.Y. 10027 USA

Published in Great Britain by Cassell, London

Cataloging-in-Publication Data available through the Library of Congress

ISBN: 0-8077-3501-9

Typeset by Colset Pte Ltd, Singapore
Manufactured in Great Britain by Redwood Books, Trowbridge, Wiltshire

99 98 97 96 95   1 2 3 4 5

Contents

To Jo

Series Editor's Introduction

In Britain and Australia, they call it teaching. In the United States and Canada, they call it instruction. Whatever terms we use, we have come to realize in recent years that the teacher is the ultimate key to educational change and school improvement. The restructuring of schools, the composition of national and provincial curricula, the development of benchmark assessments – all these things are of little value if they do not take the teacher into account. Teachers don't merely deliver the curriculum. They develop, define it and reinterpret it too. It is what teachers think, what teachers believe and what teachers do at the level of the classroom that ultimately shapes the kind of learning that young people get. Growing appreciation of this fact is placing working with teachers and understanding teaching at the top of our research and improvement agendas.

For some reformers, improving teaching is mainly a matter of developing better teaching methods, of improving instruction. Training teachers in new classroom management skills, in active learning, cooperative learning, one-to-one counselling and the like is the main priority. These things are important, but we are also increasingly coming to understand that developing teachers and improving their teaching involves more than giving them new tricks. We are beginning to recognize that, for teachers, what goes on inside the classroom is closely related to what goes on outside it. The quality, range and flexibility of teachers' classroom work are closely tied up with their professional growth – with the way that they develop as people and as professionals.

Teachers teach in the way they do not just because of the skills they have or have not learned. The ways they teach are also grounded in their backgrounds, their biographies, in the kinds of teachers they have become. Their careers – their hopes and dreams, their opportunities and aspirations, or the frustration of these things – are also important for teachers' commitment, enthusiasm and morale. So too are relationships with their colleagues – either as supportive communities who work together in pursuit of common goals and continuous improvement, or as individuals working in isolation, with the insecurities that sometimes brings.

As we are coming to understand these wider aspects of teaching and teacher development, we are also beginning to recognize that much more than pedagogy, instruction or teaching method is at stake. Teacher development, teachers' careers, teachers' relations with their colleagues, the conditions of status, reward and leadership under which they work – all these affect the quality of what they do in the classroom.

This international series, Teacher Development, brings together some of the very best current research and writing on these aspects of teachers' lives and work. The books in the series seek to understand the wider dimensions of teachers' work, the depth of teachers' knowledge and the resources of biography and experience on which it draws, the ways that teachers' work roles and responsibilities are changing as we restructure our schools, and so forth. In this sense, the books in the series are written for those who are involved in research on teaching, those who work in initial and in-service teacher education, those who lead and administer teachers, those who work with teachers and, not least, teachers themselves.

Teacher development is often portrayed as a process of human development, involving personal growth and adult learning, individually and with others. While this is a worthy aspiration and while these aspects of teacher development can be achieved in practice, the real world of schools is also a political world, a world of power and influence, bargaining and negotiation, assertion and protection in which one's own developmental needs must be pursued in tune with the needs and wishes of others and sometimes despite them. Teacher development must therefore take place within the micropolitical realities of schooling. It is these micropolitical realities that Joe Blase and Gary Anderson address in this book.

In a book of impressive conceptual and empirical scope, and one that draws on literature from both sides of the Atlantic, Blase and Anderson describe how the micropolitics of educational leadership in particular impact upon the working worlds of teachers. Politics, for them, are not confined to the higher echelons of policy-making. They are everywhere in schools – in classrooms and in staff lounges, in interactions with principals and parents, children and colleagues. Nor are politics ubiquitously negative. The micropolitics of schooling can of course be cynical, controlling and calculative, but they can also be positive, empowering and collegial.

Through a critique of the micropolitical realities of many kinds of leadership that are closed and transactional, authoritarian and adversarial, pseudoparticipative or superficially transformational in character, Blase and Anderson develop a vision of leadership for teacher development that is open, honest, collaborative, inclusive and democratic. It is a vision that goes beyond other forms of leadership – moral, instructional or transformational – that currently abound in educational writing, towards a truly inclusive and collaborative notion that is empowering for all.

Blase and Anderson's book is not gratuitously celebratory of successful schools. It does not devote most of its space to ideal models and atypical instances of success. It describes the gritty micropolitical realities of teaching and leadership that most of us have experienced and will recognize. Through these, it will force readers to confront their own practice. It will make it difficult to hide behind superficial realizations of collaboration or empowerment and to pursue higher goals, more democratic and inclusive visions that can already be seen in the realities of what some school people currently do. Blase and Anderson's book is real and it is practical. Teachers and leaders alike will identify with it. All those who search for robust solutions of real improvement and who wish to pursue positive politics in their schools will undoubtedly benefit from reading this text.

Andy Hargreaves

Preface

In 1992, I was approached by Andy Hargreaves about writing a book that would bring together under one cover the results of several of my studies on the micropolitics of teachers' worklife. I felt that the research on teacher micropolitics had important implications for leadership theory which I wanted to explore at greater length. Gary Anderson and I had just finished a collaboration for ATE's Teacher Education Yearbook and I felt that between my own background in symbolic interactionism and Gary's background in critical theory we could together explore how the micropolitical research might inform leadership theory. We were particularly interested in helping administrators-in-training to cope better with the micropolitical world that they were about to inhabit. Gary found in the micropolitical data a solution to some conceptual problems he had encountered in the current debate over transactional and transformative approaches to leadership. The result was the micropolitical leadership matrix described in the first chapter. This matrix combines the open and closed styles of leadership from my research on teacher micropolitics with Burns' transformative and transactional approaches (Burns, 1978).

In addition, the micropolitical leadership matrix is an attempt to provide a template for conceptualizing and interpreting the vague reform discourse that is currently being heaped on school practitioners. Unfortunately, terms like 'empowerment', 'restructuring', 'school-based leadership' and 'participatory decision-making' are used just as often to camouflage the exercise of hierarchical power as they are to generate concepts that challenge power relations in schools and communities (Anderson and Dixon, 1993).

Because of the 'messiness', or complexity, of school micropolitics, we have made descriptive, qualitative data about micropolitics in schools central to each chapter. These data range from single case studies of individual schools to broad-based, open-ended qualitative teacher survey data. As a result, readers are treated to an insider's view of school micropolitics. A description of the current literature relevant to understanding the critical aspects of life in schools and a discussion of implications for school leadership are also presented. We hope this is a book from which academics, reform advocates, principals and teachers will benefit.

Joseph Blase
University of Georgia

Acknowledgements

This book has required a great deal of work and patience from our secretary, Linda Edwards. We are deeply grateful for her support. Thanks also to Jo Blase, Cheryl Smith and Art Crawley for their fine editorial assistance. Finally, we wish to thank students at the University of New Mexico for the feedback on an earlier manuscript of this book.

Chapters 1-6 in this book have been adapted from the following previously published work:

Chapter 1:

> Blase, J. (1990) Some negative effects of principals' control-oriented and protective political behavior, *American Educational Research Journal*, 27(4), 727-53.

Chapter 2:

> Blase, J. (1991) Everyday political perspectives of teachers toward students: the dynamics of diplomacy. In J. Blase (ed.) *The Politics of Life in Schools: Power, Conflict, and Cooperation*, pp. 185-206. Newbury Park, CA: Sage.

> Blase, J. (1987) The politics of teaching: the teacher-parent relationship and the dynamics of diplomacy. *Journal of Teacher Education*, 38(2), 53-60.

Chapter 3:

> Blase, J. (1987c) Political interactions among teachers: sociocultural context in the school. *Urban Education*, 22(3), 286-309.

Chapter 4:

> Blase, J. (1989) The micropolitics of the school: the everyday political orientation of teachers toward open school principals. *Educational Administration Quarterly*, 25(4), 377-407.

> Blase, J. (1991) The micropolitical orientation of teachers toward closed school principals. *Education and Urban Society*, 23(4), 356-78.

Chapter 5:

Blase, J. (1993) The micropolitics of effective school-based leadership: teachers' perspectives. *Educational Administration Quarterly*, 29(2), 142–63.

Blase, J. and Blase, J. (1994) *Empowering Teachers: What Successful School Principals do*. Newbury Park, CA: Corwin.

Chapter 6:

Anderson, G.L. (1991) Cognitive politics of principals and teachers: ideological control in an elementary school. In J. Blase (ed.) *The Politics of Life in Schools: Power, Conflict and Cooperation*, pp. 120–38. Newbury Park, CA: Sage.

Glossary

Leadership Styles

Open and Closed Leadership Styles: The terms open and closed indicate ends on a continuum which represents *degrees* of closedness or openness. Although no leader possesses characteristics of only one style, the micropolitics data suggest that most leaders have a dominant style.

Open Style: Describes a leadership style characterized by a willingness to share power. Open leaders are also characterized by teachers as more honest, communicative, participatory and collegial than closed leaders.

Closed Style: Describes a leadership style characterized by an unwillingness to share power. Closed leaders are also characterized as less accessible, less supportive, more defensive, more egocentric and more insecure than open leaders.

Leadership Approaches

Transactional and Transformative Leadership: The terms transactional and transformative refer to ends on a continuum which represent the degree to which leaders are transactional or transformative with regard to the goals and direction of the organization.

Transactional Leadership: This approach to leadership is largely based on exchange relationships between leaders and followers. In return for effort, productivity and loyalty, leaders offer tangible and intangible rewards to followers. This approach is oriented to creating an environment that remains essentially static and supportive of the status quo.

Transformative Leadership: This approach to leadership involves a relationship oriented towards fundamental change, the object of which is the raising of the consciousness of leader and follower alike. Transformative leadership is concerned largely with end values.

Power Relations

Power Over: Leaders achieve goals through their control of resources, persuasiveness, and hierarchical position over followers. The power-over approach is strongly influenced by the bureaucratic tradition. Power is exercised *over* followers.

Power Through: Leaders achieve goals through the motivation and mobilization of followers. The power-through approach is strongly influenced by the human relations and organizational development traditions. Power is exercised *through* followers.

Power With: Goals are achieved through the collaboration of leaders and followers. Leadership and followership may shift depending on the issue. The power-with approach is strongly influenced by the feminist, participatory and workplace democracy traditions. Power is exercised *with* followers.

Introduction

Research on teachers has for decades documented a basically conservative professional orientation. Although oases of innovative schools exist, the average classroom remains highly bureaucratized, and teachers work under the constant threat of judgement and criticism from every direction. Recent research on schools as workplaces has shown that when a culture of collegiality and trust is fostered in a school, teachers feel freer to take risks in and out of the classroom. The micropolitical research reported in this book demonstrates that a school's micropolitical culture is, in part, a reaction to the type of leadership present in the school. Indeed, a negative and reactive micropolitical culture is, in large part, a response to a particular type of leadership exercised by principals.

Leadership has clearly become a 'hot topic' in educational literature in recent years, and prescriptions for 'empowering' approaches to leadership fill the pages of academic and practitioner journals. Unfortunately, most of these prescriptions ignore the root word of the overused and abused term 'empowerment'. Only the micropolitical literature places the notion of *power* at the centre of its analyses. For this reason the micropolitical literature does not demonstrate the naiveté that characterizes most leadership theories in regard to power and politics. Micropolitics deals with the realities that teachers negotiate on a daily basis. Thus, research that documents the micropolitical world of teachers, principals and students and their parents provides a solid base from which to rethink leadership theory. Blase writes:

> The micropolitical perspective on organization provides a
> valuable and potent approach to understanding the woof and
> warp of the fabric of day-to-day life in schools. This perspective
> highlights the fundamentals of human behavior and purpose.
> Micropolitics is about power and how people use it to influence
> others and to protect themselves. It is about conflict and how
> people compete with each other to get what they want. It is
> about cooperation and how people build support among
> themselves to achieve their ends. It is about what people in all
> social settings think about and have strong feelings about, but
> what is so often unspoken and not easily observed. The

micropolitical perspective presents practicing administrators and scholars alike with fresh and provocative ways to think about human behavior in schools.

(Blase, 1991, pp. 1–2)

PERSPECTIVES ON MICROPOLITICS

Early work in the area of micropolitics began in the fields of public administration and management as a direct challenge to traditional-rational models of organization discussed by Weber (1947), Taylor (1947) and Fayol (1949), and systems theories developed by Parsons (1951) and Getzels and Guba (1957). Burns (1961) was among the first theorists in public administration to discuss organizations as political systems. He argued that organizational life consists of cooperative and conflicting elements; individuals and groups are 'at one and the same time cooperators in a common enterprise and rivals for the material and intangible rewards of successful competition with each other' (Burns, 1961, p. 261). Burns contended that both aspects of organizational life are necessary and that political coalitions and political obligations were the 'exchange currency' of organizational life. Early studies by Strauss (1962), Cyert and March (1963) and Pettigrew (1973), among others, further challenged traditional apolitical models of organizational functioning.

It was not until the 1980s that theoretical and empirical work in micropolitics proliferated in the fields of both management and education. Although there are several approaches to micropolitics, all emphasize the strategic use of power in organizations for the purposes of influence and protection. In management, Bacharach and Lawler (1980) define politics in organizations as 'the tactical use of power to retain or obtain control of real or symbolic resources' (p. 1). These writers describe a political model of organization that emphasizes the power and conflict dynamics of coalitions within a framework of bargaining relationships and bargaining tactics. More broadly, Pfeffer (1981b) defines organizational politics as 'activities taken within organizations to acquire, develop, and use power and other resources to obtain preferred outcomes in a situation in which there is uncertainty or dissensus about choices' (p. 7).

In education, British and American writers such as Hoyle (1986), Ball (1987) and Blase (1991) have discussed different perspectives on micropolitics. Hoyle states:

> Micropolitics is best perceived as a continuum, one end of which is virtually indistinguishable from conventional management procedures but from which it diverges on a number of dimensions – interest, interest sets, power, strategies, and legitimacy – to the point where it constitutes almost a separate organizational world of illegitimate, self-interested manipulation.
>
> (Hoyle, 1986, p. 126)

Ball's (1987) perspective on micropolitics stresses group-level analysis and conflict dynamics. Ball writes:

> I take schools, in common with virtually all other social organizations, to be *arenas of struggle*; to be riven with actual or potential conflict between members; to be poorly coordinated; to be ideologically diverse.
>
> (Ball, 1987, p. 19)

Blase (1991) has developed a comprehensive definition of micropolitics from a review of the relevant literature. He writes:

> Micropolitics refers to the use of formal and informal power by individuals and groups to achieve their goals in organizations. In large part, political actions result from perceived differences between individuals and groups, coupled with the motivation to use power to influence and/or protect. Although such actions are consciously motivated, any action, consciously or unconsciously motivated, may have political 'significance' in a given situation. Both cooperative and conflictive actions and processes are part of the realm of micropolitics. Moreover, macro- and micropolitical factors frequently interact.
>
> (Blase, 1991, p. 11)[1]

Some perspectives on micropolitics suggest that aspects of political action in organizations may be inconsistent with espoused organizational policies, goals and values (e.g. Ball, 1987; Blase, 1988a; Greenfield, 1984; Mayes and Allen, 1977; Pfeffer, 1981b). For example, Mayes and Allen (1977) define politics as 'the management of influence to obtain ends not sanctioned by the organization or to obtain sanctioned ends through non-sanctioned influence means' (p. 675). Similarly, Greenfield (1984) argues that in a society that recognizes and values plurality, disagreement and contention among individuals and groups will exist. Since educational settings are primarily contexts for the expression of 'individual willfulness', educational leaders can be expected to engage in 'persuasion, calculation, guile, persistence, threat or sheer force' (Greenfield, 1984, p. 166) to achieve preferred ends. All in all, micropolitical perspectives have emphasized the dialectical, interactive, multidirectional, strategic, conflictive, ideological and interpretive/perceptual aspects of organization as they relate to the use of power.

THE MICROPOLITICS OF EDUCATION

Research in the micropolitics of education has only recently begun. However, there have been noteworthy accomplishments during the last several years, particularly in understanding relationships between teachers and school principals

3

or heads. For instance, Ball (1987) has described the major styles – interpersonal, managerial and political – used by British school heads to control teachers. Such control typically resulted in fatalism and frustration, and occasionally satisfaction. Ball also alludes to the tactics and 'ploys' teachers use (e.g. visibility) to further their career goals. Anderson (1991) has discussed how administrators (in one suburban school) influenced teachers through the manipulation of language and ideological control. He underscores the subtle but powerful effects of 'cognitive politics' and its ability to contain and marginalize collective action by teachers in that school district (see Chapter 6). Corbett (1991) has studied the effects of community influence on one high school's discipline policy and how a principal's attempts to pre-empt central-office and parental intrusions inadvertently led to a redistribution of political power away from teachers to parents and students.

Only a few studies of cooperative/consensual political relationships between teachers and school principals or heads have appeared in the micropolitical literature. Smylie and Brownlee-Conyers (1990) have studied innovative working relationships between school principals and teacher-leaders in one school district and described strategies employed by both groups to shape working relationships. In a study of the micropolitics of leadership in an elementary school, Greenfield (1991) discovered that effective leadership by both the school principal and teachers relied heavily on moral sources of influence: a commitment to serve children dramatically affected the development of cooperative political relationships between the principal and teachers and also among teachers themselves.

Other administrator–teacher relationships are highlighted in an earlier article by one of us that explores the politics of favouritism (Blase, 1988a). A comparative study of two elementary schools in one school district by Noblit *et al*. (1991) demonstrates the powerful effects of existing school-level micropolitical structures on school reform. Hargreaves (1990) has discussed the dramatic implications for teachers' work of an administrative perspective on time.

Other micropolitical research in education has focused on: relationships between new assistant principals and teachers (Marshall, 1991; Marshall and Mitchell, 1991); relationships between a superintendent, principal and teachers (Kline-Kracht and Wong, 1991); relationships between a department head and teachers (Sparks, 1988, 1990); collegial relationships among teachers (Hargreaves, 1991); teacher–student classroom interaction (Bloome and Willett, 1991); race and gender (Marshall, 1991); and teacher induction (Schempp *et al*., 1993).

TEACHER WORKLIFE STUDIES

Indeed, although significant strides have been made in understanding the political nature of teachers' relationships with school principals (and heads), and some studies have produced valuable insights about teachers' relationships with other stakeholders, micropolitical research in education is still in its infancy. However, evidence of the political aspects of teachers' relationships with others has also been apparent in what is loosely referred to as teachers' worklife research. Although this research has specifically focused on a plethora of topics – such as satisfaction, professionalism, efficacy, commitment, classroom control, authority/power, status, gender, deskilling, autonomy, strategies, collegiality and culture – findings from this line of inquiry illuminate many aspects of teachers' political relationships with others. The following review highlights those aspects of the worklife literature that have particular relevance for understanding teachers' micropolitical relationships with students, parents, faculty and school principals.

Teachers' Relationships with Students and Parents

In the studies discussed in Chapters 2 and 3, we point out that problems related to academic instruction and social control (i.e. discipline) frequently provoke political interactions between and among teachers, students and their parents. The teachers' worklife literature has consistently emphasized the centrality of these two factors in teachers' relationships with students and parents (Becker, 1980; Connell, 1985; Dreeben, 1970; Fuchs, 1967; Gitlin, 1983; Hoyle, 1969; Jackson, 1968; Lieberman and Miller, 1984; Lightfoot, 1983; Nias, 1989; Sarason, 1982; Veenan, 1984; Wilson, 1962). For example, Lortie (1975) found that the achievement of social and moral outcomes with students was quite important to teachers. Other studies have reported that control of students is frequently more important to teachers (and administrators) than the achievement of academic goals (Willower *et al.*, 1967). Cusick (1983) discovered that in the high schools he studied, student control was so problematic that maintaining 'good relationships' (i.e. 'cordial' relationships) with students was more important than academic instruction or adhering to policies and procedures. Similarly, McNeil's research on high schools (McNeil, 1983, 1986) uncovered administrators' and faculties' inordinate concern about controlling students and the profound adverse effects of such an orientation on teaching and learning in the classroom.

The worklife literature also reveals that teachers use a variety of strategies to influence students to achieve instructional and social goals. In fact, Pollard (1985) argues that 'good' teaching is fundamentally manipulative; teachers attempt to get students to internalize and pursue goals defined by teachers. Good teaching is associated with acting ability, communication skills, ability to give praise, and other such factors. Pollard describes four major strategies (open negotiation, routinization, manipulation, domination) that teachers used to control students.

Waller (1932) examined techniques such as command, punishment,

5

manipulation of interpersonal and group relationships, appeal and temper used by teachers to maintain classroom control and discipline. For example, Waller explored teachers' use of 'controlled anger' in dealing with student behaviour problems. McPherson (1972) describes strategies that teachers employed to influence and control students, including praise, blame, competition, labelling, and development of standardized classroom operating procedures. Hargreaves (1979) provides an in-depth examination of teachers' attempts to use the strategy of policing (e.g. control of student talk and articulation of rules and display of hierarchical relations) for student crowd control in the middle school.

Woods (1990) observed that teachers devised several 'survival' strategies – socialization, domination, negotiation, fraternization, absence or removal, ritual and routine, occupational therapy and morale boosting – to control incidents and to 'avoid', 'mask/disguise', 'weather', and 'neutralize' classroom incidents. McNeil (1986) describes several defensive teaching strategies, e.g. mystification, omission and simplification, which teachers employed to control students.

A few teacher worklife studies have yielded descriptive data relevant to understanding political interactions between teachers and parents. The results of several comprehensive studies point out that teachers typically view relationships with parents as distant, distrustful and hostile (Becker, 1980; Lortie, 1975; McPherson, 1972; Waller, 1932). Such characterizations have been attributed to the different perspectives of teachers and parents regarding the student. Waller (1932) wrote that teachers and parents 'wish [the student] well according to different standards of well-being. Parents and teachers want to do different things with the child' (p. 68). Like Waller, Lortie (1975) and McPherson (1972) interpret teacher–parent enmity in terms of the conflict between universalistic expectations (required for group life) and particularistic expectations (related to individual needs). Teacher–parent conflicts are considered inevitable because they result from differences linked to primary (e.g. intimate) and secondary (e.g. impersonal) group affiliations (Bates and Babchuk, 1961).

Conflicts between teachers and parents can be exacerbated when parents' 'own ego feelings, or their own projected ambitions' (Waller, 1932, p. 68) become involved in responding to a child's progress in school. Naegle (1956) notes that teachers often learn the 'guilty secrets' of the families of their students and that such knowledge can strain relationships with parents. Teachers' judgements about grades and the values they choose to emphasize in socializing children may contradict those of parents (Lortie, 1975).

In addition to conflicts that stem from differing perspectives on the student, teacher authority and parental authority regarding school matters are often overlapping and unclear. Thus, teachers and parents each believe that they have the right to determine educational practices in the school (Dreeben, 1968; Lortie, 1975; McPherson, 1972).

As suggested, the research cited above links teacher–parent conflict with interactions concerning subject matter and student discipline. The studies reveal that parents attempt to elicit 'special favours' for their children in each of these areas. The parents' inclination to 'interfere' in school matters, to challenge the teacher's authority – and to do so in ways that violate interpersonal and professional norms for reasonable, productive and supportive interaction – further undermines the teacher (Becker, 1980; Connell, 1985; Lortie, 1975; McPherson, 1972).

Consequently, teachers develop ways to deal with parents. Connell (1985) found that teachers infrequently responded to parental pressure through genuine power-sharing. Generally, teachers responded defensively; they often created 'tokenistic' ways of involving parents in the school (i.e. a 'public relations exercise') or worked to minimize contact with parents. Connell also found that the teachers' general view of education – particularly if their view emphasized intellectual growth, rather than the transfer of skills or the transmission of culture – often 'pitted' them against parents.

McPherson (1972) and Becker (1980) have described teachers' attempts to establish common bonds of parenthood and invoke bureaucratic rules to deal with critical and obtrusive parents. McPherson (1972) identified other devices such as politeness, avoidance, conferencing and forming coalitions with students to deal with parental challenges to decisions about student promotions, group placement, instructional material and practices that departed from the 'tried and true'. Waller (1932) remarked on the efficacy of projecting a stable, friendly and judicial disposition to disarm 'irate' parents. Lortie (1975) and McPherson (1972) note that teachers often develop coalitions with school principals to protect themselves from intrusions by parents.

Teacher–Teacher Relationships

Several teacher worklife studies have shed light on the micropolitical dynamics of the teacher–teacher relationship. Such studies have emphasized the significance of classroom autonomy and non-interference norms for relationships among teachers (Becker, 1980; Cusick, 1983; Lortie, 1975; McPherson, 1972; Nias, 1989; Rosenholtz and Simpson, 1990). Lortie (1975) also describes the importance of norms related to friendliness, sociability, support (i.e. responding to requests for assistance), sharing (e.g. ideas, work supplies and materials) and meeting school-wide obligations.

Becker (1980) and McPherson (1972) highlight the salience of faculty loyalty and solidarity norms (*vis-à-vis* students and parents) as well as support (cathartic and therapeutic). Becker describes norms about handling discipline, the amount of work teachers should accomplish and attitude towards school principals. Cusick (1983) found that although teachers usually did not work together they tended to unify and exhibit 'open hostility to attempts to encourage their cooperation or change their behavior' (e.g. mainstreaming special education students). Teachers also worked to build support among faculty for their personal curricular and extracurricular interests. From a study of a primary school,

Pollard (1985) describes how humour among teachers helped to reduce the impact of both external (e.g. from managers, parents, advisers) and internal threats from the classroom.

Other politically relevant findings about relationships among teachers have appeared in the worklife literature. Beale (1936) notes that teacher ostracism was used to elicit compliance from unconventional teachers – 'Few like to get the reputation of being a crank' (p. 599). Nias (1989) learned that to preserve their core ideals, teachers engaged in impression management to gain the support of their colleagues. Nias also notes that internal promotions and unequal power in decision-making increased hostility among the faculty.

Teacher–Principal Relationships

The studies discussed in Chapters 1, 4, 5 and 6 focus on micropolitical interactions between teachers and school principals. The teachers' worklife literature has generated a great deal of politically relevant information about this relationship.

The importance of the school principal (or head) in shaping political relationships with teachers is discussed throughout the worklife literature. Lieberman and Miller (1984) write: 'The principal (especially in the elementary school) makes it known what is important, what will not be tolerated, and in a strange way, sets the tone for tension, worth, openness, and fear' (p. 28). Sikes *et al.* (1985) recognize that heads in Britain have substantial freedom in organizing their schools and that variation in their leadership – i.e. their philosophies, values and personalities – results in considerable differences in the atmosphere of the school.

Lortie (1963) and Dreeben (1970) argue that, for a number of reasons, the school principal's formal authority *vis-à-vis* teachers is limited, at least in comparison with managers of other types of organizations. Close control by administrators is impeded by the 'cellular' structure of the school (teachers teaching in separate classrooms) and the value teachers place on attaining intrinsic rewards in their work with students. As a result, Lortie maintains, 'control over teachers is accomplished through selection-socialization and subtle mechanisms which refine bureaucratic rule' (Lortie, 1963, p. 10). Lortie also emphasizes that principals are the ultimate authority on student discipline and make decisions about the allocation of space, materials and equipment – decisions that strongly influence teachers' working conditions.

Although principals' authority in the school is considered 'supreme', teachers expect principals to make allocative decisions fairly. Sikes *et al.* (1985) found that in some British schools teachers believed that school heads unfairly used appointments and promotions to develop 'latent status hierarchies' to support their own orientations. Violations of norms for fair and equitable treatment have been linked to decreases in teacher morale, increases in teacher stress, teacher role conflict and teacher alienation (Becker, 1980; Blase, 1984, 1987a, 1988a; Cusick, 1983; Nias, 1989; Sikes *et al.*, 1985).

In an early seminal study of freedom in teaching, Beale concluded that the rights of American teachers were systematically violated by school principals:

> The principal's power over the teacher and the importance of a
> good standing with him leads to submissiveness to his will ...
> the general climate of schools and the undemocratic rules under
> which they are administered tend to make principals autocrats
> and teachers yes men.
>
> (Beale, 1936, p. 602)

Questions about the loyalty or character of teachers usually led to dismissal. Beale (1936) concluded that 'a liberal minded principal may be the best friend that freedom in teaching has' (p. 605).

The teachers who Nias (1989) studied indicated that administrative inefficiency, poor communication, lack of clear goals and the means to achieve them, and inadequate supervision adversely affected their work environments. Blase (1987a) describes several characteristics of principals that teachers viewed as 'closed and ineffective', including inaccessibility, lack of knowledge/expertise, indecisiveness, lack of direction, lack of follow-through, authoritarianism, non-support/avoidance of conflict, favouritism, unwillingness to credit/reward, criticalness and use of intimidation. Such characteristics were correlated strongly with increases in teachers' feelings of frustration, anger, insecurity, confusion and apathy, as well as negative affects on key aspects of the teachers' performance with students. Fuchs (1967) describes actions by principals that routinely violated professional and interpersonal norms (e.g. overloading teachers with extra responsibilities) and led to feelings of exploitation and alienation among teachers.

Connell (1985) found that although Australian principals have been expected to use 'more consensual', 'open textured' methods (in contrast to unilateral control) in working with teachers, the result has been a pseudo-democratic stance on the part of many principals. School administrators maintained control by chairing committees, controlling agendas and avoiding contentious issues. Hunter (1979) also demonstrated how a school head maintained control of decisional processes through indirect means, despite the existence of a democratic governance structure. Hunter argues that the consultative structures designed to facilitate faculty participation also 'keep the head informed' (Hunter, 1979, p. 129) and actually increased his control and substantiated his claim that he alone had a global view of the school. Hunter underscores the importance of taken-for-granted assumptions that make up the political culture of the school (e.g. the staff's acceptance of an advisory rather than power-sharing role in decision-making) in explaining the head's control.

There is little doubt that school principals wield power over teachers through formal and informal means. However, evidence from teachers' worklife studies suggests that some school principals use leadership styles that depart from strict domination and subordination of teachers. The resulting teacher behaviour contradicts simplistic portrayals of teachers as conservative, compliant and submissive (e.g. Lightfoot, 1983). Blase (1987b, 1988b) discovered that those principals whom teachers defined as 'open and effective' (e.g. accessible, consistent, knowledgeable, communicative, decisive, problem oriented, supportive, participatory/consultative, fair, rewarding and delegatory) tended to be highly 'interactive' with teachers rather than unilateral, arbitrary and authoritarian. Their leadership affected teacher motivation, involvement, morale and performance, and was also linked to the development of productive and open relationships between teachers and students, teachers and teachers, and teachers and parents. Lortie (1963) contends that bureaucratic control of teachers is not possible, and, consequently, principal–teacher relationships are frequently characterized by 'exchange' instead of domination. Little (1982) discovered that in successful and adaptable schools, 'reciprocation' (defined as equality of effort and equal humility) was an important property of administrator–teacher interaction.

The work of Hanson (1976) further indicates that the bureaucratic authority is inadequate in explaining political dynamics between school principals and teachers. Hanson discovered that administrators and teachers controlled different 'spheres of influence' or decision zones in the schools he studied, and that each sphere was characterized by relative degrees of power, autonomy, decisional discretion and legitimacy. Hanson also found that administrators and teachers developed informal tactics to influence one another even in their own sphere of influence. Principals, for example, tried to control teachers by manipulating their concept of 'professional' behaviour; teachers formed coalitions with colleagues and took stands on issues at faculty meetings.

Other worklife studies provide additional evidence of the variability of teachers' responses to school principals. Biklen (1988) describes several ways in which teachers react to administrators, including unhappy compliance, the stand-off, silent non-cooperation and the open challenge. The typology of Brieschke (1983) of teacher role enactment describes three major orientations – elite, reinforcement, fringe – to school principals. Other researchers have emphasized the subtle ways in which teachers resist administrative control of their work (Apple, 1986; Becker, 1980; McNeil, 1983; Zeichner and Tabachnick, 1984). In fact, Bridges (1970) theorizes that teachers typically use strategic tactics to influence administrators, including, for example, exchange, bargaining, threats, bluff, flattery, exercising influence through significant others, providing biased information and dramatizing involvement.

Other teacher worklife studies provide further insight into teachers' micropolitical relationships with school principals. Several writers have demonstrated the importance of principals' 'buffering' from a range of organizational and external intrusions (Becker, 1980; McPherson, 1972; Rosenholtz and Simpson, 1990). Rosenholtz and Simpson (1990) found that buffering by principals was related strongly to new teachers' work commitment. More concretely, teachers expect principals to use their authority to support them in conflicts with students and parents. Teachers lose respect for principals who fail to support them and in some cases view these principals as 'cowardly' (Becker, 1980; Cusick, 1983; McPherson, 1972). Cusick (1983) reports that a failure on the part of administrators to support teachers in dealing with student discipline undermined significantly the academic programmes of three high schools. In general, teachers appear to respect and are willing to extend loyalty to principals who use a 'light rein' with them (Lortie, 1975, p. 200) and who make their authority available to protect them and to help them achieve instructional goals and rewards (Blase, 1987b; Lortie, 1975).

Studies of teachers' perspectives consistently emphasize that although significant differences exist in the leadership orientation of school principals and result in profoundly different effec ᷉ on teachers, few principals exhibit a fundamentally democratic-collegial style of leadership. Most principals are oriented towards control of teachers, although the strategies they use to achieve such control range from openly directive and authoritarian to diplomatic and subtle (Ball, 1987; Blase, 1993; Johnson, 1984).

THE MICROPOLITICS OF EDUCATION: FROM DESCRIPTION TO PRESCRIPTION

Micropolitical research, building on the politics of education and teacher worklife research that preceded it, represents an important lens through which to view school life. Its importance is equal to that of bureaucratic, open systems and human relations perspectives, the popularity of which have been long-standing within the school management literature. None of these perspectives alone is sufficient to understand school life. Each one illuminates different phenomena and provides different prescriptions for leadership.

Traditional organizational theories of schooling lack a grounding in the day-to-day realities of school life. Because of this lack of grounding, many of their elaborate prescriptions and recommendations for leadership assume a rational, predictable and controllable world that does not exist in schools. Partly for this reason school practitioners have not found these theories to be very useful in understanding the highly politicized internal and external contexts of schools.

Political theories of school life have tended to suffer from the opposite dilemma: although they provide rich descriptions of the realities of day-to-day life in schools, they have been less successful at providing school practitioners with models of leadership that help them to survive politically *and* create a democratic, humane environment. Micropolitical accounts of schools often leave teachers and administrators with little more than the satisfaction that finally educational researchers are tapping into the messy political realities of school life. In this world practitioners on a daily basis must make judgements and decisions that affect their lives in profound ways.

Unfortunately, few studies of the politics of schools have much to say about how to break the vicious cycle of destructive political behaviour or how to move beyond the mere management of conflict to seeing it as significant behaviour that can lead to needed changes. Too often, conflict is viewed as a symptom to be managed rather than a reflection of deeper issues that may have gone unexamined or been silenced. The study of micropolitics provides us with a unique opportunity to elaborate a model of leadership based on the political realities of everyday school life. An important agenda of this book is to explore what a theory of leadership grounded in micropolitics would look like and how it might guide teachers and school administrators in their day-to-day decision-making.

MICROPOLITICAL LITERACY AND EDUCATIONAL PRACTITIONERS

We all know something about micropolitics. Any staffroom of any organization is full of talk about organizational micropolitics. In schools we experienced micropolitics as students; we learned how to engage in classroom politics with our classmates and our teachers. Later, much of our teacher training in classroom management became a series of lessons about classroom politics, but this time instead of resisting teachers, we were controlling students. Once we mastered the micropolitics of the classroom (which often consisted of nego-tiating some kind of 'deal' with students), we became increasingly aware of the micropolitics of the school, in which the major players were parents, adminis-trators and other teachers. Most of us coped as best we could, but our most com-mon response tended to be to retreat into our classrooms, where we had at least the illusion of autonomy.

The data we report in this book demonstrate the coping strategies that teachers have developed to protect themselves when they encounter the world of school-wide micropolitics. In conventional bureaucracies in which control is exercised hierarchically, these strategies may suffice in that they allow teachers and principals to achieve a tolerable coexistence. However, increasingly teachers and principals are being asked to set common goals and work col-laboratively towards their realization. Teachers are being asked to play a larger role in school-wide decision-making, and principals are expected to take a larger role in the classroom as instructional leaders. This means that a greater level of micropolitical literacy is required for teachers, principals, parents and students to work together authentically rather than politely tiptoe around each other.

Part of political literacy is becoming aware of what we already know so that it can be dealt with openly (Argyris *et al.*, 1985). The other part is a more in-depth understanding of the increasingly sophisticated and subtle ways in which power is wielded in educational settings. To develop a greater level of micropolitical literacy, it is first necessary to understand something about how power operates.

THEORIES OF POWER

How people wield power and influence others has been a central focus of works of philosophy from Plato's *The Republic* through Machiavelli's *The Prince*, and on up to Foucault's *Power/Knowledge*. Contemporary theories stress the less visible ways that power is used and the ways in which power is often structured into social relations so that it does not appear to be 'used' at all.

Political scientists agree that power is exercised when A gets B to do what B would not otherwise do. A classic study of power and politics was Dahl's (1961) *Who Governs?: Democracy and Power in an American City*. In their critique of Dahl's book, Bachrach and Baratz (1962) point out that Dahl limits his consideration of the exercise of power to formal, observable decision-making arenas. They argue that sometimes, however, power is exercised by what they call 'non-decision making'. In other words, some conflicts are organized into demands that gain access to the political system and others may simply be eliminated. For example, backstage manoeuvring often takes place in which deals are made and potential critics are silenced. In this way many issues never reach decision-making arenas, and, according to Bachrach and Baratz, we must study the ways in which this form of non-decision-making takes place.

Although Bachrach and Baratz's approach to the exercise of power is more subtle than its forerunners, in that it emphasizes the behind-the-scenes exercise of power, it is, according to Lukes (1974), still mired in a definition of power that is essentially behaviouristic. In other words, power is exercised overtly or covertly by individuals in specific situations that are, at least theoretically, observable.

Lukes (1974) argues that power is also exercised in ways that are far more amorphous and difficult to observe. He states that 'in shaping their perceptions, cognitions and preferences in such a way that they accept their roles in the existing order of things' (Lukes, 1974, p. 24), people's grievances can go unrecognized. More recent work by Foucault (1977) argues that power is 'structured into' the activities, events and social relations of bureaucratic organizations. The implications of these different theories of power for micropolitical theory and leadership theory serve as a cornerstone of this book and therefore are a recurrent theme throughout.

Power in relationship to others consists of a tripartite structure expressed in terms of 'power over', 'power through' and 'power with'. Authoritarian forms of leadership tend to be based on 'power-over' assumptions, which associate power with domination and control; one enhances one's own power at the expense of others. This vertical or hierarchical approach views power as a scarce resource. Competition for power pits people against each other in zero-sum power contests. These assumptions about how power operates in schools are rampant among teachers and especially educational administrators.

There are, however, alternative assumptions that can form the foundation of one's leadership approach. According to these alternatives, power or the ability to act does not have to be a scarce resource, nor does it have to be based on zero-sum assumptions – certainly not in interactions between human beings. One alternative is the notion of 'power through', which is a primary assumption underlying more 'facilitative' approaches to leadership. In a 'power-through' model, goals are accomplished through motivating individuals and groups who feel a sense of ownership in organizational goals. The extent to which organizational members are involved in formulating these goals has been the subject of organizational change and programme implementation research over the last two decades (Crandall *et al.*, 1986). 'Power-through' models generally are used to implement policies that originate at higher levels of the educational hierarchy. Both educational practitioners and policies and programmes are expected to mutually adapt to each others' needs. The move to shared governance models at the school building level is creating greater local input into this process. 'Power-through' assumptions are clearly an improvement over 'power-over' assumptions and create a less alienated teacher workforce as we will see in subsequent chapters.

A third alternative, which we advocate in this book, might be termed a 'power-with', 'power-together' or 'power emerging from interaction' alternative (see Chapter 7). The Stone Center at Wellesley College has developed a 'power-with' model in the context of women's empowerment. In discussing this model, Surrey describes empowerment as necessarily a relational, i.e. 'power-with', process:

> Recently the concept of group empowerment has begun to appear in the community psychology literature [Rappaport, 1984] and in writing on methodologies for oppressed groups to gain political and social power [Freire, 1972]. These writings, describe widely diverse ends and means of empowerment ... For the present, we define psychological empowerment as: the motivation, freedom, and capacity to act purposefully, with the mobilization of the energies, resources, strengths, or powers of each person through a mutual, relational process. Personal empowerment can be viewed only through the larger lens of power through connection, that is, through the establishment of mutually empathetic and mutually empowering relationships. Thus, personal empowerment and the relational context through which this emerges must always be considered simultaneously.
>
> (Surrey, 1991, p. 41)

A 'power-with' model, which is inherently relational in context, represents a challenge to traditional, hierarchical approaches to leadership that encourage administrators not to develop close relationships with subordinates. The 'power-with' model also empowers 'subordinates' and other stakeholders to expect democratic participation as a right, rather than to view it as a privilege at the discretion of administrators.

TOWARDS A MICROPOLITICAL LEADERSHIP MATRIX

The study of school micropolitics and our increased understanding of how power is exercised in social institutions enable us to map out the ways in which different approaches to leadership affect the life of teachers in schools. This map illuminates important but subtle distinctions that are often lost in discussions of leadership, site-based management and teacher empowerment. In this section we discuss two basic types of leadership *style*: open and closed. This is followed by a discussion of two basic approaches that relate to the ends or *goals* of leadership: transactional and transformative. Finally, we present a matrix that depicts these various styles and goals.

Leadership Style: Open and Closed Principals

In the context of a micropolitical analysis, leadership style refers to types of political strategies employed by leaders and the forms these strategies take. In the following chapters, we demonstrate the impact of open and closed leadership styles on the nature of institutional micropolitics. At the closed end of the open-closed continuum, power is wielded in fairly direct ways, and micropolitical interactions with teachers are generally characterized by avoidance, defensiveness and protection. As we move towards the other end of the continuum, we find that more open forms of diplomacy are the norm. However, in schools with open leaders, power is wielded in more indirect ways. Thus, more subtle and ideological forms of control are often characteristic of the open style.

Leadership Goals: Transactional and Transformative Leaders

Leadership *styles* are generally adopted as a means to achieving larger *goals*. These larger goals may be to legitimate the institution to its publics, to maintain the status quo, to restructure the organization in a particular way, or to advocate greater equity and social justice. These ends or ultimate goals are seldom made explicit in administrative training programmes, but they represent what is sometimes called the leader's vision, values or platform. How leaders define their overarching goals also depends on how they conceive their social role as leaders. Some are activists and view themselves as social advocates, moving their school towards challenging a status quo that they view as unacceptable. Others see themselves as neutral public servants who are simply

15

supposed to maintain the status quo while tinkering with selected aspects that may need improvement.

This latter conception is sometimes referred to as 'transactional leadership' (Burns, 1978). Transactional leaders tend to view everything in terms of explicit and implicit contractual relationships. This type of leader relies heavily on contractual conditions of employment, disciplinary codes and reward structures. The politics of transactional leadership take place within a kind of marketplace school culture in which material, psychic (e.g. praise) and symbolic (e.g. larger office) goods are exchanged. Most of the data in this book reflect this type of leadership, referred to in the sociological literature as 'exchange theory'. When this type of leadership and followership become part of the school culture, the higher purposes of the educational enterprise often get lost or distorted amidst political bargaining. Transactional leaders can adopt either closed (authoritarian) or open (facilitative) administrative styles.

Those leaders who exhibit a more proactive style and attempt to move a school towards a larger vision or set of ultimate goals are referred to by Burns (1978) as transformative leaders. According to Burns:

> Such leadership occurs when one or more persons engage with others in such a way that leaders and followers raise one another to higher levels of motivation and morality. Their purposes, which might have started out as separate but related, as in the case of transactional leadership, become fused. Power bases are linked not as counterweights but as mutual supports for common purpose. Various names are used for such leadership, some of them derisory: elevating, mobilizing, inspiring, exalting, uplifting, preaching, exhorting, evangelizing. The relationship can be moralistic, of course. But transforming leadership ultimately becomes moral in that it raises the level of human conduct and ethical aspiration of both leader and led, and thus, it has a transforming effect on both.
>
> (Burns, 1978, p. 20)

It is important to point out that all leaders, even transformational ones, engage in transactional leadership to some degree, and as Burns (1978) makes clear, occasionally transactional leaders might tap into a larger vision embedded in the wants of followers. In the context of discussing opinion leaders, Burns states:

> It is possible that transactional opinion leaders will appeal to fundamental, enduring, and authentic wants, to deeply seated latent needs, and even to followers' convictions about morality and justice. Opinion leadership and followership in the context of the marketplace, however, does not readily lend itself to such

substantial appeal or to creative, self-fulfilling responses as characterize transforming leadership.

(Burns, 1978, p. 21)

Transactional leadership, in reality, seldom raises issues related to urgent social realities. Even in schools with open leaders, transactions tend to be around narrow, individual concerns (see Chapter 4). Blase (1989) found that 'the political objectives of teachers tended to focus on individual rather than group concerns; there were only a few instances in which teachers acted directly on behalf of others' (p. 390).

Transformative leaders can adopt a closed or open leadership style. Closed transformative leaders often rely on their charisma and what they view as the moral rightness of their positions. Open transformative leaders blur the distinction between leadership and followership and attempt to find common purposes through authentic dialogue.

The Micropolitical Leadership Matrix

The micropolitical leadership matrix depicts two key dimensions of analysis, one representing micropolitical leadership styles and the other the overarching goals of micropolitical leadership (Figure 1.1). These are presented as two independent dimensions and, as such, represent the open–closed continuum of leadership style and the transactional–transformative distinction within leadership theory. It should again be noted that these approaches are seldom found in pure form, and should not be used as rigid categories. Rather, they are conceptual models meant to serve merely as aids in the analysis of school micropolitics and leadership.

Closed Transactional Approach: Authoritarian Leadership

The research data that we present in this book demonstrate that in accommodating themselves to the closed leadership styles of principals, teachers' actions may inadvertently reinforce such styles to gain goals such as greater autonomy. A vicious circle frequently results in which mutual adjustment and alignment, negotiation and confrontation produce and reinforce a closed school climate characterized by fear, distrust and avoidance.

Principals in such schools attempt to avoid, disable or ignore teachers, suppress dialogue, and exercise control through formal structures and the enforcement of policies and rules. This leadership style, prevalent among the closed principals described in our studies, is a classic authoritarian style in which, at least, the 'rules of the game' are fairly clear to both teachers and principals. Transactions tend to be formalized or 'by the rules'. Negotiation is minimal and tends to be achieved covertly, not openly.

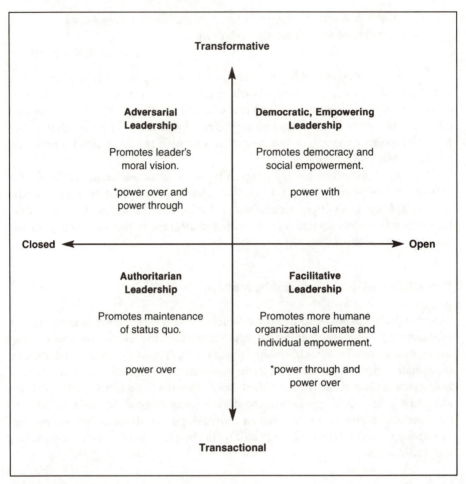

Figure 1.1 Micropolitical leadership matrix.

Closed Transformative Approach: Adversarial Leadership

Another leadership style characterizes some closed principals but was less prevalent in the studies reported in this book. These principals, although fundamentally authoritarian in style, tend to be more proactive and engage in politics more publicly and with a greater *appearance of openness*. They also tend to be more confrontational and aggressive in achieving their goals. Ball (1987) calls this leadership style adversarial. Adversarial principals are closed, not in the sense that they avoid conflict, but in the sense that they rarely share power. They are transformational in that they have strong ideological commitments that they promote aggressively. As Ball indicates:

There is a recognition of competing interests and ideologies in the school, and these are allowed to enter the formal procedures of discussion and decision-making. Decision-making is described by participants in the language of confrontation. They speak of 'rows', 'battles', 'challenges'. Here, then, headship is very much a public performance; the emphasis is on persuasion and commitment.

(Ball, 1987, p. 104)

Although it appears that the adversarial style would create a climate that would encourage more open, honest and proactive micropolitical interactions, this is rarely the case. In fact, this type of leadership approach simply tends to intensify teachers' use of defensive strategies (see Chapter 1). According to Ball (1987):

In the adversarial mode the assertion of control rests upon the skills of the head as an active politician and strategist both in the conduct of leadership, the use of talk and in the choice of issues, allies and opponents, and so on. The reliance on a social style and the public exchange of views means that any challenge to the head's authority must be a challenge to the person, or at least their views. The head is of necessity closely identified with the issues and ideologies being advocated. None the less, challenges are an accepted part of the form of micropolitical process generated by the adversarial style. The important point is the head's ability to handle, to deal with, these challenges. Crucial to this is the awareness, cultivation and use of allies. The head's allies, and opponents, come to be recognized as a part of the normal terrain of competing interests and ideological divisions among the staff. Allies must be encouraged, at times rewarded; opponents must be neutralized or satisfied, as the occasion demands.

(Ball, 1987, pp. 106–7)

Because adversarial leaders are in control of an organization's overarching goals, even though they allow some dissent within unilaterally defined limits, they represent a model that is often referred to as paternalistic. Often, along with an aggressive bargaining style, paternalistic leaders win allies through a warm, charismatic and dynamic style. Donmoyer (1983) provides a classic example of this type of principal in his portrait of Carmen Guappone, an affectionate but dominating figure who, through harsh bargaining and lots of hugs and backslapping, created a model school centred around the fine arts. The Guappone case will be elaborated in the following chapter as an example of adversarial leadership. Portraits abound of these high-energy, paternalistic leaders, many of whom have created outstanding educational programmes.

Both the authoritarian and the adversarial styles of leadership represent a view of power as 'power over'. Principals using these styles tend also to exercise power in more traditional ways, both through decision-making in public arenas and the avoidance of decision-making, i.e. using behind-the-scenes manoeuvres to keep issues off the agenda so that they never reach decision-making arenas. Towards the open end of the continuum, power tends to be exercised in more subtle and less visible ways, such as those identified by Lukes (1974) and Foucault (1977) and discussed in a previous section. Because adversarial leaders are often highly motivational, they often also exercise power *through* the mobilization of efforts by teachers and other stakeholders.

Open Transactional Approach: Facilitative Leadership

The categories of open and closed are limited because they do not take into consideration how power is wielded and for what purposes. For example, open 'human relations' styles of leadership are now routinely regarded as more effective mechanisms of bureaucratic control (Ferguson, 1984). Open principals, as described in Chapters 4 and 5, have succeeded in using less reactive and more diplomatic micropolitical strategies. However, teachers and principals in open leadership schools also indicated that leaders were willing to employ tactics that were indirect, subtle and somewhat covert. Such tactics are considered manipulative because the 'target' remains unaware of the influence (Blase, 1989, p. 389).

Although some forms of micropolitical manipulation are probably inevitable in organizations, regardless of leadership style, its potential danger lies in the fact that leaders often employ a discourse of change while maintaining the status quo. This often involves authorizing superficial or local change so that deep and macro-level changes do not occur. After summarizing the literature that finds traditional human relations techniques suspect, Ferguson concludes:

> Human relations strategies work better on people with middle-
> class educational and cultural backgrounds, who are more
> responsive to cooptation than to direct coercion; such strategies,
> as Richard Sennett notes, operate to 'soften' the demands of
> authority without changing them, to 'mystify what the boss
> wants and what the boss stands for'.
>
> (Ferguson, 1984, p. 69)

This type of leadership – also referred to as 'cultural' or 'facilitative' leadership – is the style of choice for the current site-based management and restructuring movements. It often appropriates a discourse of change and participation while engaging in bureaucratic manipulation towards pre-established goals. This style is an improvement over approaches to leadership that represent a 'power-over' orientation in the sense that there is increased opportunity for participation and a more humane and professional school climate. Nevertheless, such an orientation locates the real power outside the school and community because power exercised by achieving goals *through* motivation of others still depends on a hierarchical system in which overall goals are determined at the top.

Open Transformative Style: Democratic/Empowering Leadership

This approach is democratic in its processes of decision-making as well as in its fundamental concern with goals of equity and justice within educational institutions and in the broader communities. Because of the emphasis on a 'power-with' approach to decision-making, micropolitics becomes a genuine exchange of opinions in which virtually anything can be questioned or challenged without fear. According to Ferguson:

> Genuine political activity, as opposed to bureaucratic manipulation, is ideally a creative process by which individuals order their collective lives. It requires an open public space in which common interests can be defined, alternatives debated, and policies chosen. It engages individuals in an active, self-creative process involving both cooperation with and opposition to others. Politics in this sense entails the empowerment of individuals and groups, so that they are able to do things collectively that they could not have done alone.
>
> (Ferguson, 1984, p. 99)

Democratic/empowering leadership represents a shift from an emphasis on leadership as management – e.g. managing the school culture or managing diversity – to an emphasis on leadership as a form of empowerment. In this model, Maxcy contends that

> teachers need not look to a particular role player (e.g. administrator) to empower them. Rather, empowerment points to the capacity of individuals in *collaboration* to empower themselves. Power is not so much transferred as it is *released* through interpersonal transactions
>
> (Maxcy, 1991, p. 155)

This form of empowerment does not simply leave teachers alone to be autonomous professionals within their own classrooms, but engages them in a larger mission of student and community empowerment. It recognizes that, in fact, autonomous teachers can be a barrier to student and community empowerment. Maxcy (1991) points out that empowerment contains a moral dimension: 'to empower is to inculcate a *potential* to do harm' (p. 152). The literature is full of analyses of how school professionals through subtle (and not so subtle) forms of micropolitics disempower students and their parents (Malen and Ogawa, 1988; Weatherley and Lipsky, 1977).

Democratic/empowering leadership defines democracy as more than mere participatory management or teacher empowerment. Democracy is closely identified with issues of equity and justice at all levels of institutional and social life. Unfortunately, the field of education and particularly the subfield of educational administration tend to promote very narrow definitions of democracy and empowerment, both in terms of who is viewed as worthy of holding power and in terms of what issues are legitimate for power-sharing.

THE REMAINING CHAPTERS

These four approaches to leadership are further developed throughout this book, as data from several studies of micropolitics are discussed. Part 1 (Chapters 1 to 3 examines closed administrative styles and their impacts on teachers, students and parents, and Part 2 (Chapters 4 to 7) discusses open administrative styles and their effects on teachers, students and parents.

In Chapter 1 we focus on data that delineate the micropolitics of authoritarian, control-oriented principal leadership. In Chapter 2 data about micropolitical interactions among teachers, students and parents are discussed from the standpoint that teacher empowerment cannot and should not occur at the expense of the school's students and their parents.

Micropolitics between and among teachers is the subject of Chapter 3. Too often, research refers to 'teachers' as if they represent a monolithic group. It is impossible to understand a school's micropolitics without an understanding of how teachers relate to each other as individuals and as members of informal political factions and coalitions.

Chapter 4 presents data that illustrate the unique ways that teachers respond to open versus closed principals. In this chapter we examine the impact of a school's formal leadership on the micropolitical 'culture' that develops in a school.

How open principals affect the micropolitical world of teachers is examined in Chapter 5. The first study discussed develops the notion of normative-instrumental leadership, an effective leadership approach found in traditional schools. The second study provides data on leadership drawn from shared governance schools.

Chapter 6 presents case study data that illustrate how open administrative leadership styles, through the manipulation of cultural, symbolic and ideological dimensions of school life, may lead to more sophisticated forms of control of teachers.

The final chapter considers how schools might move to a democratic, empowering form of leadership in which power is shared throughout the school.

NOTE

1. This definition of micropolitics includes both legitimate and illegitimate forms of *power* (Ball, 1987; Blase, 1990; Mayes and Allen, 1977; Morgan, 1986). Goals that individuals and groups pursue may be interests, preferences or purposes (Bolman and Deal, 1984; Comstock, 1982; Morgan, 1986; Pfeffer, 1981b; Zaleznik, 1970). Political actions may include decisions, events and activities. Differences or discrepancies may be related to needs, values, beliefs, goals and ideologies (Bolman and Deal, 1984; Gronn, 1986; Hoyle, 1986; Mangham, 1979; Miles, 1980; Morgan, 1986).

   Consciously motivated actions may be intended, calculated, strategic or purposive. Unconsciously motivated actions may refer to routine action, lack of decision-making, negligence, non-action, habitual actions resulting from socialization, and actions that prevent others from exercising influence (Bachrach and Baratz, 1962; Galbraith, 1983; Goffman, 1972; Hall, 1972; Hardy, 1987; Kriesberg, 1973; Lukes, 1974).

   Political significance may refer to the consequences or import that actions have for others. Such actions and their effects on others are also considered to be part of the politics of an organization (Lofland, 1976; Mangham, 1979).

   Political action includes both conflictive and cooperative processes and structures, although certain types of political actions and purposes may be more closely identified with one than with the other (Blase, 1989; Burlingame, 1988; Burns, 1961; Mangham, 1979; Morgan, 1986; Townsend, 1990; Wamsley and Zald, 1973).

   Finally, the organization's external environment interacts with its internal political domain – each influences the other (Ball, 1987; Iannaccone, 1975; Meyer and Rowan, 1978; Wamsley and Zald, 1973).

PART ONE

CLOSED, CONTROL-ORIENTED LEADERSHIP: THE MICROPOLITICS OF SUBORDINATION

Part 1 of this book provides descriptive data and analytical categories that describe school principals with a closed, control-oriented approach to leadership. This approach is represented on the micropolitical leadership matrix in both the authoritarian and adversarial quadrants.

The distinction between an open and closed approach to leadership is important because the kind of micropolitical culture that results from each form of leadership is qualitatively different. The three chapters that comprise Part 1 of this book describe aspects of the micropolitical culture of schools that result from authoritarian and adversarial approaches to leadership. Most readers will recognize the micropolitical strategies employed by teachers as ones they themselves have used to survive in authoritarian social organizations, including families, churches, factories or schools.

One of the important findings of the micropolitical studies reported in this book has to do with the effect that control-oriented administrative behaviours have on the micropolitics of organizational cultures. Social institutions are not inherently bureaucratic, hierarchical and control-oriented. Rather, the behaviours, structures and values supported by those entrusted with formal institutional power contribute to these characteristics. This book shows that teachers tend to develop patterns of social interaction that are often in direct response to principals' leadership styles.

The closed, control-oriented leadership described in these chapters not only creates negative interaction patterns between principals and teachers, but also affects the ways in which teachers relate to students and parents. Just as teachers are in a subordinate relationship to principals, students are in a subordinate relationship to teachers. In poor neighbourhoods parents may also feel subordinate to teachers; in more affluent areas teachers may feel subordinate to parents. In the hierarchical, control-oriented, power-over world of most schools, subordination is a constant fact of life. It spreads the negative interaction patterns that teachers develop to cope with principals to all social relations within the school. To the extent that closed, control-oriented administrative styles are used by principals, the dynamics of subordination will continue to dominate the school's micropolitical culture. Ferguson (1984) writes: 'When one is a subordinate, one does what must be done in order to survive in a world largely beyond one's control. Oppression distorts one's abilities and self-understanding, silencing authentic speech' (p. 26).

The result of control-oriented leadership is subordination and the dynamics of subordination result necessarily in unauthentic behaviours based on the need to survive. The following three chapters document the micropolitical dynamics that are unleashed by closed, control-oriented principals.

Chapter 1

Negative Effects of Authoritarian and Adversarial Approaches to Leadership
Leadership as 'Power Over'

> Top-down, hierarchical relationships foster dependency. Teachers learn not to move without orders or permission from the principal; principals learn that they cannot leave 'their' building, lest it disintegrate. This dependency immobilizes and distances teacher and principal when what they need to accomplish their important work is maximum mobility, responsibility, and cooperation.
>
> (Barth, 1988, p. 146)

One of the most important findings of the research presented in this book is how control-oriented behaviours on the part of principals affect the micro-politics of the school culture. Teachers, in particular, tend to develop patterns of social interaction that are often in direct response to principals' leadership styles. Both the authoritarian and adversarial quadrants described in the micro-political leadership matrix are based on an orientation to power that stresses *control over* subordinates. The data in this chapter are largely based on principals who exhibited an authoritarian approach to administration. In the final section of the chapter data drawn from case studies of adversarial leaders are presented.

The study of authoritarian leadership focused on teachers' perspectives on school politics. An open-ended instrument was used to collect data, which were analysed according to principles for inductive analysis and qualitative inquiry. Of the 902 teachers who participated in the study, 276 chose (without any direction from the questionnaire) to describe specifically what we refer to in this chapter as control-oriented (manipulative) and protective political strategies used by principals. This chapter describes only this portion of the data and only these types of political strategies and tactics and their consequences for teacher work involvement and performance. In addition, the research data are briefly discussed in terms of Etzioni's compliance theory (Etzioni, 1961, 1975) and Barnard's theory of authority (Barnard, 1948). (See Appendix for a detailed discussion of the research problems and procedures.)

The strategies described are common to both authoritarian and adversarial models of administration; however the principals in this study exemplify, more directly, the authoritarian quadrant of the matrix. Descriptive statements and conceptual understandings derived from the data indicate that the use of control and protective strategies by principals has a negative impact on fundamental aspects of teachers' work in schools.

Although all principals do not employ control-oriented and protective tactics in their everyday political interactions with teachers, the findings of this study do indicate that some principals, in the teachers' view, may rely rather heavily on the use of control tactics. The conservative notion of authority prevalent in the state where the participants of this study were employed, the fact that unions are quite weak in this state because collective bargaining is prohibited by law, and recent legislative mandates may help to explain the use of control by some principals.

So far, only Ball (1987) has completed systematic empirical work on the 'political' practices of heads of (British) schools viewed from the perspectives of teachers. For example, Ball reported that the authoritarian type typically used tactics such as insulation, concealment and secrecy; the adversarial type was described as relying on public performances of persuasion. Ball found that the control orientations of school heads resulted in satisfaction for teachers who were content with existing political realities, fatalism for those cut off from influence relationships, and frustration for individuals with 'intense preferences' who continued to try to influence decisions.

In other (non-political) research, school principals have been seen as manipulating sanctions and rewards associated with resource distribution, administrative assignments, appointments and advancement opportunities in order to control teachers (Becker, 1980; Blase, 1988a; Cusick, 1983; Johnson, 1984). It has also been discovered that principals manipulate teachers' concepts of 'professionalism' (Hanson, 1981) and use 'participatory rhetoric' (Hunter, 1980, p. 213) to gain teacher compliance. Greenfield (1984) argues that educational leaders can be expected to engage in 'persuasion, calculation, guile, persistence, threat or sheer force' (p. 166) to achieve their ends.

More specifically, some empirical attention has been given to the problematic exercise of authority by principals and its consequences for teachers. Johnston and Venable (1986) found that authoritarianism in principals was inversely related to teacher loyalty. Others have linked authoritarianism, harassment and coercion in school principals to negative outcomes for teacher motivation, commitment, creativity and risk-taking behaviour (Ball, 1987; Blase, 1987a; Nias, 1989). McNeil (1986) discovered a strong relationship between control-oriented school administrators, teacher alienation and the development of 'defensive teaching' (i.e. the simplification, fragmentation and mystification of school knowledge) in the classroom.

However disturbing such images may be, external pressures for a control orientation mean that some educational leaders (in varying degrees) will employ, intentionally and unintentionally, political tactics that teachers define and respond to quite negatively. The general organizational literature (Barnard, 1948; Burns, 1978; Etzioni, 1961, 1975; Goldner and Ritti, 1977; Katz and Kahn, 1978) and some literature on political behaviour in schools (Ball, 1987; Blase, 1988a) point out that such actions may result in deleterious consequences for both the individual and the organization, particularly if these actions are perceived to violate professional values and expectations (e.g. equity or fairness). The data that we present in this chapter describe concretely some of the adverse effects that occur when the use of power by school principals is defined by teachers as violating basic personal, professional and organizational values.

The more general theoretical work of Barnard (1948) and Etzioni (1961, 1975) highlights the critical relation between how superordinates exercise power and how subordinates perceive that exercise of power. Both authors argue that subordinates' perceptions of authority and power determine, in large part, how they respond to superordinates in their degree of compliance, their affective responses and so on. In examining the nature of authority, Barnard focuses on the distinction between the authority of position (i.e. the rational-legal rights granted to superordinates) and the authority of leadership (i.e. a superordinate's rights of influence based on knowledge and human relations skills).

In effect, Barnard contends that how subordinates respond to super-ordinates – whether they confer 'authority' – is a function of how both types of authority are exercised: The 'determination of authority' (Barnard, 1948, p. 174) in this sense always ultimately remains with subordinates. Subordinates grant authority or legitimacy (i.e. the 'rights' of influence) and respond accordingly to superordinates whose actions are perceived to be consistent with organizational purposes and values as well as with personal and professional standards. In the final analysis, authority is based on acceptance or consent by subordinates. Among other things, subordinates can be expected to reduce 'indispensable con-tributions' (Barnard, 1948, p. 165) such as their time and energy to the organiza-tion if the actions of those in authority contradict organizational values and their personal interests.

More directly, Etzioni (1961, 1975) investigated the relationship between superordinates' use of power in organizations and subordinates' perceptions and responses. He theorized that compliance patterns in organizations result from an interaction between the dominant type of power used and subordinates' domi-nant type of involvement (i.e. their affective and cognitive orientation towards power).

Because schools (like religious and political organizations) are normative organizations, Etzioni argues, the use of certain types of power, such as coer-cion, may be considered incongruent with the psychological dispositions of teachers and thus have significant negative consequences. The data discussed in this chapter do indeed indicate that when teachers perceive that principals misuse power, this has a negative effect on their involvement in work as well as on the stability of the school as a whole. For example, the use of sanctions by some school principals was experienced as 'unfair' and 'punishing' and tended to violate teachers' expectations and values regarding responsible professional behaviour. According to the data, such sanctions had profound effects on teacher morale, expression, pride, trust and performance and resulted in feelings of anger, depression and anxiety.

Political Tactics Used by School Principals

The political behaviours employed by school principals were analysed in terms of two strategies that emerged from the data: control and protection. Tactics dominated by a control orientation were defined by varying degrees as manipulative. Such tactics were seen as deceptive, self-serving and narrowly conceived. Control tactics were perceived as highly proactive and unilateral, rather than bilateral. The direction of influence was from principals to the teachers, and the ends were seen as predecided and non-negotiable. Not uncommonly, control tactics were experienced as coercive. They were defined as forceful, stressful and punishing. The control strategy and its related tactics were employed by principals almost entirely with teachers. In this sense it should be considered a central aspect of principals' internal political orientation.

The second category of micropolitical tactics used by school principals was dominated by protective considerations. In contrast to the control strategy, the protective strategy reflected greater reactivity on the principals' part. In this sense, principals used protective tactics primarily to reduce their vulnerability to various forms of pressure, such as criticism and demands from administrative superiors, community members, parents and, to a lesser extent, influential teachers. Clearly, protective tactics are a significant dimension of the external political orientation of principals. However, our data indicated that protective considerations were also strongly related to the use of control tactics with teachers. That is, the pressure and nature of external demands seemed to contribute both directly and indirectly to principals' attempts to control teachers. (See Tables 1.1, 1.2 and 1.3)

The Control Strategy (n = 226)

Our study revealed that principals were viewed as using *direct* and blatant tactics to control teachers. The use of *sanctions and rewards* by school principals to achieve control was discussed by 160 teachers. Teachers perceived sanctions negatively in that they defined them as 'unfair', 'punishing' and 'harsh' within the context of control discussed above. Principals used sanctions most often to control individual teachers. The implementation of such sanctions was related to the control of specific groups such as departments and associations and was frequently perceived as the predominant stance of some principals towards entire faculties.

According to teachers, principals used sanctions to manipulate resources (e.g. equipment, materials, space, funds), work factors in classrooms (e.g. class

Table 1.1 Summary of teachers' perceptions of political strategies and tactics used by principals, including reasons for use

Political strategy and tactic	n	Reasons	f
Control strategy/tactics (226)		Reasons for control	
Direct			
Sanctions/rewards	160	Elicit support	124
Harassment	17	Suppress dissent	43
Dictatorial means	7	Achieve organizational goals	24
		Personal	69
Indirect			
Accessibility	18		
Content of discussions	14		
Teacher role concept	10	Total reasons ($f = 260$)	
Protection strategy/tactics (50)		Reasons for protection	
Acquiescence	22	Demands of superintendents	
Ingratiation	19	and school board members	28
Inconsistency	9	Parental influence and	
		demands	36
		Community expectations	26
		Faculty member and faculty	
		group influence	14
		Total reasons ($f = 104$)	

Throughout this chapter, n refers to the number of teachers and f refers to the frequency of response.

loads, class size), work factors outside classrooms (e.g. strict rule enforcement, unwillingness to bend rules), opportunities for input into decisions (e.g. curricular, extracurricular), support (e.g. for change, in disagreements with parents and students), and opportunities for advancement (e.g. appointments, promotions, special assignments). The manipulation of merit salaries, evaluations and work contracts was discussed less frequently. Teachers also reported that principals used the threat of sanctions ('punishments and reprisals') to obtain compliance: 'You definitely got the impression that you would lose your job if you made the wrong move.'

For teachers seen as 'favoured', principals were still viewed as manipulating many of the factors already described, but in a positive direction. Principals rewarded certain teachers with more resources, better working conditions, leniency with regard to policies and rules, positive performance evaluations, praise/recognition and greater input into decisions. Such teachers usually referred to more involvement in decision-making in the classroom, but not in the school generally. Principals manipulated teachers to gain their compliance

Table 1.2 Effects of strategies/tactics on teacher performance

Effect		
Classroom performance		
No effect	52	(n)
Negative effects on:		
Morale	78	(f)
Classroom decisions	63	
Instruction/student behaviour	32	
Classroom resources	28	
Extra work	12	
Mixed effects	6	
Positive effects	22	
Total effects	241	
School-wide performance		
No effect	33	(n)
Negative effects on:		
Morale	42	(f)
Involvement (time, energy)	76	
Expression of thoughts	49	
Teacher–teacher relationships	57	
Teacher–administrator relationships	27	
Teacher–student relationships	6	
School pride	16	
Mixed effects	8	
Positive effects	15	
Total effects	296	

with goals/policies for the school and, to some extent, for the community. The use of rewards by principals in the manner described was identified with the development of mutually reinforcing networks of exchange with teachers ('You scratch my back and I'll scratch yours'). However, since such networks included only a small percentage of teachers in any one school, this tended to have an alienative impact on other teachers.

Some principals employed *harassment* ($n = 17$) to control teachers – frequently to 'force the teacher to leave'. Teachers reported that principals attempted to discredit them ('demean', 'ridicule') in professional and sometimes personal terms. It was evident that harassment was often used over extended

Table 1.3 Teacher feelings about strategies/tactics

Feelings	f
Anger	189
Depression	58
Anxiety	55
Resignation	27
Satisfaction	12
Total feelings	341

periods of time and was accompanied by 'surveillance . . . in order to catch you doing something wrong'.

Some teachers explained that principals employed *dictatorial means* ($n = 7$) to elicit their compliance with policy as well as their personal expectations and demands. Compared with the manipulation of sanctions and rewards, dictatorial tactics were grounded entirely in the 'force of command'.

Principals also used *indirect* and subtle means to control teachers. Indirect tactics served to reduce or eliminate opportunities for teacher influence. Tactics of this type seemed to hinder teachers in their efforts to influence policy and programmes. For example, principals controlled *accessibility* ($n = 18$). Teachers claimed that principals managed their 'approachability' ('There is the impression there that they were not interested in talking') and restricted the teachers' access to superiors ('The message was clear . . . don't go over my head').

Principals were also seen as attempting to control the *content and process of discussions* ($n = 14$) ('Only certain ideas would be tolerated . . . were thought of as worthwhile'). It was also reported that principals created pseudo ('phoney') opportunities for the participation of teachers in decisions, in part to 'give the impression' that collaborative relationships were present in schools. Teachers believed that their contributions were either ignored ('there was never any mention of it') or overruled by principals.

Finally, school principals attempted to restrict teachers' influence by manipulating the *professional role concept* ($n = 10$) of teachers to reinforce their subordinate status. Principals emphasized authority differences ('I'm the boss') and delimited teachers to a functionary role ('You are here to do a certain job').

Reasons Control tactics, although frequently used to achieve internally oriented goals, were often linked to protectionist concerns. Teachers claimed that external demands (e.g. parental expectations) frequently provoked protectionist responses in principals (e.g. acquiescence to such demands). To meet such demands, principals often used control tactics with teachers.

Teachers reported that principals used control tactics, particularly the manipulation of rewards and sanctions, to secure individual and group *support* ($f = 124$) from teachers. Support was discussed in terms of attempts by principals to reduce uncertainty regarding teacher behaviour. More concretely, principals were perceived as trying to garner support for programme and policy changes as well as to buttress 'public images' ('He wanted teachers to politic in the community for the school and its programmes'). Political tactics linked to the development of support were, in part, associated with exchange and reciprocation processes ('favours for favours') between principals and teachers. Interestingly, the data strongly implied that the existence of such exchange and reciprocation networks themselves may have actually contributed to the continuation of control efforts by school principals ('It has a life of its own . . . the system of debts and repayments creates obligations long into the future').

In addition, teachers saw principals as attempting to *suppress dissent* ($f = 43$). 'Deviations', 'challenges' and 'criticism' by teachers of principals and their policies were targeted. Several teachers reported that control tactics were used by principals to maintain existing arrangements and to achieve *organizational goals* ($f = 24$) identified with ongoing programmes and policies. The achievement of 'quality' programmes, programme 'consistency' and 'special project goals' was described.

Teachers felt that principals often used control tactics for *personal reasons* ($f = 69$). Ego satisfaction was mentioned frequently ('They love to show who's the boss', 'They engage in politics for the feeling of power', 'Some people just feel good when they are dominating and controlling others'). Principals' use of control tactics was also attributed to 'narrow and arbitrary educational philosophies that do not permit collegial relationships with faculties'. Rewarding personal friends and personal career advancement were also reported.

The Protection Strategy ($n = 50$)

Although the 'proactive' use of control tactics dominated the orientations of some principals, they were also seen to employ three major protective tactics: acquiescence, ingratiation and inconsistency. Principals used these tactics reactively to reduce their vulnerability to school board members, superintendents, parents and certain powerful teachers.

Acquiescence ($n = 22$), i.e. behaviours indicating a submissive approach to those outside the school ('They give the parents what they want'), was perceived to directly undermine 'sound educational standards': 'An influential person in the community causes our principal to make decisions that are contrary to his own feelings. This person is a big contributor to the school.' *Ingratiation* ($n = 19$), a tactic suggesting greater proactivity as compared with acquiescence, was discussed primarily in terms of efforts by school administrators to promote activities and programmes that 'satisfy the community . . . look good on paper' ('This means placing the emphasis on football, pep rallies and other nonsense'). *Inconsistency* ($n = 9$) refers to contradictory changes in day-to-day decisions and policies in response to conflicting external pressures ('The principal sways with the wind depending on which group has the most political pull at the time').

Reasons for Protective Strategies Teachers indicated that the *demands of superintendents and school board members* ($f = 28$) frequently precipitated protective responses in principals. In the teachers' view, principals often 'felt compelled' to hire relatives and friends of prominent school officials. For some teachers, *parental influence and demands* ($f = 36$) were seen as contributing to principals' use of protective tactics. Teachers accused principals of being 'overly sensitive' to parental pressure and criticism, often to the point at which student discipline and academic standards were sacrificed.

More broadly, teachers explained that protective reactions of principals were closely linked to a general concern with *community/expectations and the maintenance of a good 'public image'* ($f = 26$). Accordingly, teachers described principals as covering up 'gross deficits' in teaching performance and programmes, making decisions related to teachers that were seen as inconsistent with policy, and stressing 'high-visibility programmes [special productions, athletics] rather than substance'.

Teachers explained that the influence of teachers who were hired because of their political connections contributed to the use of protective tactics by principals and that, in addition, individual *faculty members and faculty groups* ($f = 14$) were able to 'intimidate the principal into decisions' because of internally based power that often grew from a 'favour system'.

Effects on Performance in the Classroom

Fifty-two respondents indicated that the political behaviour of school principals had *no effect* on their performance/involvement in the classroom. The no-effect response was given primarily by teachers who described the principals' use of protective tactics (i.e. tactics designed to reduce vulnerability to external pressures).

The frequency (f) of all effects – negative, positive and mixed – reported for classroom performance was 241. A total of 196 teachers pointed out that the political practices of school principals resulted in *negative outcomes* ($f = 213$) for their performance/involvement in the classroom. Negative effects appeared to be direct. To illustrate, teachers and supervisors hired for 'political' reasons without regard for competence were seen as having a direct negative influence on instruction and discipline in the school.

In discussing the adverse effects of principals' practices on *morale* ($f = 78$) teachers used terms such as *cynical, lackadaisical* and *couldn't care less* to describe their attitude toward the classroom. Clearly, the actions of principals that reflected lack of recognition and appreciation for the work of teachers were perceived to have devastating consequences:

> The administration of our school has identified a few teachers
> who receive preferential treatment ... Often these teachers are

held up to the public ... put on display ... as a personification of all positive teaching virtues. Many good teachers feel 'put down' because they can't compete with the superstars ... I feel like giving up because what I accomplish doesn't compare to others.

Teachers reported that the behaviour of principals interfered with their ability to make *decisions for the classroom* ($f = 63$). Several explained that they were 'forced to use materials and teach content [they] did not agree with'. Others indicated that materials and topics considered 'controversial' (this usually meant innovative) were severely restricted by some principals:

I feel constraints upon my teaching – I do not feel as spontaneous and open in my classroom discussions. I avoid the use of materials that might be in the least questionable, even though I do not consider them so and their value would outweigh any questionable aspects.

Teachers complained that their professional judgements were not respected; they were 'not free to modify or deviate from the curriculum when that's what is the sensible thing to do'. Others, however, disclosed that some principals forced them to ignore programme requirements:

As an eighth grade science teacher I planned to teach evolution because it was in our textbook and was part of the curriculum. ... Pressure was put on me not to teach the unit. Though the words were never spoken, it was made clear that I would not acquire the administrative position which I was seeking in the county ... Teachers in my school are very careful not to express opinions or exhibit behaviours which they know are not approved by the administration.

Teachers also indicated that classroom decisions related to curricular improvement were negatively affected by principals. For example, teachers reported that 'no matter what I do, I can't get anywhere ... there's no recognition'. Many indicated that 'the system forces you to concentrate on how you get by smoothly. It encourages loyalty, but discourages people who want changes made.' In effect, teachers reported that they were required to be 'careful' and 'avoid anything that could cause problems ... raise questions'. For many, such a stance was experienced as a 'loss of control' over the classroom.

From the teachers' standpoint, decisions associated with *instruction and student behaviour* ($f = 32$) were frequently 'sabotaged' by principals' political orientation to parents and the community. Attempts by principals to secure 'favoured treatment for football players', for instance, interfered with the instruction and discipline of students:

To accommodate parents, the principal overrules the decisions made by teachers. Teachers are afraid to punish certain students for fear of backlash from the principal . . . This established a very 'egg shell' atmosphere to work in and causes teachers to dislike certain students.

As a result, several teachers indicated that they displaced 'frustration and hostility on the kids'. Teachers also argued that 'academically oriented students suffered' in schools with principals who were more concerned, for example, with 'images' than with performance.

In addition, *classroom resources* ($f = 28$) (e.g. materials, equipment, funds, space) were perceived to be limited under control-oriented principals. Several teachers discussed this issue in terms of 'opportunities lost'. Other teachers indicated that when *extra work* ($f = 12$) during and after school (e.g. duties, committees, PTA) was 'dumped on you' by principals, this detracted from time devoted to instruction and planning.

Finally, teachers reported *mixed effects* ($f = 6$), and *positive effects* ($f = 22$), on their involvement in the classroom in relation to principals' political practices. These teachers pointed out that increased morale resulted from their 'favoured status' and increased support. Interestingly, eight of these teachers stated that their involvement in the *school* was adversely affected because trust, cooperation and respect among teachers had decreased as a result of their principals' actions.

Effects on Performance in the School

Thirty-three teachers indicated that the political practices of principals had *no effect* on their performance/involvement in the school.

The frequency (f) of all effects (negative, mixed, positive) for school-wide performance was 296. The frequency of negative outcomes reported for the school (273) was higher than that reported for the classroom (213). A total of 220 teachers discussed the *negative outcomes* that principals' political behaviours had on their performance/involvement in the school.

Teachers indicated that their *morale* ($f = 42$) was substantially and negatively affected by principals' political tactics. Teachers used terms such as *apathetic, alienated* and *less satisfied*. Principals' manipulation of sanctions and their acquiescence and ingratiation in response to external demands were frequently cited as contributing to lowered teacher morale.

Teachers reported that their *involvement* ($f = 76$) – i.e. the time and energy they devoted to school-wide activities – was adversely affected. In part, principals were seen as making professional involvement in the school 'risky' ('You knew you would be blamed if there were any problems'). Teachers who were 'improvement-oriented' appeared to be especially 'fearful' of control-oriented principals ('Improvement means change . . . he wants to preserve the status quo'). Others pointed out that their involvement was prevented, 'automatically cut off', because of lack of support from principals ('without his help we couldn't get anywhere'). Teacher voluntarism in school activities was reduced because of lack of recognition from principals ('He took all the credit to advance his own career'). Negative effects on the classroom also spilled over and affected teacher involvement in the school ('I can't get what I need for students, why should I do anything in the school'):

> The principal in this situation openly showed favouritism toward a few select faculty members: classroom duties, attendance at meetings, giving confidential information ... I found myself less interested and less willing to support school functions. If a meeting was required I was always the last to arrive and the first to go. I never went the extra step unless it was required and had an attitude of rebellion against any decision or suggestion made by the principal.

Closed principals severely restricted the *expression of teachers' thoughts/ opinions* ($f = 49$) about school-wide programmes and policies, through both formal (e.g. meetings) and informal (e.g. impromptu conversations) channels. It was apparent that the political practices of these principals limited the teachers' participation in decisions ('It was prudent to keep a low profile', 'fear turns teachers into cowards ... they won't stand up for what they believe'):

> With the possibility of negative sanctions from an administrator taken against me as a result of my freedom of speech ... you must be aware of what you say and do. There is a definite fear of free speech since someone is watching your actions and expressions. This usually splits a school into two or more groups. If the local situation is very heated then the political factors can really destroy a school.

Strong norms circumvented the teachers' inclinations towards change and their 'willingness to confront problems'. Teachers pointed out that both direct and indirect control tactics of principals (e.g. manipulation of accessibility, teachers' professional role concept) caused teachers to reduce participation in school-level decisions.

When teachers described the negative consequences of principals' behaviour on *relationships among teachers* ($f = 57$), it was apparent that cohesiveness within faculties was seriously undermined. Higher levels of resentment were associated with increased competition and conflict ('It's a dog-eat-dog situation ... everyone out for themselves'). Teachers pointed out that the development of cliques ('splits') within faculties ('favoured versus unfavoured', 'those for and against the principal') weakened faculty relations. Others discussed problems of increased exploitation ('People try to sue one another, it's not supportive') and defensive behaviour ('You stay on guard'). Finally, power imbalances ('They think they run the school') and abuse were noted:

> Principals constantly face the situation of parents requesting
> which teacher their child has ... This has led to conflict with
> other teachers. Jealousy, competition and other negative factors
> within school can arise ... All this has led to real problems and
> lack of cohesiveness.

Relationships between teachers and principals ($f = 27$) were seriously damaged as a result of control-oriented practices. Teachers pointed out that trust and respect for principals were negatively affected and that it was difficult for them to predict the behaviour of principals. This reduced the teachers' willingness to engage in actions that required symbolic and tangible support from principals. Consequently, teachers became overly cautious and compliant. Several teachers disclosed that the 'politics of the situation' frequently made an understanding of 'real goals and agendas' of the school problematic. Even those who 'played the political game' explained that they 'worried about what the payback will be'. Others, to protect themselves, attempted to 'avoid' principals altogether. Only a few reported using passive-aggressive tactics (e.g. gossip) to 'hurt the principal ... get revenge'.

Although the data strongly suggest that *teacher–student relationships* ($f = 6$) in the classroom were adversely influenced by principals, the frequency of this effect was low. In each instance, teachers indicated that student discipline and control were more difficult as a result of the principals' willingness to extend preferential treatment to students and their parents:

> It is difficult, at times, to be fair and consistent to all students
> when the principal caters to some whose parents have
> complained. It can create some very awkward situations when
> the parents or students make identical requests and you can't
> legitimately honour these requests.

Teachers reported that *school pride* ($f = 16$) suffered because of the political practices of principals. The school was described as a 'source of embarrassment', especially with regard to the community. Some teachers explained that they 'retreated to the classroom' as a result; others discussed their attempts to transfer to better schools. In addition to the manipulation of sanctions, the dictatorial style of principals was seen to have a negative affect on school pride.

Mixed outcomes ($f = 8$) for performance in the school were described by some teachers ($n = 8$), and others ($n = 15$) disclosed that the political behaviour of principals had *positive effects* ($f = 15$) on school-wide performance levels. Increased motivation and involvement in activities and decisions were associated with 'favoured' treatment.

Feelings

The total database was examined for feeling states that teachers identified with the political practices of principals. A model that one of us developed from a study of teacher stress is consistent with the emergent database and with relevant models that have appeared in the psychological literature (Cormier and Cormier, 1979). Data related to feelings were analysed in terms of five major categories: those associated with anger, depression, anxiety, resignation and satisfaction. The total number of feelings described was 341. Only feelings that were directly discussed were coded; no attempt was made to infer feelings from the database.

Anger states ($f = 189$) describe strong negative feelings directed towards others. The descriptive terms used by teachers were *resentful, hostile, frustrated, disgusted, outraged, bitter, violated, used, exploited*, and the term *angry* itself. The words *angry* and *frustrated* appeared most frequently:

> The principal thinks that if something is wrong in the school it should be 'covered up' rather than made public and corrected . . . It makes me angry . . . it stinks! I've seen incompetence and have seen children suffer because of it. Nothing is ever done, and on top of it all, anyone who tries to expose it is in serious trouble.

Depressive states ($f = 58$) describe a general feeling of being out of control. Teachers used the terms *alienated, negative, defeated, sad, humiliated, powerless, put down, left out, unimportant, unappreciated, hopeless, alone, disheartened* and *depressed*:

> Politics is the tool used by the principal to promote her self-interest as she progresses on her 'career ladder'. The principal recommends transfers of teachers who do not play the political game. Everything has to be positive or you receive a poor evaluation. . . . I feel depressed, what's the use. . . . I want to give up . . . feel guilty, apathy, rejection. . . . Play the game and win favours, ask why and you may be eliminated.

Anxiety states ($f = 55$) are considered anticipatory. Individuals experience anxiety because negative outcomes or consequences are expected. Terms used by teachers to identify anxiety states were *confused, disoriented, uncertain, uneasy, fearful, scared, nervous, paranoid* and *anxious*:

> Politics means that the rules of the school are not enforced equally throughout when dealing with staff members . . . Like I said, it makes me scared . . . that people could govern others in this way. And you know, it makes me mad, even though I could never show that outwardly for fear of losing my job. I'm just glad that I have the solace of my classroom, because there I'm peaceful and don't worry about what goes on around me.

Resignation states (f = 27) describe passive acceptance, but without depressive undertones. Such phrases as *it's a way of life, it's human nature, it's a necessary evil* and *fact of life* were used:

> People engage in political activities because they are intrinsic to human nature. If you want to excel ... or even exist ... you have to comply, be quiet about things ... It is not something you want to deal with, but it's there, it's a fact of life. The implication is that you are compelled to pay homage to it.

Satisfaction states (f = 12) refer to positive feelings. Terms such as *great, good, supported, appreciated* and *respected* were used to describe this state. Teachers experiencing satisfaction considered themselves to be 'favoured' by the principal ('I was on the receiving end'). Teachers indicating positive feelings, however, also discussed negative feeling states. Although they recognized the benefits of 'favoured' status, they expressed concern about the ethics of the principal's behaviour and about the negative implications of these practices for colleagues:

> When I was in the 'favoured' group I felt sorry for those who were not. Now I am in the 'non-favoured' group, I feel resentment and do not wish to participate in school activities.

DISCUSSION OF AUTHORITARIAN LEADERSHIP

In the previous section we have focused specifically on certain dimensions of the political behaviour of authoritarian school principals as defined by teachers. Two major strategies – control and protection – were described. We examined these strategies in terms of underlying reasons and purposes as well as in terms of their impact on teachers. Protective considerations arising from the external environment of schools were closely linked to the development of a control orientation in principals *vis-à-vis* teachers. The use of control-manipulative political behaviours by some school principals has serious negative effects on teacher involvement and performance. These behaviours undermine school-based academic and social standards. Anger was the most predominant feeling that teachers expressed in regard to principals' use of control and manipulation.

An overwhelming portion of the data supports the general conclusion that the use of control tactics by school principals (as described) tends to have profound negative consequences for teachers. Specific effects were noted for teacher classroom performance in terms of morale, decisional discretion, instruction and classroom resources. Likewise, school-wide performance was negatively affected in terms of morale, involvement and expression. Relationships among teachers, between teachers and principals, and between teachers and students also suffered as a result of the use of these tactics, as did school pride. In fewer instances, control-oriented principals had no effect, mixed effects and even positive effects on teachers.

Further examination of the control tactics described in this study indicates the superiority of direct tactics, especially sanctions and rewards, over indirect tactics (e.g. accessibility) and blatantly aggressive tactics (e.g. harassment), suggesting that principals primarily relied on strategies and tactics consistent with the legitimate prerogatives of the position. However, the study data, most noticeably data related to reasons attributed to principals' use of control (e.g. to suppress dissent, gain support), suggest that many control practices, from the teachers' standpoint, violated basic professional norms and expectations, broad educational standards and basic human rights (e.g. free speech). In other words, although most of the control-oriented practices discussed did not ostensibly exceed the boundaries of principals' authority (as did harassment, for instance), the teachers' belief that principals were motivated by purposes that conflicted with basic norms and values helps to account for their negative reactions to control. Goldner and Ritti (1977) have linked administrative political practices that violate professional values to the development of cynical knowledge in organizations.

Although specific effects for the classroom and the school have already been described, a more abstract analysis suggests that these effects can be viewed quantitatively (as generalized reductions of teacher work time and effort in the classroom and the school) and qualitatively (as decreases in teacher control of decisions, decreases in concern for improvement, and increases in the difficulty of student problems). Fully 71 per cent of the research participants reported negative outcomes for their classroom performance; 80 per cent described negative effects for their school-wide performance. In terms of qualitative outcomes, negative effects for teachers' involvement in both the classroom and the school were substantial, but those concerning the school were more significant. The importance of classroom instruction to teachers and the fact that teachers earn their major rewards from successful instruction (Lortie, 1975) may help to explain why performance in the classroom was less vulnerable to the adverse effects of principal control.

Negative effects for qualitative school-wide involvement were associated with decreases in voluntary participation by teachers in programmes, in influence regarding policies, in risk-oriented behaviour, and in respect for and trust in principals. Increases in defensive behaviour among faculty and in the difficulty of dealing with student problems were also apparent. The use of control by principals appeared to undermine overall teacher control and influence and to provoke teachers to question the 'legitimacy', or authoritative basis, of principals' actions.

A CLOSED TRANSFORMATIVE APPROACH:
ADVERSARIAL LEADERSHIP

Some of the closed principals we have just described employed a preponderance of authoritarian strategies. In this section we provide an example of a closed, adversarial principal (Ball, 1987) but one who exhibits transformative goals. First, we should point out that there is a great deal of variation within both the authoritarian and adversarial approaches. Each approach may vary in its location on the closed–open axis as well as on the transactional–transformative axis within its respective quadrant. However, this variation notwithstanding, there are clear differences between the authoritarian and adversarial approaches.

Nearly every school district has a few adversarial leaders. They tend to be bright, charismatic, highly opinionated, self-confident and high-energy people. They are always willing to engage in discussions and relish a good argument. However, when they cannot convince teachers or parents of their convictions, they often suggest that their opponents transfer elsewhere. Such principals are celebrated in the literature as effective leaders because they often galvanize a school's culture around a set of beliefs that lend coherence to the school.

Many accounts of such principals exist (Blumberg and Greenfield, 1986; Donmoyer, 1983; Lightfoot, 1983). In fact the mass media have highlighted several through television movies and magazine articles (Cook, 1988; Kirp, 1989; Schwartz, 1990). In this section we present data from a 'portrait' by Donmoyer (1983) of Carmen Guappone, a charismatic principal who created a dynamic elementary school around a fine arts theme in a rural Pennsylvania mining town.

Donmoyer (1983) describes Guappone as a man of contradictions. A former high school dropout who mined coal in his teens, he went to college on the GI bill and a football scholarship upon returning home from World War II as a decorated hero. Along the way, he completed a doctoral degree and developed a love of fine arts, which he made the centrepiece of Germantown Central Elementary School. As is the case with most adversarial leaders, parents and teachers are often divided in their opinions of his leadership. This is in part because he combines elements of openness and closedness in his administrative style.

On the one hand he utilizes a 'team management system' in which a representative from each grade level serves on a school-wide team that meets with Guappone once a week to make decisions affecting the entire school. In addition, there are daily grade-level teachers' meetings during free periods for collaborative planning. Donmoyer (1983) reports that there is a strong sense of community in the school and that 'German Central's teachers exhibit little of the debilitating sense of isolation that sociologists indicate is commonplace in most elementary schools' (p. 85). A parent volunteer in the school says, 'You don't have to be afraid to talk to him if you have something that's bothering you or even if you have something you want to try' (Donmoyer, 1983, p. 83). There is ample evidence that Dr Guappone has created a strong community among teachers, a dynamic arts programme, and a record of high student achievement in the school.

On the other hand, there is also ample evidence that behind the team management and the warm, dynamic style, there is an essentially closed orientation in Guappone's leadership:

> A parent describes a man who does what he wants no matter what parents say or do, and a school board member tells of an administrator whose record of student suspension days during the course of a school year exceeded those of all the other principals in the district – including those at the two high schools – combined.
>
> Staff members do little to provide a more consistent picture of Carmen Guappone. They obviously enjoy working for him, yet they talk both of the freedom and support he provides and of his mandates and demands. it is probably significant that many staff members alternate between calling him *Carmen* and *Dr Guappone*.
>
> (Donmoyer, 1983, p. 83)

With regard to his adversarial style, Guappone is described by Donmoyer as a fighter who uses a range of tactics:

> He is overpowering; as one of his teachers put it, 'He's a very verbal person, and if you've got him on your side, you've got something loud.' He can be vindictive; a mother who complains that the school overemphasized television production at the expense of the academic program is told that her son will never appear on television again, despite the mother's plea that her son needs the television experience to build his self-confidence. And Guappone can be, in his own words, subversive; should the superintendent do away with elementary school music, as he often threatens, thereby relegating Goldsmith (the music teacher) to a classroom teaching position, Guappone would, he says, simply reallocate resources internally so she could continue to be the school's music teacher.
>
> (Donmoyer, 1983, p. 88)

Furthermore, Guappone believes that he should be the authority in the school and should be able to make decisions without seeking permission from central office:

> I like authority, OK, and authority is something you take, not something someone gives you. And I take all I can get. And I don't really care to say that I have to ask someone. I'm the principal, and I feel that that's my decision, and I want my

teachers to feel that way, that they're my decisions. A principal
has to have authority, you know, and you just can't function
without authority. You can't tell the teacher or anyone, 'Well, I'll
have to check on it, or I'll have to do this.' And I always tell
them OK and I'm positive I can do what I want to do, you know.
I do what I want to do anyhow. [If] you just can't make a
decision, your word isn't worth anything. If I'm going to do all
the things I do, they have to look at me and know that I'm the
person that says it's OK – regardless!'

(Donmoyer, 1983, p. 89)

This near obsession with authority is balanced by a warm and friendly interpersonal style with teachers, one that borders on fatherliness. Donmoyer reports
that Guappone, in fact, frequently uses family imagery in discussing his relationship with teachers:

How can you refuse to work cooperatively with someone when
they're so good to you and so nice to you, and they care for you
so much, you know? And it is a little fatherly. How can you
refuse your father? Well, how can you refuse a principal-father
anything when you're so close to each other.

(Donmoyer, 1983, p. 90)

Donmoyer indicates that while Guappone's use of affect and paternalism
may smack of manipulation, his personal closeness with his teachers is generally
sincere. He genuinely cares about his staff, and his fatherly approach only
'works' when staff feel he is being authentic. Clearly, many teachers would fight
to keep Guappone as their principal, should the school board seek to fire him,
a scenario that seems likely given all the enemies he has made in the community
and at central office. A German Central teacher sums it up;

In spite of the differences I have with him, I still like him as a
person and I think I work for him for that reason. He's a friend,
too. He gets involved with us, you know. He comes in the room
and sits down and just has a nice conversation with us. And he
likes you. And he talks to you and treats you like a person, not
like he's the boss, even though he says he's the boss and I call
him the boss and he is. He's not one that can't be touched.

(Donmoyer, 1983, p. 93)

Although this case is in no way representative of all adversarial leaders, it
contains many characteristics common to this approach. Adversarial leaders
may use their persuasive and charismatic skills to create wonderful educational
programmes for children, as was apparently the case at German Central. However, these skills can also be put to use to create rigid and punitive programmes,
based on whatever idiosyncratic 'vision' or 'moral imagination' the principal may

subscribe to. Critiquing this model of transformative leadership based on the personal moral vision of a leader, Maxcy claims:

> There is a real danger that moral imagination qua authority may become the narcissistic vision of 'inspired' leaders, unchecked by democratic consensus or external criteria of rationality.
>
> (Maxcy, 1991, p. 118)

While Guappone has set up a 'team management system' for decision-making, there is much evidence in the case study to indicate that the most important decisions are reserved for the principal. Furthermore, team management systems that are set up at the discretion of principals can as easily be dismantled, should they begin to become too empowered.

Ironically, some of the most outstanding educational programmes in the country have been forged by closed, transformative principals. Given the excessively bureaucratic nature of our current educational system and the multiple special interests that impinge on the school site, perhaps the current educational environment can only be dealt with effectively by individuals with strong wills and clear moral visions of 'their' schools. Given the current nature of the system, it may appear that only through subversion and manipulation can transformation be achieved at the school site. This image of the Marva Collins-like, street-level manager confronting a rigid bureaucracy is also an appealing and heroic image for many Americans who are rightly frustrated with a public school system badly in need of transformation.

Several problems arise, however, from the teachers' perspective. First of all, an inherent dependency is created in relationships with closed transformative leaders. Quite commonly in such cases, the 'transformed school' enters a period of crisis when the adversarial leader leaves. These leaders tend to leave for diverse reasons. The most politically astute principals use their reputations and the accolades they receive from the press to move on to 'bigger and better' things. The less astute ones are either let go by school boards or superintendents for insubordination or are transferred to another school to keep them from building a powerful political base at their site. As Miles and Huberman (1984) have documented, 'careerism', in the sense of administrators creating an innovative programme that becomes a stepping stone to a higher position, is one of the major threats to the institutionalization of innovations.

Once the adversarial leader departs, teachers must learn to deal with a new principal who has a different vision. A new cycle of micropolitical manoeuvring begins, and this is often the impetus for teacher transfers. Teacher empowerment cannot be achieved with a closed leadership style, even one with transformative goals. It can only be achieved when the line between leadership and followership becomes blurred. We will return to this idea in Chapter 7, in which we discuss an *open* transformative approach to leadership.

CONCLUSION

In this chapter, we call attention to the problematic nature of administrative control practices within the context of school settings and teachers' perspectives. The present data, and relevant theoretical work (Barnard, 1948; Etzioni, 1961, 1975), suggest that strong control structures and practices, as we have described them, may actually interfere with teachers' abilities to teach successfully. More specifically, increased use of certain types of power on the part of educational administrators (e.g. remunerative and coercive) may actually contribute to forms of teacher involvement (e.g. calculative and alienative) that are inappropriate to the educational and social goals of schools.

Chapter 2

The Everyday Political Perspectives of Teachers Towards Students and Parents

> Over the years you learn that being political means surviving.
> You are open to criticism from all sides ... You are a sitting
> duck ... Parents are among those who will attack you when little
> Johnny has a problem ... They raise questions about your
> personal life or what they heard you said in class. You learn to
> be careful ... more conservative ... to protect yourself.
>
> (A Teacher)

In the previous chapter we discussed the impact of control-oriented leadership on teachers' relations with principals. This chapter discusses the political perspective of teachers as it relates to their relationships with students and parents. Interviews were used to collect data from teachers who worked in one urban high school in the southeastern United States. Data analysis conformed to guidelines for grounded theory inquiry. (See Appendix for a description of the research problem and procedures.) In this chapter, we present descriptions and conceptual ideas gleaned directly from the data.

Interpersonal politics is considered an important subset of organizational politics (e.g. Ball, 1987; Hoyle, 1986). Specifically, in the context of the present database, the concept of interpersonal politics underscores teachers' vulnerabilities and sensitivities associated with day-to-day interactions with students and parents in the schools. These sensitivities, we discovered, contribute to the development of a calculative orientation in teachers, consisting of self-monitoring and timely adjustments of behaviour to deal effectively with others. In general, interpersonal politics in schools focuses on the strategic exercise of power for purposes of both influence and protection (Blase, 1987c).

To date, little research has been published that examines the teacher–student or the teacher–parent relationship from a micropolitical perspective. However, as noted in the Introduction, a review of the findings of several (non-political) case studies points to some similarities with the results of the present study. For example, the present study indicated that the teachers' political stance towards students stemmed, in large part, from problems related to academic instruction and social control (i.e. discipline). The centrality of these factors to teachers' perspectives on work is well established in the teachers' worklife literature

(Becker, 1980; Cusick, 1983; Lieberman and Miller, 1984; Lortie, 1975; McPherson, 1972; Pollard, 1985; Waller, 1932).

Lortie (1975) discusses the importance of achieving social and moral goals with students. Other studies have reported that control of students is frequently more important to teachers (and administrators) than the achievement of academic goals (Willower *et al.*, 1967). Cusick (1983) found that the problematic nature of student control precipitated an inordinate concern on the part of administrators and teachers with maintaining 'good relationships' with students, to the point where academic instruction was seriously sacrificed. McNeil (1986) describes the deleterious results of principals' and teachers' emphasis on controlling students.

In a more limited way, the worklife literature also reveals that teachers use a variety of tactics to influence students to achieve instructional and social goals. Pollard (1985) argues that 'good' teaching is fundamentally manipulative; teachers attempt to get students to internalize and pursue goals defined by teachers. Good teaching is associated with acting ability, communication skills and ability to give praise. Pollard found that teachers used strategies such as negotiation, routinization, manipulation and domination to control students. Waller (1932) examined how teachers use anger to cope with student behaviour problems. Devices that teachers employed for protective purposes, e.g. the search for coalitions with pupils and cooperative parents and the importance of rule books in protecting teachers from criticism, are discussed by McPherson (1972).

In addition, this literature reveals, often implicitly, the significant influence that parents and school administrators have on the teacher–student relationship. For example, Blase (1988a) and Lortie (1975) discuss the stress and conflict that results when parents attempt to seek 'special favours' for their children from administrators. Blase (1987a) examined the devastating effects that non-supportive administrators have on teachers in conflicts with parents and how such conflicts affect the teacher–student relationship.

The professional literature characterizes teachers' relationships with parents as distrustful and even hostile (Becker, 1980; Lortie, 1975; McPherson, 1972; Waller, 1932). Such problems have been attributed to the different perspectives of teachers and parents regarding the student. Waller (1932) wrote that teachers and parents 'wish [the student] well according to different standards of well-being' (p. 68). McPherson (1972) interpreted teacher–parent enmity in terms of the conflict between universalistic expectations (required for group life) and particularistic expectations (related to individual needs). Within each of these perspectives, conflicts are considered inevitable, since they result from differences linked to primary (e.g. intimate) and secondary (e.g. impersonal) group affiliations (Bates and Babchuk, 1961).

For the most part, the research cited above identifies teacher–parent conflict with interactions concerning subject matter and student discipline. Parents' inclination to 'interfere' in school matters, to challenge the teacher's

49

authority – and to do so in ways that violate interpersonal norms for reasonable, productive and supportive interaction – contributes to the adverse effects experienced by teachers. Studies also indicate that teachers develop methods (e.g. establishing a common bond of parenthood, invocation of bureaucratic rules) to deal with critical and obtrusive parents (Becker, 1980; McPherson, 1972). Such methods are not inconsistent with strategies that teachers defined as 'political' in the present study.

RESULTS

In the beginning years, the data suggest, teachers were preoccupied with developing competencies (i.e. knowledge and skill) associated with instruction, control and social relations with students. Teachers had 'strong' values and held idealistic (i.e. naive) expectations for administrators, teachers, students and parents. Through experience with each of the aforementioned reference groups, teachers became increasingly sensitive to the political considerations associated with interaction in the school.

The data indicate that learning to 'play the game' for purposes of survival at work was central to socialization outcomes in teachers. The study findings support the conclusion that conflicting values, beliefs and goals of different reference groups provoke significant changes in the perspectives of teachers over the long term – many of which teachers themselves define as having political implications for their work.

Overall, it was discovered that the development of a political perspective in teachers stemmed primarily from a sense of vulnerability to criticism and threat from others. In the school studied, many teachers indicated that they worked in a 'fishbowl', that their actions were incessantly scrutinized by others, and that disagreements with others tended to cause strong reactions. In addition, teachers learned that their actions were often misinterpreted. Not infrequently, professional and personal information about teachers was distorted in the school and the community. Teachers indicated that, among other things, insecurities (e.g. personal defensiveness, turf battles), inconsistent agendas, conflicting ideologies and variation in role responsibility and role interpretation contributed to the distortion effect. According to the data, teachers construct a political self that stems from influence (proactive) and protectionistic (reactive) concerns.

Although the expectations, demands, attitudes and behaviour of the teachers' role set (i.e. administrators, students, faculty and parents) contributed to political changes, the effect of students and parents was considered of particular significance in this sense. Within this framework, the teachers' political orientation varied in relation to whether parents were considered supportive (e.g. 'They listen and want to help') or unsupportive (e.g. 'Many are unreasonable . . . irrational').

The politics of being a teacher, in part, grow out of the problematic nature of relations with students and parents. A political perspective is developed to *influence* students and parents on substantive issues and to *protect* the teacher from student and parental criticism. Clearly, many dimensions of the teachers' political perspective *vis-à-vis* students and parents grow out of tensions surrounding classroom instruction, student discipline, extracurricular involvements of teachers and teachers' personal-life matters. In the following section, these issues are described in terms of the teachers' political orientation.

Instruction

Influence In terms of influencing students in the area of instruction, teachers noted the importance of developing and maintaining the 'appropriate' social and psychological distance between themselves and students. For example, through trial and error, teachers learned to make emotional and behavioural adjustments that allowed them to remain 'in touch' with the individual needs of students: 'Each kid is a little different . . . requires a different approach. After a while you learn to handle every situation.'

Generally, teachers described a diplomatic political approach, in which they emphasized friendliness ('If we are not on a friendly basis, we're not going to have anything to do with each other') and empathy ('If you're an empathetic person, you're going to have patience and understanding because you deal with fragile minds . . . These are people for whom you may be the only source of caring'). The importance of introspection to making the necessary interpersonal adjustments was stressed: 'You need to understand yourself . . . watch yourself very carefully to be in touch with the cues kids give off or you won't develop politically.' Tactfulness and timeliness were also factors teachers described in relation to influencing effectively students' instructional behaviour: 'All students are unique, idiosyncratic – you need to know when to come on and back off . . . increase and reduce the pressure without offending.' The data suggest that a diplomatic approach enhanced teachers' 'reputations' and status with students: 'I want to have a good reputation as a teacher. It's important to me to be well thought of by students . . . I put up everything – art work, projects. I even put up D and F work.'

Although diplomatic tactics were the most salient means of influencing students on instructional matters, teachers also benefited from the use of rational methods. For example, teachers relied on instructional goal statements that were clearly articulated and periodically reiterated, as well as detailed and defensible instructional rationales. Teachers also disclosed that the 'selective' but limited use of coercion, especially threats, was important to their political repertoires:

> I've got 35 in a classroom and there's a lot of bull. I say to them
> I'm still the boss and this is my show and that means that you're

> going to do it my way. I don't like to nourish an image that is
> stern and dictatorial ... that keeps everything at a distance ...
> but sometimes, ya know, that's what's needed.

Overall, it was apparent that teachers struggled to project a respectable image and to create a reputation that students would view as authoritative: 'They need to know that I am the teacher.' In so doing, it was evident that they tried to balance control-related considerations with a need to remain sensitive to and accessible to students who had instruction-related problems. This was especially important because the factors associated with such problems (e.g. drug abuse, non-supportive parents) were often not easily discernible within the day-to-day context of the classroom.

In addition to the factors already discussed, several other considerations contributed to the development of the teachers' diplomatic political orientation towards students. Students themselves often directly solicited the support (e.g. advice, recognition of need) of teachers. This, in turn, increased the teachers' willingness to maintain an approachable and accessible stance:

> The student comes to me and is uncertain as to whether they can
> do the work ... they take the initiative to point out their
> interests and weaknesses and ask you to respond in some way to
> help them because they want to be successful in your class.

Many students were also seen as quite sensitive and even 'fragile' ('Their egos are so fragile at this age ... they are so easily embarrassed'), thus provoking a need in teachers to respond. Teachers reported that an open diplomatic style permitted them to 'keep in touch' with students and to make timely adjustments in their approach: 'You need to listen to kids, to their points of view ... to know when to joke, when to use sarcasm, those kinds of things ... pick up on their feelings and how they're responding to you.'

An open diplomatic style was associated with the responsibility to motivate students, many of whom were otherwise indifferent or recalcitrant: 'You have to have a rapport with students to know what teaching strategies work ... see how they're reacting ... when to increase the pressure, when to change what you're doing.' Teachers believed that most students did not value academic work; diplomatic means were required to 'persuade' students to take their work seriously: 'Time is spent presenting reasons ... they need to know why they're doing this or that work.' This was particularly true because few students realized the relevance of academic work to their future:

> So often they can't see the relevance of what they're learning to
> their future lives. You try to make them aware of alternatives ...
> convince them that they're preparing for the future ... get them
> to think about what they are passing up, what they are casting
> aside.

A few teachers, most of whom were affiliated with the special education programme, described their influence roles in terms of the interventions they made on behalf of students who were in conflict with regular students and regular classroom teachers: 'You're always on guard for what other people say about your students ... My students receive a lot of derogatory comments.'

Protection According to the study data, teachers developed a protective political stance towards students primarily because of their vulnerability to pressure in three instructional areas: grades, homework and the discussion of controversial topics. Teachers explained that they were 'compelled' to compromise educational standards, the principles of sound instruction, as well as their 'professional judgement'. As a result, teachers made accommodations that were defined as conservative ('low risk', 'cautious', 'guarded'): 'You tiptoe and tread lightly ... you maintain a lot of control to do things that are not offensive to students.' Such an approach, teachers pointed out, helped to reduce criticism from students and their parents.

With regard to grading and homework, teachers worked to protect themselves from students who, with the support of their parents, challenged decisions and actions. Students and parents were accused of using intimidating tactics (e.g. complaining to school administrators) to obtain 'favoured treatment'. Parental attempts to coerce teachers to change grades and reduce the amount of homework were seen as 'unfair', 'unethical' and 'irrational'. Such demands were defined by teachers as 'hurting the student in the long run'. To reduce their vulnerability, teachers 'documented all grades', notified parents and other relevant individuals (e.g. school counsellors) of student progress (or lack thereof), held parent conferences, and offered to support the student's effort to improve. The data strongly argue that failure to engage in appropriate protective political actions was tightly linked to increased teacher acquiescence to parents: 'I told her [the parent] that he hadn't turned in his homework and hadn't passed his tests. The counsellor pointed out that we should have let her know sooner ... I was in a box.'

Although political actions such as those identified above were useful in protecting teachers, the school principal's support of the teachers' authority to determine grades (for classes and individual students) was considered crucial to the teachers' response to parents. A highly respected science teacher discussed the problem of 'curving' grades for classes dominated by minority students:

> You definitely get the feeling that you will get the ax ... If kids
> fail they [administrators] say you're not a good teacher ... To
> please the parents ... you're supposed to pass the kids regardless
> of whether they're willing to work or not. Some teachers will
> adjust the grading curve. I have been labelled a 'trouble maker'
> because I refused.

Another described the problem in terms of individual students:

> It has been my experience that parents have argued that their
> child deserves special treatment and that I should be
> sympathetic to their particular problems and I could make
> exceptions ... or the parents would make trouble for me ... I
> knew that if I didn't satisfy the parent, somebody above me
> would.

From the teachers' standpoint, parents of gifted students seemed to be the most
unreasonable and aggressive when faced with problems:

> The kids have to be reevaluated every two years. If they are not
> doing what they need to be doing, then the test scores are going
> to go down. You're dealing with all kinds of parents who think
> their children are potential geniuses. They can become very
> angry and they can be very threatening.

The teachers' belief that administrators held them unduly responsible for the
problems of students ('It's your fault if the kid flunks') seemed to increase their
acquiescence to student and parental pressure. Therefore, teachers sometimes
changed grades for individual students and 'curved' grades for entire classes
of students. Those who taught 'fundamental' students (e.g. slow learners)
experienced greater pressure, particularly from administrators, partly because
of the disproportionate number of black students in these classes. Although
some, especially science teachers, adamantly refused to compromise themselves
(i.e. to change grades or reduce homework requirements), even these teachers
stated that such resistance was politically unwise: 'You become vulnerable to
criticism ... attack ... [and] lose in the end.'

In addition to the grading problem, fine arts teachers described other
subject-related issues from which 'power plays' with parents emerged. First, the
teachers' political sensitivities were linked to demands for 'favoured' treatment
of students in music ('In performing groups, the chair they sit in, who is playing
second violin, is important') and art ('You have to think about whose work you'll
display'). Second, the problematic nature of financial support further affected
the teachers' political stance. The data suggest that the lower status of fine arts
programmes (as compared with academic programmes) meant that funding from
year to year was uncertain. This, and the perception that a programme was
judged by the community primarily in terms of 'shows' and 'performances', made
teachers feel especially vulnerable. An art teacher remarked:

> You have to show what you're doing in the classroom ... I will
> do what I need to do to move my programme forward. I'm so
> dependent on money! Everything we do goes up in the hall ... I
> do it in the community ... to get high visibility ... The
> community at large likes to think that they are supporting a
> good programme.

As a result, for some teachers, political actions designed to create and maintain student and programme 'visibility' were essential to the acquisition of material and symbolic support.

Athletic coaches, too, were subjected to pressures from some parents, in this case, to 'play a kid'. Interestingly, however, coaches, as compared with the classroom teacher, did not seem to feel as intimidated by such pressures. Perhaps the pressure to win games helped modify the impact of parental demands.

Finally, it was apparent that teachers employed a protective political stance to deal with controversial topics and value disparities that 'crop[ped] up' in their classes. Interestingly, teachers claimed that such topics were directly relevant to course content and, for the most part, stemmed from questions initiated by students. Teachers who had worked at other high schools indicated that what was defined as 'controversial' varied somewhat from one situation to another: 'In a small town where I worked you didn't criticize what was happening at the mill.' Nevertheless, teachers reported that they were especially vulnerable to criticism that stemmed from class discussions of religion, politics, sex (e.g. dating, pregnancy, abortion) and evolution. Discussions of local business practices and community events had also provoked criticism: 'Parents will complain to the principal ... the superintendent ... One parent marched into my classroom ... asked me if I taught evolution.'

In the teachers' view, problems were exacerbated because the content of a teacher's remarks was often distorted by students. Although discussion and actions connected with basic values (e.g. respect, responsibility, cooperation) were pursued openly and aggressively, controversial issues, which usually 'cropped up' in class as a result of student-initiated questions (related to abortion, sex, religion and drug use), were approached 'carefully', conservatively and pragmatically.

In light of the probability of distortion and the 'irrational' (emotional and unproductive) nature of many confrontations with parents ('People react very strongly to little things'), most teachers used materials and planned lessons in ways that would reduce their vulnerability. Some teachers avoided discussions of potentially controversial subjects altogether: 'My job could be jeopardized for expressing the truth.' Others developed diplomatic strategies in class (e.g. humour, non-verbal) and out of class to ensure that important value issues would not be avoided entirely. one teacher explained:

> When I send permission slips home for novels the kids are going
> to read – I teach *Chocolate War* and *One Flew Over the Cuckoo's
> Nest* but also I teach *Hamlet* and *Macbeth* and the *Wife of
> Bath* ... I do not tell the parents that some of these novels are
> controversial ... I couch them between these heavy-duty things
> like *Hamlet* and *Macbeth*, hoping that parents will go ahead and
> approve everything on the list.

For the most part, however, being political, in a diplomatic sense, meant being 'objective'. In class, teachers presented what they believed to be the major perspectives on an issue: 'I want to present all the theories on the origin of life ... and say now these are the facts, you examine it ... rather than being arbitrary and authoritarian.' Teachers reported that they identified their position on an issue ('The kids are entitled to know your opinion'), especially when asked to do so. In many instances, teachers explained that the kind of structure demanded by 'political realities' affected negatively the freedom, spontaneity and creativity necessary to explore the 'most exciting and meaningful questions' associated with a topic. Teachers pointed out that to minimize problems with students and parents, critical examination of legitimate academic topics (e.g. capitalism versus communism) was at times avoided.

On the positive side, it was evident that the teachers' political sensitivity to parents stimulated 'reflection' on what was done in class. Teachers claimed that a reflective orientation reduced the probability of inadvertently demeaning students and parents ('You can avoid hurt feelings') and served to build better working relationships. It should be mentioned that despite the teachers' diplomatic approach, the value problem was not infrequently viewed as a no-win situation: 'You're between a rock and a hard place ... If you teach one concept over and above another you're going to get it from the other end and vice versa.'

On the whole, being political in terms of values meant 'analysing the morality of the situation' and making the necessary adjustments for survival. Such adjustments, the data suggest, varied somewhat from school to school (most of the teachers studied had worked in other schools) and from class to class: 'With sharp kids you can talk more liberally ... they can weigh things out. With basic classes you are very conservative.'

Discipline

Influence Teachers reported a number of factors that accounted for their influence orientation towards students in the area of discipline. School principal support was particularly important in this regard: 'If I know he's [the principal] behind me ... I will be more honest, straightforward ... my involvement with discipline changes with the level of support.' Students' attempts to manipulate teachers were also seen as contributing to the teachers' political approach: 'I have to be careful ... I may be playing into Jason's hands ... he wants to be suspended.' Special difficulties related to the behaviour of lower level students were described as well: 'They get bored ... want to play around.'

Although factors such as those referred to above increased the teachers' motivation to control students, other factors seemed to temper inclinations along these lines. Once again, the perceived fragile nature of students was salient: 'You don't discipline them in class ... in front of others ... their egos are fragile ... they're easily embarrassed by things.... You can go overboard.'

Teachers disclosed that their efforts to discipline students were also constrained by the fact that school administrators occasionally punished students 'too severely' for infractions of discipline: 'Sometimes students are unfairly victimized by administrative sanctions ... you don't want to get the kids in more trouble than they deserve.'

Moreover, the teachers' general stance toward students – based on sensitivity and openness – was associated with greater understanding of the complex nature of student discipline problems. This served to increase the teachers' supportive posture towards students: 'You become a listening ear ... take on a problem-solving role ... There are serious problems behind discipline; they [students] may have no one else to turn to.' Frequently, this meant that teachers spent extra time with students outside of class. In the event of serious problems, being political for some teachers was described as baby-sitting: 'Sometimes I hold their hand until the juvenile authorities come.'

Paradoxically, an empathetic political stance towards discipline required teachers to depersonalize relationships with students in varying degrees: 'To deal with some of their (the students'] problems you learn to take things less personally ... to protect yourself emotionally.' As with instruction, teachers believed that political interactions were motivated by the need to persuade students of the relevance of their school behaviour to the future: 'They don't see how what they're doing in school is relevant to their futures.'

Finally, it should be mentioned that certain teachers gained an 'added edge'; they derived additional 'authority' over students from other school-related roles:

> Being a coach the students sort of look up to you as they would
> an administrator. Kids look to coaches as more authoritative
> than the normal teacher. Kids will recognize and associate more
> with a coach ... It's easier to earn respect ... and tell kids what
> you expect ... get follow through from the kids.

Protection A number of factors were related to the development of a protective diplomatic orientation towards students whose behaviour was problematic. Teachers feared parental criticism and reprisals for initiating disciplinary actions: 'I don't want to do anything to cause parents to jump down my throat, call me a liar.' Among other things, teachers were blamed for negative favouritism ('picking on the child'), unreasonable punishment (paddling, suspensions), improper supervision ('There would not be a problem if you were doing your job'), and false accusations ('They think their child can do no wrong'). The problem of parental reactions was exacerbated if students proved to be particularly vindictive: 'They [the parents] cussed me out for everything they could think of ... He was sitting there in the corner smiling, looking at me.'

When administrative support was inconsistent, teachers seemed to become more tentative and 'cautious' in their approach to discipline: 'Uncertainty means that anything could happen and often did ... You can't predict the result.' In addition, teachers reported that school administrators encouraged teachers to handle their own discipline problems: 'You are made to feel there is something wrong with you if you need assistance from the front office.' The need to earn the students' respect and teacher's self-pride ('I don't want to go to anyone else to try to deal with this problem. There is a certain sense of pride in handling it myself'), as well as racial considerations ('There are always racial overtones here when a black student is the problem'), also seemed to increase teachers' protective tendencies.

To reduce their vulnerability, teachers sometimes ignored problems identified with individual students; more commonly they used conservative discipline strategies. For instance, teachers attempted to forestall discipline problems by clarifying, justifying and periodically reinforcing their expectations regarding classroom behaviour. Teachers also refrained from public disciplinary actions to avoid student embarrassment.

When confronted with problems, teachers conformed meticulously to written procedures: 'Fortunately, I followed the procedure and had a witness and all that.' Careful documentation of problems was also described: 'The teacher won't get far on her own veracity ... it will be interpreted as your fault. . . . You keep a log ... use pink slips.' To warrant certain actions, teachers solicited the timely assistance of other individuals (e.g. school counsellors), especially if a problem had the potential of 'mushrooming beyond control'.

Although severe discipline problems were experienced as stressful, the data indicate that 'borderline' problems were also potentially troublesome over the long run: 'There's that kid who talks constantly ... makes that little smart comment ... disrupts everybody else. This could happen every day.' Because no explicit norms governed such problems, they were viewed as politically quite difficult: 'They [administrators] have no clear guidelines for these students ... there's no black and white.'

Extracurricular Involvement and Visibility

Influence Teachers reported that providing leadership in the area of extracurricular activities helped to expand their influence with students. This was particularly true when the roles they assumed were highly visible and when students benefited directly:

> I'm in charge of graduation at the end of every year. When I get
> up in front of those seniors and they give me their attention ...
> the juniors, freshmen, and sophomores will see me too, and I'm
> sure that it's passed around through word of mouth that
> Mr _____ says this and says that ... it's another case of my
> gaining respect.

Teachers sponsored clubs, chaperoned events, attended evening and weekend activities, worked on the school newspaper, and volunteered for committee work. Extracurricular activities in which teachers did not assume a leadership role (e.g. chaperoning and attending school events) also produced some political payoffs: 'Anything you do that students are interested in can earn you respect . . . if they like you too, there's nothing better than that.'

On a more concrete level, teachers claimed that extra involvement provided opportunities for influence not available in the classroom. Alternative settings permitted increased frequency of interaction as well as more meaningful interaction as teachers and students assumed different roles: 'There's greater openness . . . communication in other situations, the opportunity for positive influence on kids is tremendous.' Teachers explained that their extra involvement had the effect of enhancing expectations and values related to 'helping others', 'hard work' and 'responsibility'.

Protection At the same time, extracurricular teacher involvement was related to increased vulnerability to criticism from students, as well as from parents and administrators who intervened on behalf of students. In effect, teachers claimed that increased involvement with students was associated with the increased potential for conflict – 'things that provoked adverse reactions in others'.

> If you do anything outside of your basic teaching job you are increasing your vulnerability . . . Coaching is an admirable job . . . but so many things can happen . . . a kid drops dead on the field from running too many laps . . . somebody gets his feelings hurt because he didn't start and parents go to the principal.

According to teachers, the problematic nature of involvement in extracurricular activities increased, in part, because of the high potential for information distortion in the school:

> I had a situation when I was in charge of the Key Club . . . Some kids had left the club meeting . . . picked up beer and liquor . . . and went to the graveyard and sat around drinking and the cops came up and took them all to jail . . . Some parents said that the last I knew, my kid was on the way to a meeting that was supposed to be run by Mr _____ . . . I just don't know what they do at the Key Club . . . I don't know if maybe Mr _____ got them that beer.

Problems related to discipline, teachers disclosed, were exacerbated when students 'lie[d] to their parents to avoid punishment'.

For protection, some teachers avoided additional involvements; others attempted to reduce their vulnerability to students and parents by creating strict guidelines and rules for student participation in extracurricular activities:

> If you can't come up with a system to cover yourself . . . you get out. Everything hinges on how people perceive what you are

> doing with students ... and whether they are going to hold you
> to blame for problems and accidents. I have yet to find a safe
> way to protect myself ... You don't always even get the chance
> to explain yourself.

Some teachers meticulously informed parents of activities and, when necessary, solicited their consent.

Personal Factors

Influence Ironically, teachers reported that conformity to conservative norms – both formal and informal – regarding personal demeanour (e.g. dress, hairstyle) and adherence to conventional values (e.g. social responsibility and respect for authority) increased their acceptance as role models among students. Furthermore, teachers believed that students were impressed when teachers' verbal communication and behaviour were consistent: 'Home life, TV, ... kids don't learn respect for what adults say.... There's too much inconsistency ... they get confused, learn to distrust everybody.' In effect, the special status available to teachers who were perceived as 'role models' created additional opportunities for day-to-day influence.

Several teachers disclosed that to become an acceptable model, they were required to manufacture an image: 'You suppress your political views ... I am an atheist but I go to church.' Most teachers, however, indicated that although they were more 'liberal' as beginning teachers, over the years they had gradually internalized conventional values: 'If you don't accept these expectations personally, your life will be miserable.'

Among other things, being a 'positive role model' meant having additional opportunities to provide help to students ('A listening ear ... to be a problem solver') confronted with personal (e.g. drug abuse, pregnancy) as well as school-related problems. Consequently, teachers who cultivated their status as role models tended to present themselves as friendly, accessible and sensitive to student needs:

> The friendlier you are, the more they like you, the more you can
> help them out. Like, if a kid has family problems, you want to be
> there for him. The kid has problems drinking or there's a
> girlfriend ... There could be all kinds of stuff going on.

Protection Personal considerations – parental expectations and fear of parents – contributed to teachers' feelings of vulnerability and the development of a conservative approach to students and parents. Many, particularly those who lived in the community in which they taught, compared being a teacher to 'living in a fishbowl'. About half of the teachers studied resented the 'constant scrutiny' and 'watchful eye' of the community:

> College does absolutely nothing to prepare you for the kind of
> public figure you are going to end up being. The community has
> a stereotype of teachers ... they must act within certain boun-
> daries of behaviour ... Politically, you have to define the way
> you come across to people within the constraints of their
> stereotypes ... Let's say I was an atheist, this is something I
> could not go around and advertise.

Consequently, teachers were quite selective about involvements in the community; for example, involvement in social activities – forms of entertainment
(e.g. drinking, dancing) and participation in events and clubs – was pursued in
such a way as to minimize risks:

> You have to make concessions in your public exposure outside of
> school insofar as the kind of company you are seen with, the
> kind of activities you are involved with ... Whether or not you
> feel that its right or wrong, you find yourself drinking in bars
> across town ... or going out of town ... Since you are in direct
> contact with kids, parents are always suspicious that you are
> modelling the wrong values ... You have to be very careful ...
> hold a lot inside.

Some indicated that they attended church and participated in community
activities because of community expectations: 'You have to play the middle of
the road ... just as a politician would, as a preacher would.' A couple of teachers
explained that since they were unmarried, they lived with mates outside of the
town in which they worked: 'I would probably get fired if anyone knew.' Teachers
reported suppressing their views regarding local politics, as well as information
about their personal and professional selves. The possibility of communication
distortion was again a prominent theme in this dimension of the data:

> You don't tell them your personal problems, faculty problems or
> problems with administration. The potential for people to
> misunderstand is great ... Information is spread and your
> problems are compounded ... It's all political because it's part of
> how you're perceived.

Indeed, the politics of conformity (at least overt compliance) regarding the
teachers, personal lives seemed to be more acute for those who taught in small
towns. Nevertheless, teachers who had worked in suburban and other urban
areas reported that they were by no means insensitive to the politics surrounding their personal lives. The data point out that anonymity and privacy were not
easily achieved by such teachers.

For most teachers, the expectations of parents were seen as compelling: 'It's
more than making concessions, you're gonna be miserable if you don't believe in
what you're doing ... the concessions you have to make.' For some, however,

being political meant developing a conservative facade; they complied overtly with community expectations and learned to hide their true selves. The data suggest that personal expression was sacrificed to enhance one's professional reputation, to achieve respect and prestige with parents. Although some teachers deeply resented the personal compromises they were required to make, most, after years of experience, were able to acclimatize themselves:

> There is a power structure and if you don't meet that power
> structure they will either get rid of you or you'll be on the
> negative side and you will get negative reinforcement. . . . I am a
> Morman. It hasn't been difficult for me as a person to fit within
> those structures.

Principal Support

Overall, the data suggest that the willingness and ability of principals to support ('backing up') teachers in confrontations with parents increased the probability of having rational and productive interactions. Supportive principals, for example, encouraged teachers 'to talk with the parent . . . and not only when there were problems'. Politically, principal support was seen to enhance teachers' discretion, authority and ability to influence parents.

With principal support, teachers reported that they were more 'honest' and 'straightforward'. Hence, meetings, conferences and telephone conversations with parents tended to produce better communication, i.e. 'an understanding of a student's problems . . . on both sides'. Indeed, the data suggest that there was less suspicion and defensiveness, greater consensus regarding decisions and goals, and an inclination on the parents' part to 'cooperate with the school . . . for the child's sake'. Teachers indicated that some principals 'went out into the community . . . visited homes of students with problems' and attempted to solicit parental support. Actions of this nature were related to a positive disposition in parents:

> Parents have more understanding . . . they are less defensive . . .
> more supportive . . . Community involvement is a tremendous PR
> tool . . . it helps parents understand what I'm trying to do in the
> classroom.

In essence, the data argue that principal support for teachers caused parents to respond more positively and rationally to the school and its expectations. Teachers were able to make decisions and pursue goals compatible with professional ethics and school standards: 'I was more demanding . . . that's not the case when [parents] want A's and B's for no effort at all.' In general, principals who displayed a strong interest in teacher–parent relations were considered instrumental in reducing obstacles to communication and cooperation.

Conversely, lack of support from principals appeared to be a prominent factor that negatively influenced the teachers' political orientation to parents. The unwillingness of principals to 'stand behind' teachers in confrontations with parents regarding the discipline and instruction of students tended to make teachers overly cautious, defensive and acquiescent. (Few instances of teacher aggression were noted in the data.) This, in turn, was viewed as making interactions with parents 'artificial' and 'non-productive'.

Teachers reported that dealing productively with irrational or irate parents was impossible if such parents perceived principals as unsupportive of teachers: 'These parents don't bother with the teacher if they know the principal can be manipulated around to their side.' With unsupportive principals, it was politically feasible for teachers to avoid contact with parents to protect themselves from unwarranted criticism and abuse: 'I was afraid to talk with parents.' When compelled to communicate with 'angry' parents, teachers suggested that lack of support limited chances that their decisions would be treated seriously. Principals were occasionally viewed as weak or incompetent by the community. In these cases, teachers explained, the parents were more distrusting and suspicious, and generally less cooperative.

SUMMARY AND CONCLUSION

In this chapter we examined teachers' micropolitical relationships with students and parents. We argued that the micropolitics of being a teacher result, in part, from teachers' sense of vulnerability to students and their parents, particularly in such areas as classroom instruction, student discipline, extracurricular involvements and personal-life matters. In each of these problematic areas of work, teachers construct a political orientation that permits protection from and influence with students and parents. This chapter demonstrates that principal support strongly affects teachers' general sense of vulnerability and whether they emphasize the politics of influence or protection.

Perhaps the most difficult challenge facing schools as they move to restructure and share power is bringing their non-professional constituencies into the process of shared governance. Many more studies are needed that describe the complex micropolitical interactions among student, parent and teacher subcultures in and out of schools. Administrator–teacher–parent–student interactions have never been easy, but these interactions promise to become more numerous in restructured schools. In the following chapter we present data from another micropolitical arena that has received little attention from researchers – the micropolitical interactions that occur among teachers themselves.

Chapter 3

Political Interactions Among Teachers
Implications for the Sociocultural Context of the School

> I thought that doing a good job in the classroom was all I
> needed to do ... I was very surprised after a couple of years to
> learn that I did not have the support of other teachers ... There
> are all these complex considerations ... you develop a deep
> awareness of and behave differently as a result. For me this
> mostly meant establishing good relations just for support,
> someone to talk to, to share ideas with, to get advice from ... for
> sheer survival.
>
> (A Teacher)

Too often, the term 'teacher empowerment' is used as if teachers are somehow a homogeneous and monolithic group who share a common set of values, goals and aspirations. Although there are, perhaps, some general professional cultural norms that most teachers would subscribe to, there are also many differences among teachers with regard to teaching philosophies, personal goals and values, and political interests. This creates in most schools a complex set of micropolitical interactions among teachers. In this chapter, we see how variations in principals' leadership style affect micropolitical interactions among teachers. Of special interest is how the authoritarian and adversarial styles negatively affect micropolitical relationships among teachers.

The research discussed in this chapter examines the politics of the teacher–teacher relationship, from the teachers' perspective. Unstructured and semistructured interviews and observations were employed to gather data from teachers in an urban high school in the southeastern United States. This chapter focuses on how teachers define and interpret significant aspects of the politics of their interactions with other faculty. Descriptive categories and concepts constructed directly from the data are presented. (See Appendix for a description of the study discussed here.)

Only a handful of qualitative studies have reported data (usually limited to a few sentences) that have relevance to understanding political aspects of interpersonal political action among teachers. For example, Lortie (1975), in a comprehensive study of teachers in Massachusetts and Florida, discovered the importance of norms related to friendliness, sociability and support (e.g.

assistance to others) among teachers. Becker's study (Becker, 1980) of Chicago public school teachers uncovered the significance of norms linked to non-interference (in another's classroom) and control (of students) in accounting for the informal status and prestige of teachers. McPherson (1972), in an examination of collegial relationships in one elementary school in Massachusetts, describes the salience of norms associated with faculty loyalty and solidarity (against parents), as well as support (cathartic, therapeutic) and non-interference. Cusick's study (Cusick, 1983) of three high schools in the Detroit area indicates that teachers worked to build support (e.g. cultivated sponsors among faculty) in pursuit of personal curricular and extracurricular interests.

RESULTS

The study discussed in this chapter uncovered both positive and negative forms of political interaction among teachers. Negative political transactions were linked to the teachers' use of aggressive and manipulative tactics, usually to attain individual (self-centred) ends at the expense of others. This mode of interaction was interpreted as contributing to the development of *dissociative* (fragmented) sociocultural patterns.

In contrast, positive political transactions were linked to the use of diplomatic strategies and mutually beneficial outcomes. Here, individual ends were also seen as important; however, there was a conscious concern with presenting oneself in ways that would lead to the development of reciprocal relationships characterized by mutual (two-way) assistance and support. This mode of interaction contributed to the development of *associative* sociocultural patterns. In the school studied, both patterns of micropolitical action seemed to emanate from tensions surrounding core values and school contextual issues.

Teachers reported that the process of developing political awareness was experienced as traumatic: 'I was burned ... took a long time to recover.' Interestingly, the evolution of a political perspective in teachers, particularly a 'diplomatic' orientation (the dominant orientation in the research site), was linked to increased empathy, tolerance and patience:

> You learn to accept differences in personality ... ambitions ...
> and goals. You recondition yourself, learn to pick up on people's
> problems, concerns ... establish rapport. You try to get your
> communication going for the good of the whole.

The approach (style, demeanour) employed in interactions with others was considered critical: 'Most of us are pretty fragile. We don't like arrogance ... browbeating ... we want to be treated with respect.' For these and other reasons, teachers learned to 'play the game ... get along' with other faculty in order to survive in the workplace.

Broadly speaking, formal organizational factors (e.g. time constraints that determined frequency of political interaction) and informal sociocultural factors (e.g. administrator values, teacher beliefs, parental expectations) appeared to influence the development of the teachers' perspective:

> There are many reasons why you become political ... For example, you quickly learn that you are fair game ... Students, parents, administrators will be quick to criticize you for the smallest off-the-wall things. You make adjustments, learn to protect yourself, you're cautious about what you say and to whom ... You become more calculating ... plan your moves and learn to anticipate consequences.

The Impact of Principals and Department Chairpersons

Though several factors seemed to influence the character of political interaction among teachers, the orientation of school principals and department chairpersons was especially salient in the present data. Teachers had worked with four principals at the high school during the 10 years preceding the study. Ineffective leadership (as defined by teachers) at either the school or department level appeared to provoke negative political interactions and consequences. Effective leadership promoted positive political interactions and consequences among teachers:

> The principal influences everything ... It's more than how I relate to teachers ... it affects everything across the board: motivation, morale, feelings, relations with students ... parents ... how you relate to kids ... Effective principals are ones who make a positive climate ... An ineffective person can destroy everything.

For instance, principals who practiced favouritism towards 'selected' teachers precipitated feelings of anger, jealousy, suspicion and futility among the faculty. Competition among teachers (e.g. for resources, status, recognition), ingratiation (e.g. brown-nosing), avoidance, and sabotage of 'chosen cohorts', created further splits in the faculty; cliques formed around in-group and out-group alliances. Some teachers retreated to the classroom.

Other dimensions of school-based leadership also appeared to affect faculty political interaction adversely. The data demonstrate that ambiguous organizational goals, inconsistency in policy and rule enforcement, and non-support of teachers, in confrontations with students and parents, for example, resulted in anger, confusion, uncertainty, impotence and reduced work motivation on the part of teachers. Such leadership factors were viewed as negatively influencing communication ('We only talked with trusted colleagues', 'There was constant bitching'), support ('You isolate yourself ... It's every man for himself') and friendliness within the teachers' group. Overall, such outcomes increased the probability of unproductive political interaction and conflict.

In contrast, equitableness (non-favouritism), clear goals, viable goal-setting processes and rational (analytical) approaches to problem-solving – characteristics that teachers associated with effective school principals – were perceived as enhancing faculty political interaction. To illustrate, equitable treatment of teachers helped reduce informal status differences among teachers ('We're all important') and increased the importance of identification with the school as a whole ('We have a feeling of responsibility to others').

Friendliness on the part of principals was seen as promoting friendly interactions among teachers. By initiating luncheons and parties for faculty, the principal facilitated open relations characterized by more authentic interactions among faculty. Teachers explained that the benefit of friendly and open relations 'spilled over' into their political interactions. Similarly, recognition and praise of individuals and groups enhanced esteem, camaraderie and morale ('We are all built up') – factors that were interpreted as increasing solidarity among faculty.

Clearly, the research data suggest that the different orientations of school principals had different effects on the teachers' political demeanour. Principals viewed as effective by teachers seemed to enhance positive interpersonal transactions and the development of associative patterns; increased cohesion associated with increased communication, trust, respect, support and collaboration were evident. Teachers noted that they were more diplomatic in their interactions with one another as a result. Obversely, principals who were defined as ineffective seemed to diminish the quality of interpersonal political processes and contributed to the development of dissociative patterns; decreased cohesion, reflected in distrust, suspicion, non-support and poor communication, was apparent. Teachers indicated that they engaged in what were considered negative forms of political behaviour with other faculty (e.g. confrontation, passive-aggressiveness, ingratiation, acquiescence).

The orientation of department chairpersons also appeared to have an important influence on politics among teachers. This was true despite the fact that in the research site such individuals had limited responsibility and authority for curriculum development and teacher evaluation. Nevertheless, responsibility for scheduling and room assignments, coupled with the general status and symbolic nature of the position, was sufficient to influence political transactions among teachers:

> The department head has a lot to do with working relations in the department ... Ours has set a cooperative tone ... We help each other out ... lesson plans, handouts, readings, films, ideas ... You never ask anything in return when you help others but you know it will be reciprocated.

Department chairpersons who were perceived as equitable ('Schedules are made rationally'), supportive ('She's very sensitive to your problem'), friendly and personable ('We can talk . . . laugh') and facilitative ('You can see she wants us to work with each other') encouraged diplomatic transactions. Among other things, increased cohesion seemed to be linked to increases in support (e.g. sharing materials, cooperative problem-solving), socializing and trust – factors related to positive political interactions and associative patterns:

> If the department chairman isn't fair, objective . . . it will affect
> your resources . . . your teaching load . . . your reputation (they
> will give you credit for the messes . . . the problems) . . . They can
> affect the whole teaching environment. All this makes a
> difference in your politics . . . how you relate to other teachers,
> whether you are supportive or don't give a damn.

In contrast, department heads who were viewed as inequitable ('He made sure his buddies got the better courses'), non-supportive ('. . . was gossiped about'), unfriendly ('He himself is aloof . . . no attempt to encourage cordial relations') and non-facilitative ('Never did Mr _____ try to bring us together') negatively affected morale, support and communication within the faculty. Negative (dissociative) forms of political action (e.g. confrontation, ingratiation) resulted in negative consequences for intrafaculty relations.

Protection and Influence: Two Themes

A preponderance of data implies that teachers develop an acute sensitivity to both positive (e.g. praise) and negative (e.g. punishment) forms of control and manipulation by others. As indicated in an earlier chapter, teachers believed that they worked in a 'fishbowl'; their personal and professional lives were continuously subject to scrutiny and distortion in the school and in the community. In their view, 'distortion of the facts' was related to a diversity of perspectives (e.g. values, goals, beliefs) and a reliance on perceptual ('soft') data obtained indirectly (usually 'through the grapevine').

Therefore, with regard to one another, teachers learned to tailor their political actions to reflect *protectionistic* and *influence* concerns. Protectionistic actions are designed to avoid and/or ameliorate the impact of the threatening behaviour of others, e.g. criticism, gossip, rejection and sabotage. At times, threatening behaviours (e.g. gossip) were perceived as aggressive. Within the framework of the present database, protectionistic actions are considered reactive.

> Being political is watching what you say and do . . . being careful
> about criticism. If you say 'that person is an absolute fool and
> can't teach' . . . it gets back to them. You have alienated them . . .
> They will sabotage you. They could be in a position to really
> screw things up for you.

Influence responses, on the other hand, were constructed to persuade, support and facilitate other teachers. This category of responses is considered proactive. The objective was to build reciprocation:

> Politics mean being quiet, some of it is listening, some of it is
> biting your tongue ... Well, for me in this position [gifted
> teacher] it means letting them [teachers] know I am not trying to
> encroach on their territory ... or threaten them. I am not in
> competition with them just because I dabble in several
> areas – art, mathematics. I want to use them as resources so I
> approach them very carefully.

Positive and Negative Interpersonal Politics

As noted, the data suggest that the processes, strategies and purposes of political transactions among teachers can be described as positive or negative; the terms 'associative' and 'dissociative' refer specifically to the consequences of intrafaculty politics and the impact of such politics on the sociocultural context of the school.

Positive interpersonal politics refers to work-related interactions that increase cohesion among faculty. Politically, giving support and controlling the expression of negative emotions were identified with this category. In general, tactics analysed in terms of positive politics were specifically defined as diplomatic. Negative interpersonal politics, in contrast, refers to actions that decrease cohesion in the school. Confrontation, passive-aggressiveness and ingratiation are prominent examples of this response set. Either type of political action was perceived to stem from protectionistic or influence concerns, but usually associative consequences are more closely related to the latter, and dissociative consequences to the former.

In general, the data indicate that positive political actions, and in particular 'diplomatic' strategies, were most prevalent among the teachers who worked at the school under investigation. The overriding consequence of interpersonal diplomacy was the development of a sociocultural context consistent with norms of reciprocation (Gouldner, 1966). In other words, the politics of diplomacy were consistent with the norms of equitable exchange and mutual benefit. Diplomatic actions, such as support among teachers, promoted networks of indebtedness and mutual assistance among faculty:

> Some faculty members will have more influence over
> administrators than other faculty members. As a music teacher
> it's important that I cultivate relationships with influential
> faculty ... Then, maybe sometimes they're more likely to say
> [to an administrator], 'well, why don't you do something for
> music' ... Being political has come to mean much more than the

> performance or the 'show' fine arts people worry about to
> impress others ... to get support.

In the teachers' view, diplomatic political interactions were defined as essential to the curricular and extracurricular work performance of teachers. In
reference to the quality of interaction, teachers believed, 'It's not a matter of
better or worse ... it's the difference between a working and non-working
situation'.

Positive Politics and Teacher Diplomacy

Diplomatic political transactions among the faculty were reported in terms of
a specific set of values, activities and actions that grew from protectionistic and
influence concerns and that served to build reciprocal networks among teachers.

Control of Self According to teachers, being diplomatic was related to limiting
the expression of negative emotions and aggressive forms of behaviour. Frequently, this meant 'biting your tongue ... and smiling', despite one's feelings.
Regardless of the issue, loss of control ('You don't lose your temper') and/or
aggressiveness usually resulted in serious damage to one's reputation. Given the
possibility of misunderstanding and negative distortion, managing one's reputation was not unproblematic. As a whole, teachers tended to avoid or withdraw
from those who failed to display composure in their interactions.

In attempting to manage themselves politically, most teachers conformed
to norms of conventional politeness. This, in the teachers' view, helped reduce
the deleterious effects generated by negative feelings and differences in values
and goals among teachers. Politeness norms were seen as enhancing rapport
among teachers and appeared to increase the stability, predictability and
longevity of working relationships among them: 'There are so many problems
that crop up. We can really make life miserable for each other'. In light of the
daily stresses that continuously threaten teacher–teacher relationships, it is
apparent that politeness was often negotiated with great difficulty. The phrases
'It's all in how you approach people' and 'We need to work at practising good
human relations' are revealing.

Friendliness In addition, teachers emphasized the politics of friendliness,
expressed in terms of smiling, touching, joking and small talk. A friendly
demeanour was also viewed as a way to reduce anxieties linked to individual differences. As a central aspect of diplomacy, friendliness seemed to increase the
probability of two-way interaction (bilateral influence), emphatic communication, support and consensus.

Support According to the data, support was central to diplomatic faculty interactions. Generally, support – its scope, intensity and frequency – was a more salient feature at the departmental level. As might be expected, support grew out of common interests and problems. It was a prominent theme within individual departments for roughly 70 per cent of the teachers studied. For others, often because of ineffective departmental leadership, supportive interactions and positive interpersonal political relationships were less common.

For teachers highly involved in activities in the school and in the community, the politics of diplomacy and the combined goals of protection, influence and reciprocation were significant. This was especially true for fine arts and special education teachers, who were 'forced' to develop informal support systems. Because their programmes were located outside of the regular curriculum, these teachers explained that they did not benefit from regular budgetary status. It appears that leadership responsibilities transacted in the complex dynamics of the school organization and the community made teachers acutely aware of differences in perspectives and the problematic nature of material, human and symbolic resources. In discussing positive forms of political interaction, teachers indicated the importance of 'getting along' and building mutually beneficial support networks with others.

Politically, to protect themselves from criticism and rejection and to reinforce conditions for continued influence and reciprocation, teachers engaged in several kinds of supportive activities.

Support referred to *sharing* materials for instructional purposes. In most cases this meant loaning handouts that could be used by a faculty member for instruction. At times, teachers loaned whole lesson units or 'all the materials covering a subject'. In this way the burden of teaching, especially outside of one's areas, was alleviated. In one case, for example, a teacher distributed a package of new instructional materials obtained at an educational conference.

Support was described in terms of *services* that teachers provided for other faculty. Here, the amount of time associated with a service was the critical factor. Spending time on behalf of another increased the recipient's degree of freedom and flexibility in a job largely controlled by strict constraints of time and place. Teachers 'covered' classes, detention hall, and bus and lunch duties for colleagues. Administering makeup tests was also cited in the data. Sometimes, the services of other teachers were requested because of their special status or skill. Coaches were often asked to 'talk to', 'counsel' or 'threaten' student athletes for misbehaviour or lack of motivation.

Praise/recognition was defined as a critical aspect of support and the politics of exchange and reciprocation. Teachers believed it was important to recognize colleagues for their successes and accomplishments (e.g. appointment to a state-level committee). Sometimes, this required attending activities (games, productions) sponsored by faculty members. As compared with the impact of other types of support, receiving praise/recognition appeared to enhance directly the prestige and reputation of the teacher. The politics of recognition allowed teachers to share in the successes of others. This, in turn, seemed to increase the level of integration among teachers.

Support meant *advising* other teachers about issues related to the instruction and control (discipline) of students. Advice on coping with school administrators and policy was also considered important. Typically, advice was solicited and given in a 'low-keyed' manner. It was important to be 'positive, not to criticize . . . raise the teacher's defenses . . . or go to the point . . . [that] what you say discredits a colleague'. Recommendations and solutions to problems were offered tactfully, in an effort to build reciprocal relationships.

Support also referred to giving *therapeutic* advice. In light of the daily stresses of working in the high school, teachers' feelings, needs and values were frequently the focus of attention. Teachers seemed to 'learn a lot about themselves' and to be able to enhance their self-esteem as a result of consultations with other teachers. Therapeutic support also served a cathartic function: 'Really, I just have to blow off steam now and then'.

Gratitude was cited as a significant aspect of support. This was particularly important, since teachers rarely received gratitude from students, parents or administrators for their work: 'You seldom get a "thank you" in this profession'. Therefore, within the social and cultural context of the school, demonstrating gratitude was important to diplomatic interactions.

Support was also linked to *empathy*. Many teachers felt alone, isolated and misunderstood by others. For example, differences between teachers and students (e.g. maturity, interests) created a need to be understood by others who shared similar perspectives. Although work-related problems were most significant in this regard, empathic support was also important to discussions of teachers' personal problems. Empathy linked teachers to other adults and created opportunities to express true feelings in a setting dominated by routine, rules and professional protocol. Interestingly, empathy helped teachers survive duties perceived as distasteful; such duties often required behaviours and dispositions inconsistent with key values and thus demeaned the professional and personal self of the teacher.

Negative Politics

Although the bulk of the data collected from teachers in the research setting was conceptualized in terms of positive interpersonal politics, ample data were available regarding some dimensions of negative political interactions among teachers. To reiterate, the latter were more closely associated with self-serving purposes and behaviour defined as offensive, e.g. ingratiation, confrontation and passive-aggressive political action. The data suggest that actions of this type tended to disrupt the school and resulted in reduced cohesion. Lower levels of trust, support, friendliness and morale, as well as increased conflict and alienation, were linked to negative political actions.

Although teachers viewed these types of actions as having adverse consequences, they believed that such actions were, at times, important for protection and/or influence purposes. This was particularly true in situations in which school principals were seen as ineffective. Specifically, in the context of the present data, negative political actions among teachers were promoted by the following.

- *Ingratiation*: 'sucking up to the committee chairman'
- *Flaunting*: 'She makes sure everybody knows what she's done'.
- *Spying*: 'There are ways of providing information to the administration ...'
- *Criticalness*: 'teachers who put you down to look good'
- *Aggressiveness*: 'They're belligerent and overbearing ...'
- *Lack of involvement*: 'There is little concern ... the paycheck is their goal'.
- *Self-centredness*: 'He will talk about himself ... no interest in anyone else'.
- *Non–supportiveness*: 'Some teachers aren't willing to help ...'
- *Incompetence*: 'can't control the kids or teach for that matter'
- *Aloofness*: 'You only associate with certain colleagues ...'

Given the dominant political culture of the school (i.e. associative), many teachers defined negative factors as 'unpolitical': 'It's not wise to avoid helping others here'. However, positive and negative political factors probably exist in all schools. While one set of factors may be dominant, the data intimate that both sets of factors interact, and each appears to sustain the other.

SUMMARY AND CONCLUSIONS

The results of this study point out that teachers construct a political perspective towards their work environment. They develop values, beliefs, purposes and strategies that they themselves define as political as a result of their work experience. This chapter has described what being political means, specifically as it relates to interpersonal interactions among teachers.

While this category of interaction is shaped by many factors, the present data point out that the behaviours of school principals and department chairpersons were particularly important in setting the political 'tone' of the school. In adjusting to effective administrators, teachers developed a positive political orientation towards others, which resulted in positive, supportive, collaborative, integrative and reciprocal political interactions. In contrast, ineffective administrators provoked a political orientation that resulted in non-supportive, non-collaborative, fragmented and self-oriented interactions. Both sets of conditions seem to grow from central concerns regarding protection and influence.

The terms *associative* and *dissociative* have been used here to describe the divergent effects of each pattern of interaction for the social and cultural structure of the school.

In a more speculative vein, we postulate that positive and negative interpersonal political transactions and associative and dissociative conditions (as described) probably coexist in all schools. (The degree to which either set of conditions is prevalent in a particular setting would require empirical investigation.) In fact, at an abstract level, the study data strongly indicate that changes both in the perspectives of teachers and the social and cultural structure of the school may emerge from 'tensions' surrounding core values (norms) that characterize the situation. For example, in the school investigated, support was a core value around which tensions built; it served as a key reference point to which teachers (and others) oriented themselves. That is, various teachers interpreted and behaved somewhat differently regarding the support issue. Although supportive interaction was dominant in the school studied, apprehensions linked to non-support (rooted in teachers' past experience) and instances of non-support gave this issue a volatile, problematic quality.

If the work context of a particular school (at least those dimensions of context influenced by teachers) can be defined, for example, in terms of core values such as support, autonomy, fairness, participation and friendliness, then meanings associated with such values can be expected to change over time, as a result of external and internal events. In part, the teachers' interpersonal political perspective in a given school may describe how teachers orient themselves with regard to these values. More generally, meanings generated by this process of orientation can be expected to affect the social and cultural structure of the school: associative purposes and actions of teachers contribute to associative social and cultural structures, and dissociative purposes and actions contribute to dissociative structures. Both types of structures vary dramatically in relation to the leadership style of school principals.

Erickson (1976) describes a model of culture consistent in a general sense with the notion that interpersonal processes and cultural changes may emerge from processes linked to what are considered core values in a particular organizational setting. (It is possible, of course, to think of some of the core values mentioned above as more or less generic to public school teachers.) Erickson (1976) theorizes that 'the mind that imagines a cultural form ... also imagines its reverse' (p. 81). Attention to one value (e.g. with regard to the present data, 'equitableness') requires attention to its counterpart (e.g. 'inequitableness'). Essentially, Erickson (1976) proposes that 'the identifying motifs of culture are not just core issues ... but also lines of point and counterpoint along which they diverge' (p. 82). Thus, each core issue can be viewed in terms of an 'axis of variation'. A given context is conceptualized as a gravitational field where core values exist, yet individuals and groups are differentiated by 'contrary pulls' built into the text of the culture.

In sum, Erickson argues that every culture can be described by 'axes of variation' associated with core values along which people's responses to significant events are apt to take place. Data from the present study are consistent with a model of organizational culture similar to that discussed by Erickson – one that gives attention to dominant behaviours and norms, and yet recognizes diversity and the precipitants to change.

PART TWO

FACILITATIVE AND DEMOCRATIC LEADERSHIP: THE MICROPOLITICS OF EMPOWERMENT

The next four chapters focus on the two quadrants on the open end of the con-tinuum of the micropolitical leadership matrix: facilitative and democratic/empowering leadership (see Figure 1.1).

In these chapters data representative of the three major movements away from authoritarian and adversarial forms of leadership are presented. The first reform wave began with the human relations and organizational development movements: these were followed by the effective schools research, which emphasized greater input from the school's stateholders and a more humane school climate. The effective schools literature in the early 1980s, however, con-tinued to promote a high-profile and control-oriented role for school principals. While administrative styles became somewhat more open, the transactional, control-oriented nature of leadership seldom went beyond making the status quo more palatable.

A second wave of school reform, which began in the late 1980s, emphasized the devolution of power to the school site and school restructuring to ensure greater participation by a wide range of constituencies, including the private sector. Restructuring allowed for the possibility that leadership might be dispersed throughout the school community and was an important addition to the previous leadership model. Now, at least in theory, principals would be obliged to include teachers, parents and others in decision-making. This model, although still located in the facilitative quadrant for reasons discussed later, is a significant step in the direction of democratic/empowering leadership.

It is hoped that a third reform movement will originate neither in state legislatures nor universities, but rather from a democratic, grassroots demand for new ways of conceiving of power and principal–teacher and professional–client relationships. The last chapter attempts to sketch out what this might look like.

In Chapter 4, data about teachers' descriptions of open principals are presented. These open principals are seen as honest, communicative, par-ticipatory, collegial, informal, supportive and demanding but reasonable in their expectations of teachers. The micropolitical orientations teachers construct with open principals are contrasted with those they construct with closed principals.

In Chapter 5, we discuss an expanded data set on teachers' perceptions of open principals and describe an approach that we call *normative-instrumental leadership*. Although this approach falls within the facilitative quadrant of the micropolitical leadership matrix, we argue that it is still very much a control-oriented approach. Its fundamental goals are highly transactional and are intended to facilitate the maintenance of current power relations through a process of exchange. This approach to leadership owes much to the human relations movement, which incorporates knowledge about group process, interpersonal relations and conflict management, but has not developed a political dimension that discusses power in a broader context of conflicting interests.

In the second part of Chapter 5, a relatively recent manifestation of open-style leadership, *shared governance*, is discussed. This second case provides data from "restructured" schools in which participatory structures have been put in place. These schools have made an effort to move towards democratic, empowering leadership, in which participation in decision-making by teachers, parents and students is viewed as a right, not a privilege. Restructuring efforts have only been partially successful at opening up participation, for reasons discussed in detail in Chapter 7.

Case study data illustrating some of the ways in which principals exercise control through managing the school's symbol system are presented in Chapter 6. We argue that open principals' use of symbolic and ideological control over teachers makes more direct, authoritarian forms of control less necessary.

The final chapter highlights the democratic/empowering quadrant of the micropolitical leadership matrix. This chapter describes the basic premises of this approach and the obstacles to achieving it in schools. Finally, a description is provided of Debra Meier's school in East Harlem to illustrate some facets of democratic, empowering leadership.

Chapter 4

The Everyday Political Orientation of Teachers Towards Open School Principals

> The structure of schools and school systems seems to discourage openness and cooperation. Principals are accountable to parents, the central office, school boards, and the state department of education. The school principal is the agent through which others seek to prevail on teachers to do their bidding.
>
> (Barth, 1990, p. 27)

In the Introduction to this book, we reviewed studies focusing on teachers, relationships with school principals. We concluded that although variations in principal leadership resulted in dramatically different effects on teachers, there was little evidence that such effects were significantly empowering and democratizing.

This chapter illustrates the foregoing conclusion; it describes the everyday political strategies teachers employ in their interactions with principals whom they themselves define as 'open' and 'effective'. The study discussed here used an open-ended instrument to collect data from 770 teachers taking graduate courses at two major universities in the United States. Of these, 404 teachers chose to describe the political strategies they used specifically with 'open' and 'effective' principals. Data related to understanding the reasons for using such strategies, teachers' feelings associated with their use, and their effectiveness from the teachers' perspective, are also presented. We also present a brief comparison of these data with another portion of the database, focusing on teachers' political orientation to 'closed' and 'ineffective' principals. (See Appendix for a complete discussion of the research procedures used in this study.)

RESULTS

We present two major dimensions of the data: teachers' definitions of the working styles of open/effective school principals and teachers' definitions of the political strategies they used to deal with such principals. In terms of the former, we discuss seven factors – expectations, honesty, communicativeness, participation, collegiality, informality and support. With regard to the latter, six major political strategies used by teachers – diplomacy, conformity, extra work, visibility, avoidance and ingratiation – and three minor strategies – documentation, intermediaries and threats – are described. We also include reasons/purposes identified with each strategy, data on feelings, and teachers' ratings of the effectiveness of each strategy.

The data imply that openness in principals, as described in this chapter, contributes to the development of relatively open political orientations in teachers, characterized by the use of both proactive (influence) and reactive (protective) strategies. In addition, the data demonstrate the teachers' interest in *maximizing benefits* (such as principal support, advancement) and *minimizing costs* of interaction to obtain valued outcomes – in exchange for tangible and intangible factors such as extra work, loyalty and tactfulness. This recurrent theme in the data is discussed further throughout this chapter.

We hope that the data in this chapter will lay to rest the misconception among many that teachers represent a monolithic group characterized by shared goals and ideologies. An understanding of the diversity and micropolitical complexities that exist within teaching staffs is necessary if the empowerment of teachers is to become a reality.

The Workstyles of Open and Effective Principals

Openness was discussed by teachers in terms of principals having high but 'reasonable' *expectations* regarding teachers' job performance, professional demeanour and personal propriety (e.g. dress). Teachers reported that open principals communicated their expectations clearly, efficiently and in a timely manner. Along these lines, teachers frequently discussed expectations in conjunction with the principals' role in clarifying and implementing central-office policies. The relation between high expectations and 'modelling' by principals was underscored: 'We looked at him as a mentor . . . leads by example.'

Open principals were described as *honest*; they were considered non-manipulative in their interactions with teachers ('there are no hidden agendas . . . they don't use deception'). Such principals were seen as 'respond[ing] openly', as being 'straightforward', 'sincere' and 'trustworthy'. Teachers reported that honest principals tended to be fair and consistent: 'He doesn't show favouritism'. According to the teachers studied, honest principals also seemed to be willing to 'admit mistakes'.

Open principals were described as *communicative*; they expressed themselves in 'constructive, not offensive ways' ('She gives feedback in a non-threatening manner'). In the teachers' view, the ability to understand their 'personal and professional needs' was considered crucial. Teachers described communicative abilities in the context of their principals' willingness to engage in ('face-to-face') interaction and deal with a range of teacher-related problems and needs.

Teachers reported that open principals were inclined to be *participatory* (collaborative) in their approach to decision-making. These principals solicited input from teachers regarding a range of diverse curricular, extracurricular and organizational issues: 'She was willing to discuss any problem or matter of importance to the faculty.' Teachers' data linked participation in principals to progressiveness ('He's open to new ideas and suggestions') and a willingness to negotiate issues ('He asks if I will do a job; if there's a problem, then we negotiate'). Participatory tendencies were further associated with the inclination of principals to explain actions ('give reasons') and decisions ('It's not just, here's the way it is and he's off the hook').

Roughly half of the teachers who emphasized participation as a dimension of openness in principals claimed that their involvement in decision-making was broad (e.g. curricular, extracurricular) and direct. The remainder seemed to assume a consultative role. They gave advice and opinions, but principals made most of the decisions: 'We shared opinions within the limitations of the principal's disposition.' Other data indicated high degrees of discretion for teachers, specifically in regard to the implementation of decisions: 'He lets me come up with my own decisions about how to implement things.' Most teachers suggested that the principals for whom they worked reserved the right to some final decisions: 'Bottom-line decisions are made by her when necessary.' Generally, the data indicated that principal–teacher interaction was dyadic; occasionally, small group meetings were used as a viable forum for participation. Only one teacher reported that her principal used a formal questionnaire to solicit input.

Open principals were described as *collegial*; such principals actively created relationships with teachers that minimized 'status differences' ('It was a partnership, we were co-workers') and promoted teacher autonomy and authority, particularly in relation to instructional matters (e.g. teaching style, materials). Direct supervision by collegial principals was minimal: 'She lets me do my job, doesn't get involved unless asked.' When supervision did occur, teachers explained that principals tended to 'ask' them to do things rather than to 'tell' them what to do. To be sure, this was more than tactfulness: 'We could disagree and say so.' Notwithstanding, teachers reported that they had substantial discretion/autonomy in the classroom. Many teachers indicated that they also enjoyed substantial autonomy in their performance of 'delegated', noninstructional assignments as well.

According to teachers, *informality* was a characteristic of open principals; such principals were perceived as polite ('courteous'), friendly ('personable', 'pleasant'), calm ('mellow', 'relaxed', 'easygoing', 'unpressured') and loose ('doesn't get hung up on details . . . rules'). Several discussed the importance of humour and timing in relation to informality. Teachers frequently qualified their descriptions, indicating that 'being informal does not mean that he [the principal] is wishy-washy'. Rather, open principals were viewed as 'maintaining authority' but in 'human . . . unoffensive ways'. Again, the data indicated that informality helped reduce status differences and contributed to open relationships between teachers and administrators.

Teachers emphasized the centrality of *supportiveness* in their descriptions of open principals. Specifically, teachers linked support to the willingness of principals to 'stand behind' teachers in their confrontations with students and parents, particularly with regard to issues related to student discipline and student academic performance: 'My principal supports teachers down the line when challenged by parents, students, the public or any other outside agents.'

Supportiveness and the accessibility of principals were, in the reports of teachers, directly interrelated. Accessible principals responded in a timely way to the professional and personal needs of teachers: 'He has a 'real' open door ... I'm free to drop in and discuss personal ... professional matters.' Principal accessibility also served a crucial symbolic function for teachers: 'Most of all I need to know I can count on him ... he's always there if the need should arise.'

In the teachers' view, support was further related to the visibility of principals throughout the school: they maintained a 'presence' in the school (e.g. hallways, cafeteria) and in the classroom. Consequently, such principals were perceived as possessing knowledge and expertise; they were 'aware' and 'well-informed' regarding school matters. Visible principals tended to maintain relatively 'familiar relationships' with faculties and students.

Teachers reported that supportive principals directly provided them with relevant and timely information. In addition, by encouraging teacher participation in special seminars, conferences and in-school staff development programmes, they indirectly helped teachers to obtain meaningful information and knowledge, which, in turn, contributed to their self-esteem and professional growth: 'He empowers me through information.'

Support was further associated with praise and recognition for teachers and their work: 'He is always appreciative, quick to praise.' Positive and timely feedback to individual teachers for 'special strengths ... accomplishments' was considered quite important. There was considerable evidence to suggest that most of the praise/recognition that teachers received was for contributions made in response to specific 'requests' by principals.

Support was linked to the willingness of principals to follow through with appropriate material and technical resources, again, in a timely fashion: 'He sees to it that materials are available to work with ... accommodating my needs and desires.' Principals who followed through in this respect were considered 'proactive' and 'facilitative'; they assisted teachers in achieving curricular and extracurricular goals.

According to the data, support was frequently exhibited through empathy for the teachers' personal life ('The principal understands our situations away from school too') and professional life ('He shows a personal interest in my teaching'). This, teachers explained, directly affected teacher morale and satisfaction and was further associated with the development of productive collegial relationships: 'He's easy to talk to because I know he cares about my feelings and concerns.'

Teachers discussed tactfulness as a dimension of support, primarily in terms of the ability of principals to give 'constructive' negative feedback. This type of feedback, teachers indicated, was usually given privately and in 'low-keyed ... non-threatening' ways: 'He's very tactful, not overbearing when my work is not up to par ... doesn't criticize directly.' Some teachers indicated that their principals only expressed negative criticism non-verbally: 'The principal moves about quietly, displays displeasure through facial expressions only.'

Teachers believed that supportive principals employed a collaborative problem-solving orientation. In part, this meant that principals made themselves readily available to teachers: 'He tells me to let him know if he can be of assistance.' Administrator collaboration was identified with strong skills in understanding and conceptualizing problems and with the use of 'implementation processes which get results'. At the same time, it was evident that collaborative principals maintained a sensitivity to teachers: 'She never made us feel incompetent because she had to help.'

Supportive principals were seen as well organized and efficient in their use of time, particularly with regard to faculty meetings and expectations surrounding paperwork: 'They take teachers' time seriously ... work to minimize waste ... at faculty meetings ... help reduce paperwork.' Well-organized principals protected teachers' planning periods and instructional time from intrusions.

We should note that although the principals described by these teachers were considered open and quite effective, some *negative* data were reported (14 teachers made some critical statements regarding their principals). Not surprisingly, teachers who made negative comments also tended to rate their principals slightly lower on both the openness and effectiveness scales. Briefly, these teachers described their principals as authoritarian ('listens but many times seems to have made up his mind'), coercive ('He often acts as a ramrod and tries to push his ideas through') and inaccessible ('He is unavailable when teachers need to talk to him'). Teachers also identified conflict avoidance ('she has a difficulty facing conflict ... correcting subordinates when necessary') and lack of interest in instruction ('Doesn't keep a close check on instruction as much as keeping the carpet clean') as negative qualities of some open principals for whom they worked.

A brief summary of teachers' perspectives on 'closed and ineffective' principals discussed in Chapter 1 points to significant differences relative to the characteristics described above. Generally, closed principals were characterized as authoritarian (they were considered controlling and tended to prohibit/limit input, questions and criticism), inaccessible (they had low visibility in the school) and non-supportive (teachers focused almost entirely on obtaining material support – symbolic and technical support were seldom pursued or obtained by teachers).

Closed principals were seen as egocentric (arrogant, aloof, braggarts), indecisive (they avoided or delayed decisions unnecessarily), insecure ('easily threatened'), unfriendly (cold, impersonal), overly negative, intimidating and tending to avoid conflict. Not surprisingly, such a configuration of characteristics provoked a political orientation in teachers that was itself quite closed and dominated by protective (reactive) considerations.

Teacher Political Strategies

We describe in this section the six major political strategies and three minor strategies used by teachers in interactions with open and effective principals.

Diplomacy Diplomacy was clearly identified with proactive and positive forms of influence, although protective considerations (e.g. avoidance of conflict) were not entirely absent. Above all, political considerations included the favourable presentation of self: the maintenance of composure and the display of self in a 'professional' and straightforward ('honest') manner.

Diplomacy was defined largely in rational terms. In their interactions with principals, teachers revealed that they used a systematic approach that, upon analysis, consisted of three major components. To begin with, teachers presented their definitions of problems; they frequently attempted to demonstrate graphically ('to show and illustrate') problems and issues to principals. Teachers emphasized that it was critical to be fully prepared and to communicate clearly, 'without confusion or contradiction, to delineate present conditions as well as future prospects'. Second, teachers developed rationales, 'convincing reasons', a 'logic', a 'case' to substantiate their concerns: 'Reasons should be well thought-out, information . . . feelings should be given.' Teachers indicated that developing a 'case' was the most demanding part of diplomacy: 'You really need to do your homework.' And finally, teachers proposed solutions to the problems that they identified.

In each of the aforementioned areas, teachers argued that although it was important to be prepared, it was politically advantageous to 'leave room for input' from principals. For example, it was useful to describe problems/issues precisely to avoid 'distortion . . . misrepresentation'; it was also important to take an incremental and somewhat open approach with principals: 'You always approach him with concrete ideas yet leave room for his interpretation and input too.' The data indicate that honesty coupled with tactfulness were useful to minimize defensiveness in principals and to increase the probability of eliciting their understanding, cooperation and support.

Teachers directly sought the advice of principals, in some respects to ingratiate themselves (through the enhancement of principals) but, more important, to elicit their political support: 'I wanted him to take an interest in this project. . . . There was a lot of respect for his expertise.' In being diplomatic, teachers frequently used subtle tactics; they employed the 'question approach', especially with regard to generating solutions: 'Sometimes I tell him what I think we should do and let him respond . . . but usually I ask questions, "what do you think of this idea?" . . . let him respond or choose.' At times, principals were used as a sounding board: 'I just think out loud, want him to get hooked in.'

Finally, teachers discussed a host of follow-up techniques designed to ensure that principals 'wouldn't forget problems and certainly not the commitments they made'. Verbal hinting, memos and even formal letters were employed along these lines.

Teachers who reported using diplomatic tactics frequently indicated their disapproval of those tactics which they believed were strongly manipulative and deceptive. Yet curiously, such teachers indicated that they were willing to employ tactics that were indirect, subtle and somewhat covert; within the context of the professional literature, such tactics are considered manipulative, since the 'target' remains unaware of the influence (Bridges, 1970; Gilman, 1962; Tedeschi, 1972).

To illustrate, teachers created opportunities to test ('testing the waters') the interest and involvement of principals ('Sometimes I just drop by the office . . . give him the opportunity to say things'; 'I'll use informal social contact to hint about my concerns'; 'I'll come in early before anyone else arrives to comment on something'). Others simply informed principals of problems: 'There was no discussion; I just wanted to bait him.' Teachers also used impromptu opportunities to communicate their needs: 'When he came by I showed him the poor equipment . . . but I didn't say anything else, not yet.' It was apparent that teachers intentionally limited the disclosure of negative attitudes, thoughts and behaviour in the presence of principals: 'I do not remind the principal what he should or should not do . . . sometimes I'd like to though.' Finally, during interactions with principals teachers reported that they attempted to dramatize, i.e. distort the significance of requests, suggestions and problems: 'I try to make a problem seem more real than it really is.'

Teachers reported that personality characteristics were important sources of diplomatic influence. Interpersonal competencies were critical to the development and maintenance of diplomatic political interactions with principals. In addition to tactfulness, the data emphasize the significance of politeness, friendliness, supportiveness, appreciation, enthusiasm, seriousness, respectfulness and humour. Teachers claimed that such competencies helped to reduce administrator–teacher status differences and promote 'quality open relationships'. The importance of superordinates' interpersonal competencies and their effect on reducing status differences have been documented elsewhere (e.g. Blase, 1987b).

Teachers explained that tactfulness was grounded in a display of respect for the principals' authority, although servility was considered unbecoming. A diplomatic approach to principals did require, however, a willingness to accept rejection graciously: 'You have to accept "no responses to requests" . . . and give the impression that you recognized and respected his authority.' To be sure, the data suggest that teacher diplomacy was circumscribed by the teachers' perception of the authority of principals.

According to teachers, diplomacy occurred primarily through face-to-face, one-to-one interactions, although notes and formal letters were occasionally used to 'present problems and requests' or to follow up on issues. Diplomatic interaction also occurred at the convenience of principals; determining the 'receptivity' of principals was, in the teachers' view, an important strategic consideration. The political objectives of teachers tended to focus on individual rather than group concerns; there were only a few instances in which teachers acted directly on behalf of others.

The following reasons/purposes were identified with the use of diplomacy. (They are presented in the order of most to least frequently coded, a format used for all reasons/purposes described in this chapter.) Above all, teachers disclosed their need for *support* from principals. At a symbolic level, teachers sought recognition (for their expertise, competence and motivation to work) and backing: 'I need him to be on my side.' They also obtained advice (input regarding problems) from principals. Towards these ends, teachers directly discussed the significance of cultivating *open relationships*; therefore they used political approaches that engendered mutual understanding and respect: 'There is nothing wrong with trying to keep the peace and establish rapport to make for better relationships. It's a plus for the school environment.' Diplomacy was also linked to *principals' expectations* ('The principal is clear, he wants fully developed ideas ... [he] values honestly ... input'), *pragmatism* ('It works! It's effective, we both profit', 'I get my way', 'Results in better decisions', 'He listens and responds') and *change/improvement* ('I do what's best for the students ... the programme. There was a need for an algebra class').

Other reasons associated with diplomacy focused on minimizing interaction costs. These included *reduction of conflict* (teachers attempted to minimize 'defensiveness', 'hostility' and 'criticism'), *bureaucratic obstacles* ('red tape') and *poor decisions* ('by the principal operating alone'). *Professional values* ('This is my style ... I like to be able to look at myself in the mirror without flinching') and *professional growth* ('The process forces me to think things through ... understand more ... do more ... it results in self-esteem, feelings of competence') were also described. All in all, the data suggest that the teachers' use of diplomatic tactics with principals seemed to promote bilateral (two-way) influence processes. The mean effectiveness rating for diplomatic tactics was 6.26 (7-point scale).

In most cases, teachers identified diplomacy with positive feelings. Terms used most frequently to describe feelings included *good*, *satisfied*, *at ease*, *proud*, *comfortable*, and the word *positive* itself. In a few instances, teachers disclosed mildly negative feelings (*uneasiness*, *a little devious*).

Conformity Conformity refers to the display of professional and personal qualities perceived to be consistent with the formal (policies, rules) and informal (requests) expectations of school principals. Phrases such as 'I try to be on time ... on task' and 'I try to be cooperative, efficient and enthusiastic at all times', reflect the meaning of conformity to teachers. More specifically, 'timely and proper completion' of non-instructional tasks ('completing forms', 'meeting deadlines', 'missing as little school as possible') were also essential to conformity.

Teachers indicated that, in part, conformity was associated not only with the suppression of one's thoughts on significant issues ('I do not question his policies even though I may disagree') but also with the feigning of public support ('I present a supportive, positive attitude even when I don't agree'). Conformity also indicated a willingness to defend the actions of principals ('I am loyal to him; I justify his actions when I hear others criticize him').

Moreover, 'keeping the principal informed' regarding one's responses to demands/expectations was described in relation to conformity. Some teachers described the ritualistic and symbolic aspects of conformity: 'I use the words "yes sir, no sir," to show respect to him and his authority ... to show I do not consider myself equal to him. He is the boss.'

Generally speaking, the expectations of principals that seemed to provoke conformity in teachers were viewed as 'legitimate'. Occasionally, teachers disagreed with particular demands; however, they tended to respond without challenging or questioning principals. Conformity is recognized widely as a strategy used by individuals to avoid sanctions (Pfeffer, 1981b).

Analysis of the reasons/purposes that teachers described in relation to conformity indicated the importance of protective/reactive considerations; in effect there was little attempt to influence principals overtly. However, it would be a mistake to interpret conformity only as a response to the influence of external factors; it can also be considered a power strategy – one that is consistent with the principles of an exchange perspective (Jones, 1964).

Reasons/purposes associated with conformity include *principals' expectations*, *normative considerations* ('As an employee you should conform ... be loyal, that's the way it is'), *impression management* ('It makes me look good ... appear to be on top of things', 'Gives the impression that I work hard, am competent') and *job security* ('It's the best way to keep your job'). Teachers attempted to reduce interaction costs through *avoidance of sanctions* ('criticism and negative evaluations', 'gossip'). Teachers also explained their motivation to conform in terms of *benefits to others* ('students', 'the school', 'the team') and *pragmatism* ('It works'). Not surprisingly, teachers did not discuss the development of open relationships with principals as an underlying reason for conformity. It is apparent that through conformity teachers were able to gain certain benefits as well as reduce some costs of interaction (e.g. through avoidance of sanctions). The mean effectiveness score for conformity was 6.1 (7-point scale).

Teachers identified positive feelings associated with conformity. Terms such as *positive, great, fine, comfortable* and *secure* were coded. Nevertheless, the reports of several teachers pointed to feelings of slight uneasiness because of the possibility of being perceived as ingratiatory: 'I have no problem ... I'm not brown-nosing because sometimes he and I disagree and discuss this.'

Extra Work As a political strategy, teachers described extra work in terms of their willingness to assume duties and responsibilities 'beyond regular contractual requirements'. The data suggest that, for the most part, teachers worked to increase their attractiveness to principals. Teachers responded to the requests of principals for extra work and occasionally initiated involvements on their own. Politically, teachers involved themselves in activities that assisted school principals, i.e. in curricular (e.g. chaired programmatic committees) and extracurricular activities (e.g. pep rallies, sponsored cheerleading), organizational tasks (e.g. hall, cafeteria, bus duty), administrative tasks (e.g. paperwork, answering the phone) and even school maintenance ('I am fairly good in the area of maintenance', 'I look for things to do to improve the operation of the school and to prevent any maintenance problems'). Several teachers defined attendance at events (e.g. weekend games, workshops) in strategic terms.

Teachers spent time both outside of the classroom ('I work long hours outside of the classroom to do administrative work or things that would be an additional responsibility of the principal') and beyond regular school hours to achieve their political purposes. Not infrequently, teachers disclosed that extra work was accompanied by behaviours intended to dramatize their involvement (Goffman, 1959; Martin and Sims, 1956): 'I accept large amounts of extra responsibility with a smile.'

Teachers indicated that by and large they exchanged additional investments of time and energy for benefits. Principal *support* (symbolic, material, technical) was the primary political goal for the teachers' involvement in extra work. At a symbolic level, teachers sought both praise/recognition ('I want the principal's respect and want to be regarded as special ... in the principal's mind') and backup ('When regular teachers complain about some aspect of special education procedures, she backs me up'). Other exchange-related reasons expressed by teachers included *job security* ('I enjoy my work and wish to continue teaching in my present school'), *advancement* ('This experience will increase my marketability') and *influence* in decision-making. Less frequently cited (non-exchange-related) reasons included *normative considerations* ('Helping is part of my duty ...'), *inclusion* ('I want to feel important to the school and to the community') and *satisfaction* ('It makes my job enjoyable ... one that enhances my life'). The mean effectiveness score for the extra-work strategy was 6.08.

Teachers used terms such as *positive*, *good* and *great* to describe feelings connected with extra work. A few teachers described negative feelings and linked these to problems of deception.

Visibility Visibility as a political strategy refers to the display of accomplishments and involvements, both in the school and in the community. Whereas diplomatic processes seemed to be designed to enhance both teachers and administrators, visibility (like extra work) was more directly related to increasing the attractiveness of teachers to school principals. Teachers invited principals to classrooms to observe 'exceptional lessons' and they also 'publicized' the successes of particular students: 'The only strategy I consciously use with my principal is to show her the art work which my students do.'

Others cited making use of opportunities to communicate accomplishments to administrators: 'Whenever there is something exceptionally positive happening in my class . . . I make sure the principal knows about it.' Student test scores, student awards and student honours were frequently discussed by teachers in terms of visibility. Teachers acknowledged the use of 'displays' to 'impress' school administrators: 'I make use of creative displays . . . wall space and bulletin boards are designed to show subject-related materials and ideas. . . This helps inspire nice relationships with the principal.' Some teachers invited principals to meetings and activities sponsored by particular groups.

Teachers described reasons/purposes related to visibility within the context of exchange and reciprocation, particularly symbolic forms of *support*: recognition for themselves and their students ('I am proud of my students but I suppose that one reason that I am is because it reflects a bit of my abilities as a teacher'). Material support from principals ('A programme is much healthier when it is backed by the principal') was also cited in the data. Teachers also indicated that visibility was linked to *impression management*: 'I try to give the principal the impression that my class is always on target . . . which gives the impression that I am a very good teacher. It's a bit deceitful.' Non-exchange-related reasons – *normative considerations*, *personal factors* ('This is my style') and *pragmatism* – were noted in the data less frequently. The mean effectiveness score for visibility was 6.0.

With the exception of one case ('I feel a bit deceitful at times'), teachers reported positive feelings in relation to visibility. Words such as *positive*, *good* and *comfortable* were coded.

Avoidance Avoidance conceptualizes teachers' attempts to refrain from actions that they believed would be interpreted as 'threatening' to school principals. Similarly, Michener and Suchner (1972) have discussed withdrawal as a common power tactic. Generally, the data indicate that teachers avoided disagreement and criticism of principals and their policies and programmes: 'You keep your mouth shut . . . careful not to disagree.' Complaining about problems, even occasionally, was avoided: 'I don't complain about things . . . situations that aren't good . . . principals don't listen to those who complain.' Requesting the assistance of principals, particularly in matters of discipline, was minimized:

> A child had a problem with talking, blurting out, and not
> keeping a neat and tidy work area. I went through all the

assertive discipline steps several times... After his grade in conduct dropped from A to B, he then visited with the principal for harsher reprimand.

In addition, teachers suppressed potentially damaging information: 'I did something that I thought was best for me and the students but in opposition to the views she [the principal] held ... I went ahead with my actions discreetly.' Finally, some teachers indicated that they avoided face-to-face interaction with principals altogether: 'I stay out of sight to avoid questions ... more work assignments.'

Reasons that teachers discussed for their use of avoidance appeared to be grounded primarily in protectionistic considerations. Quite frequently, teachers suggested that they used avoidance to protect themselves from principals, to reduce the costs of interaction by reducing their vulnerability to formal and informal *sanctions*; they wanted to pre-empt criticism and embarrassing questions from principals: 'I do not wish to be censored ... stir my principal to anger.' Attempts to avoid *conflict* with the instructional goals/expectations of principals (e.g. standardized testing) and the use of *impression management*, in the sense defined here ('My purpose is to give the appearance that I am strong-willed and can handle my own problems') were also related to minimizing the costs of interaction. This was especially apparent for teachers who claimed that they had worked with 'insecure' and 'moody' principals.

Less frequently coded reasons reflected attempts to achieve gains. *Support* ('You avoid conflict to get support in other areas beyond discipline') and *advancement* ('... want to be recommended for an assistant principalship next year so I play the game') were discussed along these lines. *Busyness*, a non-exchange factor ('I'm too busy to get involved in the school politics'), was also coded. The average effectiveness score for avoidance was 5.3; this was the lowest mean score for those strategies reported frequently (i.e. excluding the minor strategies of documentation, intermediaries and threats).

On the whole, teachers described negative feelings in conjunction with avoidance. *Uncomfortable*, *not good* and *demeaned* were terms that teachers used. Several described mixed feelings: 'I feel dishonest somewhat but I guess it's OK. It avoids a lot of embarrassment for me.' Positive feelings were rarely coded.

Ingratiation According to the data, teachers used tactics consciously designed to elevate the self-esteem of principals. In contrast to the other strategies described, ingratiation was identified strongly with both deception and manipulation; principals were supposed to be unaware of the motives of teachers. Jones (1964) has presented a comprehensive examination of ingratiation as a general social strategy. Teachers gave praise, showed empathy and demonstrated support ('You say what they want to hear') to flatter principals. In part, this meant that teachers 'learned to read' their principals: 'I talked with other teachers who worked under him to find out what he liked.' Teachers practising ingratiation tried to be especially friendly and polite in the presence of principals; some gave their principals small gifts.

Again, most instances of ingratiation were consistent with an exchange perspective, although, as Jones (1964) suggests, ingratiators attempted to exploit the exchange process through manipulative intent and deceit. Teachers attempted to obtain *support* from principals in the form of special treatment: 'From my years of teaching experience I have found that students who are nice to me receive far more concessions from me ... Hence, I have used this mechanism with my administrator ... I usually get what I want.' Less frequently, teachers used ingratiation to enhance their *job security* and *advancement opportunities*; they also worked to reduce interaction costs, i.e. to *avoid conflict*: 'I want to keep him off my back.' The mean effectiveness score for ingratiation was 5.8.

About 40 per cent of those teachers who reported using ingratiation expressed positive feelings; strangely, the remainder failed to identify any feelings whatsoever. Other research (Blase, 1988c) has discovered that teachers' reluctance to disclose feelings about ingratiation is related to their experiencing guilt and embarrassment in using the strategy.

Documentation A few teachers described documentation as a protective political strategy. Here, keeping records about potentially troublesome problems was at issue: 'I continuously document anything relevant to my position in the event the principal ever called me on this or that.' Teachers employed documentation to minimize political costs – to avoid criticism and sanctions. The mean effectiveness score was 6.5, and positive feelings were described.

Intermediaries Teachers reported that they occasionally employed intermediaries, especially department chairpersons and other faculty, to communicate their interests to open school principals. In all such cases, the reasons/purposes that teachers described for the use of intermediaries were considered protective; teachers attempted to reduce interaction costs, i.e. to decrease their vulnerability to criticism: 'I needed to express my concern and give my principal something to think about but I wanted to keep myself from getting in any trouble.' Compared with the other political strategies discussed, the effectiveness of using intermediaries was minimal; the mean effectiveness score was 3.5.

Negative feelings were identified with the use of intermediaries. Several teachers expressed guilt in not assuming direct responsibility for their concerns: 'I don't feel good about it because I really wanted to discuss the issue with her.'

Threats In a few instances, teachers reported that they used threats, i.e. coercion ('as a last resort'), to influence principals; however, these threats did not target the principal directly: 'When there's a major problem I feel very strongly about I just close his door and threaten to walk out for a few days – I only use this when I've had it.' The teachers' goal was to *influence* the principal: 'To get my way when all else fails.' Exchange processes were not associated with the use of threats. The mean effectiveness rating of this strategy was 6.0. No feelings were described in relation to threats.

Comparisons with Data for Closed Principals

Although this chapter has focused almost exclusively on teachers' strategic interactions with open school principals, comparisons with the data set on closed principals reported in Chapter 1 reveal some striking differences. Inspection of the strategies associated with each dimension of the data suggests that in dealing with open principals, teachers were considerably less concerned with protective/reactive considerations: of the total number of strategies reported by teachers for open principals, 8 per cent reflected avoidance and 16 per cent ingratiation, whereas the corresponding figures for closed principals were 28 per cent and 42 per cent, respectively.

Diplomacy, by far the most prominent strategy for dealing with open principals, was coded for 61 per cent of the open data; rationality, a strategy roughly similar to diplomacy (i.e. there was some attempt to be open and straightforward), described only 18 per cent of the closed data set. Two relatively important strategies used with open principals – extra work and visibility – were much less important to relationships with closed principals; in fact, these strategies were only discussed implicitly for closed principals. For both data sets, strategies such as documentation, intermediaries and confrontation/threats were reported infrequently.

Further comparisons reveal that teachers engaged in substantially more interaction (avoidance was a major strategy employed with closed principals), more two-way interaction, and more complex interaction with open versus closed principals. With open principals, for instance, teachers sought material, technical and symbolic support. In relationships with closed principals, the support teachers sought was largely confined to material resources and 'permission' from principals. Also, strategies practised with closed principals were typically more covert, indirect and subtle compared with those used with open principals. Finally, teachers perceived their political actions taken with regard to open principals to be more effective as compared with those employed with closed principals.

On the whole, analysis of reasons disclosed for the use of strategies in each data set emphasized the importance of principals' characteristics in contributing to different political orientations in teachers: whereas protective considerations (e.g. avoidance of sanctions) were not unimportant to teachers' political interactions with open principals, such factors were seen as more critical to relationships with closed administrators.

Differences related to feelings associated with political actions taken with each type of principal were dramatic: 85 per cent of the feelings associated with dealing with open principals were positive, whereas 70 per cent of the feelings disclosed in relation to work with closed principals were negative. Further analysis indicated that role conflict appeared to be a more pervasive problem for teachers who worked with closed principals.

THEORETICAL IDEAS AND ANALYSES

Leadership Style

Generally, the data discussed in this chapter indicate that openness in principals was defined in terms of expectations, honesty, communicativeness, participation, collegiality, informality and support. Several studies of effective school principals, employing a variety of methodologies, have associated similar characteristics with effective school-based leadership (Blase, 1987b; Lightfoot, 1983; Lipham, 1981). Although these factors have been described separately here, the data suggest that honesty, communicativeness, participation, collegiality and support were strongly interrelated. Indeed, it was surprising to discover the frequency with which the range of principals' characteristics described appeared on individual questionnaires.

In regard to the typology of Ball (1987), the characteristics noted above are more consistent with an interpersonal control style, which emphasizes personal relationships and private persuasion, than with a managerial style, which relies on formal procedures and structuring/planning. For the former, Ball found that the task function of the school was transacted primarily through interpersonal relationships. Paradoxically, although this style was consistent with the 'preferred view of professionalism' (Ball, 1987, p. 91) held by teachers, Ball contends that the 'sinews of power' (Ball, 1987, p. 92) under such a style were often hidden. Public arenas were not used for decision-making, and teacher influence often took the form of 'lobbying' for personal views. Decision-making and policy development were frequently experienced as mysterious and unfocused and often resulted in confusion and resentment among teachers.

Although the open school principals described in this study seemed to use an interpersonal leadership style, similar negative effects were not evident. Alutto and Belasco (1972) caution that teacher satisfaction with both leadership and involvement in decision-making must be understood in terms of differential expectations: only teachers who perceive themselves to be deprived of opportunities to participate in decision-making would tend to experience dissatisfaction.

Perhaps the participants in the present study held lower expectations regarding direct and full participation in school-based decision-making and, as a result, did not experience high levels of frustration. Most of the study sample was drawn from a conservative state, one with a long history of authoritarian/ directive school leadership and a legacy of low levels of teacher involvement in policy and programme decisions (Carnegie Commission for the Advancement of Teaching, 1988). In addition, collective bargaining is prohibited for state employees; therefore unions are not considered viable agents of political action. From a political perspective, it seems reasonable to conclude that the teachers who participated in this study have been subjected to explicit and implicit forms of power. Galbraith (1983) refers to the latter as conditioned or normative power: through subtle conditioning, people come to believe that 'what is' is the way it 'should' be.

In contrast, Ball's managerial (Ball, 1987) and, more important, authoritarian styles are directly relevant to understanding closed principals and their impact on teachers from a political standpoint. In the case of the managerial style, Ball (1987) found that the head was seen as part of the school hierarchy. Control was exercised predominantly through formal structures and the enforcement of policies and rules; i.e. control was position-oriented rather than person-oriented. Decisions regarding teachers were made by others, and this contributed to alienation. In the closed data set, retreatism and alienation in teachers, as they related to characteristics of 'managerial' leaders (e.g. those who were inflexible and stressed rules and procedures), were evident.

However, Ball's description (Ball, 1987) of the political-authoritarian type seems to be most directly applicable to the closed data. In contrast to the adversarial type (who emphasizes frequent dialogue and confrontation – a style noticeably without substantiation in the present research), the authoritarian attempts to avoid, disable or ignore teachers. In ways similar to those used by closed principals, the heads of British schools drastically limited opportunities to express alternative perspectives; the goal was to suppress dialogue. Emotions expressed by administrators, in the form of anger and criticism, were used for purposes of control. Ball noted that teachers felt that they were treated as children and that this contributed to stress, compliance, dependence and alienation. At the same time, Ball pointed out, deals 'behind closed doors' with individual teachers were not uncommon.

Beyond this, the present data indicate that principal openness and closedness were directly related to a relatively open political orientation and a closed orientation in teachers, respectively. For the former, the interaction of open orientations on both sides tended to reduce 'status' differences and 'inequalities', conditions that the data suggest interfered with effective communication and the production of mutually beneficial decisions/outcomes. To be sure, this general pattern in the data is consistent with case study findings that have related open and effective leadership styles in principals and closed and ineffective leadership styles to different qualitative and quantitative dimensions of teacher work involvement (Blase, 1987a,b). For example, we have found that data available from other relevant (non-political) studies appear to be generally consistent with the findings reported here (e.g. Blumberg and Greenfield, 1986; Hannay and Stevens, 1984; Lipham, 1981).

Exchange

Finally, in varying degrees, *all* of the political strategies employed by teachers in their dealings with open principals (except the use of threats) were shaped by exchange dynamics to obtain valued outcomes. In other words, they were explicitly designed to maximize *gains* or reduce the *costs* of interaction. In terms of the former, for example, teachers exchanged tangible factors (e.g. extra work) and non-tangible factors (e.g. tactfulness, deference, humour, friendliness, support of ideas/programmes, praise/recognition) for principal support (e.g. symbolic, material, technical) and, to a lesser extent, job security and job advancement. In terms of reducing costs, teachers engaged in actions (conformity, avoidance, documentation and the use of intermediaries) primarily to reduce their vulnerability to such factors as administrative sanctions (particularly criticism) and conflict, and, to a lesser extent, to reduce principal defensiveness and bureaucratic obstacles.

By comparison, the data indicated that exchanges with closed principals were characterized by a strong concern on the teachers' part with minimizing costs (i.e. achieving protective goals). Data relevant to attaining benefits from closed principals were noticeably narrow in scope, quantitatively and qualitatively. In other words, in their relationships with closed school principals, support was sought infrequently; it was also confined largely to material goals (e.g. supplies) and 'permission' rather than symbolic support (e.g. praise) or technical support. By and large, teachers designed political strategies that were considered accommodative; these strategies were largely reactive, protective and non-threatening responses to the workstyles of principals. In effect, teachers gave less in exchanges with closed principals.

CONCLUSION

Despite the fact that openness in principals seems to be related to the development of an open political orientation in teachers, *the study data do not indicate that significant degrees of democratic professional interaction existed in schools in which teachers who participated in this study worked. Open conflict and public debate, critical self-examination and mutual decision-making were not indicated in these data or in other studies of school-based politics* (e.g. Ball, 1987). Teachers seemed to operate quite individually (almost anarchistically) in their political relations with principals: there was little evidence of collective consciousness or collective action. The political climate of the state and school leadership traditions, as well as the open principals' emphasis on 'interpersonal' dynamics, may account for the development of a predominantly individualistic political orientation in teachers. Other factors, such as physical isolation, busyness and a private classroom orientation rather than a school orientation (Lortie, 1975), may also have some bearing.

Clearly, the analyses presented throughout this chapter suggest, at best, that teachers enjoy limited access to information, responsibility and decisional power. As might be expected, the political processes described, although quite important to teachers in terms of how they defined their work, seemed to be dramatically curtailed by hierarchical, cultural and social realities. Burns (1978) has noted that leadership and followership transacted through exchange do not lead to a full understanding of needs and motives on both sides and to the development of common purposes and collective action. The following chapter explores the open orientation in more detail as well as what happens when administrators and teachers together attempt to share responsibility and power in the governance of public schools.

Chapter 5

Teachers' Perceptions of Facilitative Leadership
From 'Power-over' to 'Power-through' Approaches

> Collaborative forms of teacher development may in many instances not be empowering teachers towards greater professional independence at all, but incorporating them and their loyalties within processes and structures bureaucratically determined elsewhere.
>
> (Hargreaves and Dawe, 1990, p. 228)

In this chapter we present data from two studies, representing 'open' approaches to leadership in traditional and restructured schools. Both studies produced examples of facilitative, transactional leadership, although the first study describes open principals in largely traditional schools and the second study explores facilitative leadership in the context of schools in which participatory structures have been introduced. The first study was done between 1988 and 1990, a period when few schools had engaged in the restructuring process. The second study was done between 1990 and 1992 and drew its sample of teachers and principals from the League of Professional Schools (Glickman and Allen, 1992), a group of schools in Georgia that were undergoing intense restructuring at the time of the study.

In the first study, we see a continuation of control-oriented leadership exercised though an open leadership style. In this study, although the teachers described an open style of leadership, organizational goals were determined elsewhere, and principals were expected to motivate teachers to achieve them. Here, we begin to see less emphasis on a 'power-over' approach and more reliance on a 'power-through' strategy, in which a more motivational, productive and humane school culture is nurtured, and goals developed largely externally are achieved *through* the motivation and manipulation of groups and individuals.

The second study remains within a transactional, power-through model, but we see the beginnings of a 'power-with' approach to leadership, in which some organizational goals are decided at the school level by principals and teachers. This is made possible through the creation of shared governance structures and the introduction of site-based inquiry. The shared governance model described in this chapter has a long way to go to be a democratic, empowering site in which a power-with approach is dominant. However, the potential for teacher empowerment becomes apparent as shared governance models of school leadership gain acceptance.

FACILITATIVE LEADERSHIP IN TRADITIONAL SCHOOLS

Data for the first study were drawn from a qualitative study that examined the perspectives of 1200 teachers on the everyday strategies that principals, largely in non-restructured schools, used to influence them. The study focuses on the responses of the 836 teachers (out of the total of 1200) who specifically reported strategies used by principals whom they described as open and effective. 'Effective' in this study refers to the ability of principals to influence teacher behaviour. The data strongly suggest that open and effective principals rely primarily on normative strategies and pursue normative goals. (See Appendix for a full description of the research problem and procedures.)

Normative-Instrumental Leadership

Blase (1993) constructed the term 'normative-instrumental leadership' to capture the overall political orientation of open and effective principals towards teachers. This concept, derived inductively from the study data, refers to a political orientation in which control over teachers is central and such control is enacted primarily through a process of exchange. Open/effective principals frequently determine both the goals and means of teachers' work in schools; the use of normative strategies and goals is 'instrumental' (i.e. there is a pragmatic connection between such strategies and goals) in eliciting teacher compliance. The capacity of normative-instrumental leadership to influence teachers positively is related to its normative nature. Generally, the strategies and goals employed by effective principals are consistent with teachers' professional norms and values. The exceptions to this generalization relate directly to the use of contrived advice, coercion and authoritarianism.

In the following discussion, we outline the specific *strategies* (and some of the related *practices*) identified with normative-instrumental leadership. This concept of leadership consists of a control orientation and an empowerment orientation. Strategies identified with principals' control orientation (i.e. eliciting teacher compliance to principal-determined goals) and with the empowerment orientation (i.e. promoting teacher involvement in formal and informal decision-making) are described. Major control-oriented strategies (81 per cent of the total data) include rewards, communication of expectations, support, formal authority, modelling, visibility and suggestion. Three minor (negative) strategies are contrived request for advice, coercion and authoritarianism. The empowerment orientation includes one major strategy (19 per cent of the total data) – involvement in decision-making.

The Control Orientation

Criteria for analysing control were derived inductively from the data (Glaser, 1978; Glaser and Strauss, 1967). Briefly, a strategy was categorized as *control-oriented* when the data suggested that principals' goals or means to achieve goals were determined unilaterally and teachers indicated that they were obligated to comply. For the strategies of rewards, communication of expectations, support and formal authority, control was evident in over 95 per cent of the data. For the major strategies of modelling, visibility and suggestion, control was identified in 93 per cent of the cases. The latter three strategies were seen as less directive, and, as a result, teachers viewed themselves as having slightly more discretion. The three minor strategies of contrived request for advice, coercion and authoritarianism indicated a dominance of control. Stated differently, although teachers reported that open and effective principals used control strategies for non-control purposes (e.g. empowerment), such evidence was minimal. (The f scores described below refer to the frequency with which a strategy appeared in the data.)

Additional analyses of strategies identified with the control orientation indicated that principals influenced teachers largely through a process of exchange. Exchange was coded when it was observed that interactions between principals and teachers were based on transactions of tangible or symbolic goods. This study indicates that symbolic (normative) exchanges (Etzioni, 1961, 1975) – e.g. principal praise or support for teacher compliance – were prominent. In essence, effective principals elicit compliance from teachers through a give-and-take process, in contrast, for example, to using force. The theoretical importance of exchange processes to interaction in organizations has been widely discussed in the micropolitical literature (e.g. Bacharach and Lawler, 1980; Ball, 1987; Blase, 1991).

Rewards: Praise/Material (f = 300) Principals described the use of rewards as a particularly powerful strategy which they employed to recognize individuals as well as whole faculties for their accomplishments, especially in the classroom. Two types of rewards – symbolic (praise) and tangible – were evident. Praise is far more prominent in the data ($f = 268$), but even the material rewards that teachers identified had symbolic significance. Teachers used such terms as 'praises', 'makes positive comments', 'compliments', 'gives credit', 'shows appreciation' and 'recognizes' to describe the strategy of praise. From the teachers' standpoint, effective and open principals expressed praise regularly and used a variety of commonplace formal and informal actions to praise teachers. In addition, such principals used material rewards ($f = 32$) of symbolic significance to influence teachers' performance. These tangible rewards included food, gifts, special privileges and sponsoring social events.

Communication of Expectations (f = 112) Teachers described effective principals as spending a great deal of time and effort on clarifying and reinforcing their expectations to achieve their purposes. These expectations, derived largely from principals' personal values and goals, were consistent with the legitimate purposes of the school and formal school district policies and programmes. Words such as 'clarifies', 'emphasizes', 'expresses', 'encourages', 'wants', 'explains', 'asserts' and 'informs' were associated with the communication of expectations as a strategy. Principals communicated their expectations in formal conferences, meetings with individuals and small groups, informal conversations (in classrooms, hallways, offices) and memos.

Support (f = 137) Principals provided several forms of support. *Advice and direct intervention* related to instruction were given to 'help' teachers deal with a wide range of needs and problems. *Administrative support* refers to principals' attempts to reduce or eliminate factors that interfered with teachers' time. Specifically, principals tried to limit paperwork (by completing it themselves) and to a lesser degree the number of scheduled faculty meetings. *Student-related support* refers to a willingness on the part of principals to 'back up' teachers in their decisions regarding student misbehaviour. Principals also made available *financial and material support*, usually to meet instructional or professional growth goals of teachers.

Finally, open and effective principals provided formal (e.g. staff development) and informal (day-to-day, impromptu, casual) *supportive training* to develop practical knowledge and skill in teachers.

Formal Authority (f = 161) As a strategy, formal authority refers to exercising the legitimate rights/powers of the principalship position to influence teachers. In contrast to most other strategies discussed here, teachers viewed formal authority as a very direct form of influence in which expectations are quite explicit. Words such as 'assigns', 'tells', 'states', 'appoints', 'enforces', 'announces', 'mandates' and 'requires' were associated with principals' use of authority. About 40 per cent of those teachers who discussed this strategy viewed it as 'overly' controlling; it was therefore seen as less acceptable and the least effective in influencing teachers compared with all major positive strategies. In addition, although these teachers said they complied on a behavioural level, their thinking and feelings either remained unaffected or were adversely affected. Nevertheless, for most teachers, acceptance of formal authority was strongly related to their belief that it was used fairly.

Teachers in the sample reported that principals expressed their formal authority in direct verbal communication with individual teachers and groups of teachers, in announcements and in written statements of policy. Often principals were viewed by study respondents as using their formal authority to improve teacher performance, particularly in regard to relationships with students, lesson plans, examinations, use of instructional time, innovation and especially grading. Principal formal authority was also used to influence teachers in many non-instructional areas of work, such as grievances, attendance, new rules and policies, punctuality, deadlines and the assignment of committee work.

Modelling (f = 115) Modelling describes principals' actions that exemplify their implicit and explicit expectations for teachers: 'My principal seems to administer by behaviour versus policy. For example, he asks that we dress professionally, monitor the halls between classes, attend extracurricular activities and contribute to the United Way. He does all of these.' Three personal characteristics of principals – optimism, consideration and honesty – were coded as aspects of modelling. *Optimism* was described by respondents as a global and positive orientation. *Consideration* refers to exhibiting a sincere and broad interest in 'teachers as human beings'. *Honesty* refers to the principal's willingness to be straightforward and to demonstrate consistency between talk and behaviour.

Visibility (f = 75) Open and effective principals maintained high levels of visibility throughout the school; such visibility was used to maximize opportunities to influence teachers. Visibility was usually experienced as 'positive' and 'non-threatening'. To achieve their goals, some effective principals also maintained high visibility in classrooms ('She stops by twice each week'); others visited more sporadically. For some, participation in classroom activities was cursory; others were involved more fully.

Suggestion (f = 72) In contrast to more direct and explicit strategies, suggestion relies on interpersonal diplomacy and informal conversation. Providing alternatives/options to teachers was an important tactical aspect of suggestion. Related practices included giving advice and asking questions.

Contrived Request for Advice (f = 52), Coercion (f = 28), Authoritarianism (f = 23) Contrived request for advice refers to soliciting input from teachers, subsequently ignoring such input, and instead directing teachers toward predetermined goals. In these cases, teachers believed that principals' initial request for input was not authentic, and they reported feeling 'manipulated'. Coercion refers to the direct and indirect use of punishment or the threat of punishment to control teachers. Some principals were accused of such actions as 'reprimanding' individual teachers privately and publicly. Direct threats and questioning were also considered coercive actions. Authoritarian practices are designed to limit teachers' involvement in decisions. The principals identified with the use of any of these three strategies were clearly seen as relatively less open and less effective than other principals described by teachers.

The Empowerment Orientation

Criteria for analysing the empowerment orientation were gleaned directly from the data (Glaser, 1978; Glaser and Strauss, 1967). This orientation, as reflected in the involvement in decision-making strategy, consists of two subcategories: decision-making and authentic requests for advice. *Decision-making* was coded for this strategy when the data indicated that principals and teachers jointly assumed authority and responsibility for determining goals and means to achieve them, and/or principals empowered teachers individually and collectively to assume decisional authority and responsibility. Instances in which teachers were limited to 'giving opinions' on a narrow range of issues defined by principals, and principals took such opinions seriously but retained decisional authority and responsibility, were considered *authentic requests for advice*.

Involvement in Decision-making (f = 248) Authentic request for advice was coded for 49 per cent of the data identified with this strategy; decision-making was observed in 51 per cent of the data.

More concretely, principals encouraged teacher involvement in decision-making through both formal and informal means. They employed a variety of *formal committee/team structures* to elicit teacher participation (e.g. in restructured schools). Generally speaking, these formal teams convened regularly and included educational administrators (including department chairpersons), teachers and selected staff personnel such as school counsellors or cafeteria administrators. In some cases teachers' formal involvement in decision-making was direct; more commonly, decision-making was limited to key administrative personnel (e.g. department chairpersons, grade instructional coordinators, directors) 'representing' teachers. Although some structures seemed to focus almost entirely on problems and goals articulated by principals, others involved members fully in identifying issues and problems, developing goals and plans of action and making decisions.

Informal participation opportunities were also designed to provide legitimate channels for teachers to express their thoughts and feelings on a range of personal and professional issues. Scheduled and impromptu conversations in which principals solicited 'input' directly from teachers on particular issues were mentioned often by respondents.

The existence of formal team structures was related directly to increases in the degree of teacher involvement in actually making decisions. When teachers' participation was confined to informal channels, their role tended to be limited to giving advice. In contrast, *teachers were more directly involved in decision-making when formal participatory structures existed. However, even here, as colleagues, principals frequently influenced (but did not determine) goals, problems and topics, as well as courses of action to be taken.* This was true even for teachers who worked in schools that they referred to as 'restructured'.

Principals' Goals and Impacts of Strategies

According to the study data, the ability of principals to influence teachers is related to two fundamental factors. First, strategies used are considered *normative*; that is, they are congruent with teachers' professional norms and values (Etzioni, 1961, 1975). Second, such strategies are employed to achieve *normative* goals, i.e. goals consistent with teachers' professional norms and values. Thus, the strategies themselves are normative, and they are also applied to normative goals. For example, principals use 'visibility' (a strategy) to improve classroom instruction (a goal). Both the strategy and the goal are consistent with teachers' professional norms: principals should be visible; teachers as professionals should work to improve classroom performance. These two factors appear to explain, in large part, why the principals discussed in this chapter were reported as quite effective in influencing teachers.

To illustrate further, analyses of data point out that principals' goals focused on enhancing teachers' ability to work more effectively with students and included *support of teachers, teacher reflection (on instruction), teacher awareness of student needs, teachers' ability to deal with student discipline and programme development.* All strategies discussed in this chapter (except formal authority, contrived advice, coercion and authoritarianism) are also associated with enriching personal aspects of work and, as such, were consistent with the teachers' professional values. Goals of principals cited most frequently included *teacher satisfaction, esteem, morale and school climate*; cohesiveness and autonomy were reported in a few instances. Generally, principals' goals were described as other-oriented rather than self-oriented, a point that differentiates Greenfield's professional-collaborative 'political' style (Greenfield, 1991) (mentioned earlier) from Ball's three self-serving administrative control styles (Ball, 1987).

An analysis of the impacts of strategies further highlights the congruence of principals' goals and strategies with teachers' professional norms and values. In brief, the strategies described in this chapter produce in teachers positive *affective* impacts (e.g. esteem, pride, satisfaction, confidence, security, inclusion), *cognitive* impacts (e.g. awareness of issues/problems, reflection) and *behavioural* impacts (e.g. increased work involvement, consideration for students, innovation, creativity, follow-through, openness/positiveness, tolerance/patience and better relations with principals and parents).

Impacts consistent with teachers' norms were also linked to the use of formal authority (e.g. increased awareness, consideration for students, contact with parents); however, some negative impacts (38 per cent for this strategy) were also apparent. These data emphasize the centrality of positive feelings and the normative nature of principals' goals and strategies to understanding impacts on teachers' affective, cognitive and behavioural involvement in work. (Positive impacts were coded for 92 per cent of all relevant data.)

Summary and Discussion of Normative-instrumental Leadership

To reiterate, the term normative-instrumental leadership describes the overall strategic orientation of open and effective principals towards teachers. This concept, derived inductively from the study data, refers to an orientation in which *control* of teachers is a central goal, and such control is enacted primarily through a process of *exchange*. Open and effective principals communicate about both the ends and means of teachers' work in schools; the use of normative strategies and goals is 'instrumental' (i.e. pragmatically linked) to eliciting teacher compliance. Thus, power is exercised *over* teachers, but also *through* them, to the extent that they are motivated to pursue organizational goals.

From the perspectives of the teachers studied, eight major strategies identify what has been referred to as normative-instrumental leadership. Open and effective principals used a range of formal and informal, direct and indirect, public and private, and individually and group-targeted means to influence teachers. Although teachers only discussed one or two strategies, descriptions of these suggested that their principals used a wide *range* of the strategies discussed in this chapter. Teachers' reports also suggested that open and effective principals tend to *combine* several strategies in influencing individual teachers (and groups of teachers) to achieve particular goals. In most cases, improving classroom performance was seen as the goal and outcome of principal–teacher interaction. Effective principals were often viewed as employing a diplomatic, problem-solving orientation and as working to create (or take advantage of) opportunities throughout the school to initiate, facilitate and monitor teacher performance.

Consistent with grounded theory research, the types of power observed for the strategies constituting normative-instrumental leadership were examined to link the present database to relevant theoretical and empirical work (Glaser, 1978; Glaser and Strauss, 1967). A model of power developed by Etzioni (1961, 1975) and expanded by Bacharach and Lawler (1980) was used to analyse the entire data set. This model describes four types of power: *coercive* (i.e. use or threat of physical sanctions, generation of frustration), *remunerative* (i.e. material resources, rewards, services), *normative* (i.e. *pure* normative – manipulation of prestige, rituals, symbols; and *social* normative – manipulation of love, acceptance) and *knowledge* (i.e. control of information). (In Etzioni's original model, knowledge was considered a dimension of normative power.) This analysis demonstrated that *although politically effective principals use various types of strategies, they depend most upon normative power.* (Only contrived requests for advice, coercion and authoritarianism were not considered normatively based.)

The above analysis parallels the empirical research that implies that principals' use of positive forms of *normative* (symbolic) power is associated with beneficial outcomes in teachers. For example, Treslan and Ryan (1986) found that teachers were more responsive to influence based on principals' human relations skills and technical expertise than they were to the use of hierarchical authority. Hanson (1976) discovered that, in innovative schools, public praise by administrators resulted in modifications of teacher behaviour. The work of other researchers (High and Achilles, 1986; Isherwood, 1973; Johnston and Venable, 1986) also confirms the present study's conclusion that the use of normative forms of power by principals is effective in influencing teachers.

The study data are also consistent with the central hypothesis of compliance theory (Etzioni, 1961, 1975), which contends that in normative organizations such as schools, the use of strategies based on positive normative power by administrators may enhance teachers' *moral involvement* (i.e. an orientation based on strong positive feelings and a belief in the values of the organization). As noted earlier, analysis of the data in this study provides substantial evidence of deeper levels of teachers' affective, cognitive and behavioural involvement in their work. The critical importance of teachers' strong moral involvement to achieving educational and social goals with students has been recognized by others (Dreeben, 1968; Greenfield, 1991; Lortie, 1975; Waller, 1932; Wynne, 1987).

A comparison of normative-instrumental leadership with Burns' discussion of transactional and transformational (moral) leadership styles (Burns, 1978) reveals important conceptual differences on both counts. In transactional leadership, Burns says, leaders and followers work to achieve *individual and separate goals*. In contrast, transformational leadership, which is fundamentally *moral*, emerges from the needs, aspirations and values of followers and results in *mutuality* of purposes between leaders and followers. Moreover, followers can make *choices* among real alternatives. 'Such leadership occurs when . . . persons engage with others in such a way that leaders and followers raise each other to higher levels of motivation and morality' (Burns, 1978, p. 20). The power bases of both interact to create *mutual support* and *common purpose*. In transformational relationships, leaders and followers together define both the *means* and the *ends* of human action:

> The essence of leadership . . . is the recognition of real need, the
> uncovering and exploiting of contradictions among values and
> between values and practice, and the realigning of values, . . . and
> the governance of change. Essentially, the leader's task is
> consciousness-raising on a wide plane.
>
> (Burns, 1978, pp. 43–4)

Burns (1978) contends that 'transforming leadership is ultimately a relationship

of mutual stimulation and elevation that converts followers into leaders ...'
(p. 4).

As suggested, analysis of the present data set indicates that reported relationships between open and effective principals and teachers in this study were
grounded largely in the goal of control and such control was enacted primarily
through a process of exchange. This conclusion is consistent with Burns's notion
of transactional leadership. However, it was also argued that the control goal
and process of exchange do not explain fully the political efficacy of open and
effective principals and their positive impact on teachers. Conceptually, most of
the data fall between the idea of transactional leadership, in which exchanges
serve the 'separate' interests of leaders and followers, and the idea of transformational leadership, in which actions transform teachers into leaders who possess
decisional authority and responsibility.

On the one hand, the concept of normative-instrumental leadership, by
emphasizing teachers' moral involvement (Etzioni, 1961, 1975), extends well
beyond Burns' idea of *transactional* leadership (Burns, 1978). The open and effective principals discussed in this chapter seemed to embody core educational
values and purposes that they exemplified through everyday political actions.
In varying degrees, these principals influenced teachers to concentrate on the
higher ideal of serving students. They raised questions, examined issues, and
initiated actions that, according to the data, had a dramatic 'elevating', even
'transformative', effect on teachers. Because the specific goals and strategies
identified with open and effective principals were consistent with teachers' professional norms and values, teachers identified closely with open and effective
principals and their overall strategic orientation.

On the other hand, normative-instrumental leadership is distinguished from
Burns' notion of *transformational* leadership (Burns, 1978). Although one
strategy used by principals – involvement in decision-making – provides a
glimpse of transformational leadership, the data argue that effective school
principals typically fail to include teachers in decision-making or limit their
involvement significantly. Teachers themselves rarely identify their fundamental needs, values and aspirations. The behavioural impact data in particular provide compelling evidence that *compliance* is a typical response of teachers to
influence attempts by open and effective principals. Data regarding goals and
impacts indicate that 'control' (i.e. gaining teacher compliance to principal-
determined goals) was the aim of principals described throughout this study. In
sum, the present data argue that effective principals articulate *their* visions, set
their goals, explain *their* expectations, and, in large part, determine the means
to achieve such ends. Simply stated, teachers are normatively influenced 'to buy
into the principal's agenda'.

In fact, what some writers (e.g. Bennis and Nanus, 1985; Leithwood and
Jantzi, 1990) have called transformational leadership after Burns (1978) seems
to be closer to what is referred to in this chapter as normative-instrumental
leadership: leadership focused on control and based on exchange coupled with

the use of normative ('appropriate') strategies to achieve normatively congruent and leader-determined goals. In discussing Lee Iacocca's leadership at Chrysler, for example, Bennis and Nanus comment:

> He provided the leadership to transform a company from bankruptcy to success. He created a vision of success and mobilized large factions of key employees to align behind the vision ... He empowered them [Chrysler employees].
>
> (Bennis and Nanus, 1985, p. 17)

In both the Iaccoca example and normative-instrumental leadership, the critical process of dynamic, open and democratic interaction between leaders and others as discussed by Burns is noticeably absent, and the decisional authority and responsibility of others are limited significantly.

A number of factors probably account for the dominance of the control orientation observed among the open and effective school principals reported in this study. Some principals undoubtedly have strong needs to dominate others (Kipnis, 1976; Winter, 1973). Moreover, the bureaucratic nature of schools emphasizes rational-legal authority associated with position, policies, rules, regulations and procedures. Such control mechanisms were expanded by the legislative mandates produced during the 1980s (Chubb and Moe, 1986). A rational-control orientation to schooling has also been fostered by the school effectiveness literature and related approaches to school improvement.

Bates (1986) contends that the control orientation also appears to be prominent among many scholars in educational administration. This may be a function of strong identification with an epistemology that adheres to a 'scientific' view of administration based on the ability to produce law-like generalizations and to predict accurately (Smith and Blase, 1991). That practising administrators should work to expand their control over teachers seems to be a tacit assumption among such scholars. Hoy and Brown, for example, write:

> A major task of leaders is to get individuals to comply with their directives. Formal authority is satisfactory for eliciting certain minimum performance levels, but it is not sufficient for obtaining compliance beyond formal and bureaucratic expectations. Therefore, a basic challenge before principals is to extend their influence over their professional staff beyond the narrow limits of formal authority.
>
> (Hoy and Brown, 1988, pp. 33–4)

During the last decade in particular, many scholars of educational administration have recognized the limitations of using *direct* forms of control, primarily because of potential resistance. However, control itself has not been rejected as the dominant orientation. To the contrary, increasing control through more subtle cultural and ideological means has been advocated (Deal and Kennedy, 1984; Firestone and Wilson, 1985). In fact, there is some evidence that such forms of control have become more prominent in educational settings (Anderson, 1991; Sparks, 1988). Yet new approaches to school organization (e.g. site-based management, shared governance, participatory leadership) underscore the importance of authentic forms of democratic and transformational leadership as well (Schlechty, 1990). In the following section we explore some of the requisite conditions for beginning to move from a transactional mode to a transformative one in which the decisional authority of teachers is significantly increased.

FACILITATIVE LEADERSHIP IN RESTRUCTURED SCHOOLS

As we have seen in the first part of this chapter, many positive effects accrue to schools in which a normative-instrumental approach to leadership is employed. However, with an essentially control-oriented approach, power is exercised *through* rather than *with* teachers. The move to site-based, shared governance leadership in restructured schools is in part a recognition that teachers, as professionals, deserve a greater voice in educational decision-making.

In the second part of this chapter, we briefly describe the everyday micropolitical strategies and personal characteristics of exemplary school principals that enhanced teachers' sense of empowerment. The data discussed here were drawn from a qualitative study (Blase and Blase, 1994) of teachers in 11 schools affiliated with Glickman's League of Professional Schools in Georgia (Glickman and Allen, 1992). Each school had been affiliated with the League for three years at the time of the study.

Several generations of research on programme implementation and change have echoed the notion that teacher involvement in innovation and change efforts is crucial to their success (Fullan, 1992). More recently, reports by the Carnegie Forum on Education, Task Force on Teaching as a Profession (1986), the Holmes Group (1986) and Green (1986) began what has been referred to as a second wave of school reform. In contrast to earlier efforts, second-wave reformists have advocated fundamental changes in the governance structures of schools to enhance teacher professionalism, autonomy and empowerment. These reforms are based in part on a recognition that teachers' expert knowledge, especially in the areas of curriculum, teaching and learning, should play a major role in decision-making at the school level (Barth, 1990; Maeroff, 1988).

In a shared governance model, the role of the principal shifts to one of delegating decisions to a variety of governance councils that can be made up of a range of constituencies. These councils go under different names, such as 'school improvement teams', 'programme planning teams' and 'school restructuring councils'. In fact, a few schools are beginning to experiment with a model in which a committee of teachers replaces the principal. This section is limited to an analysis of increased participation of teachers only, since in the 11 schools studied, participation on governance committees was dominated by teachers and administrators.

In micropolitical terms, facilitative leadership, as derived from the study data, appears to be a mixture of a power-over, a power-through and, perhaps in a few cases, a power-with approach to leadership. It is *power over* in the sense that the school setting is embedded within larger, highly bureaucratic and hierarchical systems. Therefore, concerns with managing the overall impression of the school, compliance with directives and the perceived effectiveness of the principal take precedence over workplace democracy. After all, many principals correctly argue, they are the ones held accountable for what goes on in the school. When something goes wrong, it is the principal's school in spite of shared decision-making.

The aforementioned orientation is a *power-through* approach to leadership in the sense that principals are able to motivate and mobilize groups that can organize and carry out tasks that benefit the school. As more and more tasks in schools require collaboration, professional knowledge from a variety of sources can more easily be utilized for problem solving. Dunlap and Goldman (1991) have broadened the concept of power to include 'that which facilitates the work of others' (p. 7). By their definition, 'power is through other professionals rather than exercised over them' (Dunlap and Goldman, 1991, p. 23). They call this conception of power 'facilitative power' that 'is rooted in the kind of interaction, negotiation, and mutuality descriptive of professional organizations' (Dunlap and Goldman, 1991, p. 13).

In power-through models, teacher participation is still viewed as more of a privilege than a right, and most other issues remain to be negotiated, such as what kinds of decisions are included and whether participation is merely advisory. This ambiguity and managerial bias should be expected in any shared governance plan that is embedded in a top-down bureaucratic organizational structure. Hargreaves (1991) has pointed out that collaboration and participation tend to become contrived within such structures.

In rare cases shared governance schools contain some aspects of power-with leadership. These tend to be schools serving communities that have been empowered to demand the right to participate in decision-making, even in hiring and firing school administrators. Although these schools are rare, they represent a glimpse into what the democratic/empowering model discussed in the final chapter might look like.

The research on shared governance schools is in its infancy, and few schools have had many years of experience with it. A handful of recent studies of shared governance reveal the centrality of such factors as principal trust (Clift *et al.*, 1992; Lindle, 1991; Martin, 1990), respect for teachers (Clift *et al.*, 1992; Etheridge and Hall, 1991; Lindle, 1991), support for staff development (Kasten *et al.*, 1989), praise (Kasten *et al.*, 1989), vision (Kasten *et al.*, 1989), support of teachers' decisions (Clift *et al.*, 1992), listening (Clift *et al.*, 1992) and providing adequate time (Kasten *et al.*, 1989) for the development of cooperative relationships with teachers.

Studies that specifically address the impact of facilitative forms of influence on teachers' sense of empowerment are also few in number. Bredeson (1989) found several factors – listening, providing supportive resources, visibility, trust, praise, feedback, follow-through on teacher decisions and involvement – that enhanced teachers' sense of empowerment. From a single-school study, Melenyzer (1990) produced a lengthy list of principal leadership factors (e.g. vision, recognition, visibility, decisiveness, respect, support for shared decision-making, support for collegiality) that positively affect teachers' sense of empowerment.

Clearly, very little in this list of leadership factors is surprising. However, what the studies above seem to indicate is that, without such leadership factors, new participatory structures (i.e. committees, councils, etc.) will most likely become mere rubber stamps for principals' decisions. Also, as Kirby and Colbert (1992) point out, principal authenticity (i.e. genuineness) must underlie all of the above factors for teachers to feel empowered.

An open-ended questionnaire designed by the researchers provided teachers with the opportunity to identify and describe in detail characteristics of principals that enhanced their sense of empowerment. Consistent with exploratory-inductive approaches to qualitative inquiry, no *a priori* definitions of leadership characteristics or teacher empowerment were used to direct data collection. Instead, perceptual data were collected and analysed to generate descriptive categories, themes, and conceptual and theoretical ideas (Glaser, 1978; Glaser and Strauss, 1967). (See Appendix for a description of this study.)

Inductive analysis of the data generated a description of facilitative leadership that includes seven major facilitative strategies that enhanced teacher empowerment.

1. *Demonstrating trust in teachers*. Consistent with the findings of Kirby and Colbert (1992) that authenticity was an underlying theme of facilitative leaders, the notion of trust was a constant concern of teachers in the study. It was considered the fundamental element to facilitating teacher empowerment:

   > As a teacher who has worked with children for 16+ years, I feel that I do own a great deal of hands-on experience that is invaluable when assisting future curriculum changes. Not to be involved in decisions (grouping, curriculum, etc.) would be an insult and would have made me feel useless and frustrated.
   > (Kirby and Colbert, 1992, p. 17)

   However, Blase and Roberts (1994) stress that the emphasis was on decisions/actions associated with individual teachers' classrooms rather than school-wide concerns: 'She trusted me to instruct and work with my students in a manner that was compatible to the needs of my students.' 'I was trusted to make decisions about methods of instruction that would benefit my students.'

2. *Developing shared governance structures.* This strategy refers to principals' ability to create and maintain formal shared governance structures and processes. In all schools studied, governance structures dealt with school-wide curriculum, instruction and student discipline. Occasionally, governance structures addressed issues such as hiring, budgeting and scheduling.

    The effectiveness of shared governance structures in promoting teacher empowerment was related to the principals' attempts to (a) provide adequate time for committees to meet on a regular basis; (b) actively involve all faculty and staff in decision-making; (c) make available information relevant to dealing with problems confronting governance committees; (d) attend and actively participate in committee meetings as an equal member; (e) allow individual teachers to select committees of interest for membership; (f) support and implement committee decisions regardless of personal disposition; (g) develop a non-threatening atmosphere in which there was no criticism or punishment for expression; and (h) encourage the use of problem-solving approaches and action research for making decisions.

3. *Encouraging and listening to individual input.* Teachers indicated that they could tell when their input was valued and utilized by principals. They also indicated the importance of a principal's ability to listen and 'hear' teachers' words *and* feelings. Principal listening was further enhanced by a non-evaluative stance toward teachers: '[She] is so supportive of the teachers and their ability to make good decisions. She listens to us and values our opinion, not claiming to have all the answers.' A key element of encouraging input from teachers was the creation of a 'safe' environment in which teachers could speak openly without fear of reprisal.

4. *Encouraging individual teacher autonomy.* Levels of teacher autonomy varied among the shared governance schools investigated. In some schools teachers exercised what many called 'full' autonomy in the classroom; they were largely in control of instructional and non-instructional aspects of the classroom. In other schools teachers reported lower degrees of control. In all schools, both instructional and non-instructional

classroom matters were defined, at least in part, by school principals and school policies. For example, such factors as official syllabuses and curriculum, standing school policies and rules, shared governance decisions and principals' 'expectations' circumscribed individual teacher autonomy.

In spite of these limitations on their autonomy, teachers reported that the new level of classroom autonomy they possessed was sufficient for them to feel 'in control' of classroom affairs. The data suggest that, in part, the teachers' satisfaction was shaped by apparent contrasts in leadership between shared governance principals and most of the traditional principals for whom they had worked in the past.

5. *Encouraging innovation (creativity/risk-taking)*. Shared governance principals encouraged individual teachers and teacher teams to research and experiment with new teaching techniques, curricula and programmes to improve student learning. The data also indicated that creating a 'non-threatening' environment, free from fear, criticism and reprisals for failure, was especially important in encouraging innovation and empowering teachers.

6. *Giving rewards*. Shared governance principals expressed praise regularly, usually through notes of appreciation and verbal 'pats on the back'. Principals made sure that credit was given to teachers for ideas and innovations that they had initiated. Principals were aware of the different contributions that different people had made and created opportunities for all to succeed. The empowering effects of praise were enhanced by principals' recognition of the day-to-day difficulties that teachers encountered in their work.

7. *Providing support*. Support provided by shared governance principals that contributed to teachers' sense of empowerment included (a) staff development opportunities determined by the teachers themselves; (b) access to professional literature and information; (c) availability of basic resources such as time, educational materials and financial resources; and (d) assistance in problem-solving, both professional and personal.

In addition to the strategies described above, five personal characteristics of principals – caring, enthusiasm, optimism, honesty and friendliness – were mentioned by teachers as crucial to teachers' sense of empowerment.

SUMMARY AND DISCUSSION

In the first part of this chapter, we discussed the concept of normative-instrumental leadership. Although this form of effective leadership is based on principal control and teacher compliance, it relies on the use of strategies and purposes consistent with teachers' professional norms and values. However, the normative-instrumental approach to leadership is not substantially democratic. As noted earlier, under this type of leadership, principals typically fail to include teachers in decision-making or limit their involvement significantly. We also argued that normative-instrumental leadership is not equivalent to what Burns (1978) called transformational leadership. Normative-instrumental leadership can be viewed as lying at the far end of the transactional continuum in the facilitative leadership quadrant.

The second study, which describes leadership in restructured schools, moves us closer to transformational leadership. Burns (1978) indicates that transformational leadership is fundamentally moral; it grows from the values, needs and aspirations of followers, and results in mutuality of purpose between leaders and followers. 'Such leadership occurs when ... persons engage with others in such a way that leaders and followers raise each other to higher levels of motivation and morality' (Burns, 1978, p. 20). The powers of leaders and followers interact to create mutual support and common purpose. 'Transforming leadership is ultimately a relationship of mutual stimulation and elevation that converts followers into leaders' (Burns, 1978, p. 4).

Conceptually, the leadership described in the study of restructured schools is consistent with transformational leadership in certain respects even though exchange processes explain some of the underlying political dynamic between principals and teachers who participated in the study. Burns (1978) associates exchange processes between leaders and followers with transactional leadership and argues that such exchanges are designed to satisfy the separate goals of leaders and followers. Although exchange was an important aspect of facilitative leadership and teacher empowerment in this study of shared governance, principals and teachers more often pursued shared goals, especially in relation to issues of teaching and learning.

Nevertheless, it must be remembered that shared governance in the context of this study does not include students, non-certified staff or constituencies outside the school. Therefore, although the dynamics between principals and teachers evident in this study move significantly along the axis from transactional to transformative, the overall approach remains an essentially transactional, facilitative approach to leadership.

Teachers were encouraged to critically examine their classroom practices, and ethical issues and power relations within the school were discussed more openly (in comparison with traditional schools in which teachers had worked). However, as Blase and Roberts (1994) point out, there was no evidence that facilitative leadership promoted in teachers a critical awareness of classroom and school practices in the context of wider community and societal structures. As noted, the schools' communities did not participate in shared governance structures, although there was no evidence that this exclusion was intentional. Clearly, community participation should be considered as a next step in the evolution of the League of Professional Schools.

Chapter 6

Ideological Control and Open Principals
Micropolitics as the Management of Meaning

> The critical element in political maneuver for advantage is the creation of meaning: the construction of beliefs about events, policies, leaders, problems, and crises that rationalize or challenge existing inequalities.
>
> (Edelman, 1988, p. 104)

In the previous chapter we described the micropolitics of two types of facilitative leadership, the normative-instrumental leadership of the first-wave reforms of the 1980s and the shared governance approaches of the late 1980s and early 1990s. Providing structures for shared governance is an important step towards a more democratic and transformative approach to leadership. However, without a better understanding of the subtle and often invisible ways in which hierarchical control is exercised, shared governance approaches will remain firmly within a transactional model. At best, empowerment will be limited to safe and superficial forms of participation, and at worst it will become a guise under which to ensure more effective ideological control. In the current neo-conservative climate in which terms like participatory management and teacher empowerment are tossed around with ease, political literacy in the finer points of ideological control is the only way to distinguish empowerment from manipulation.

To understand the subtleties of school micropolitics, we need fine-grained, interpretive case studies. The purpose of this chapter is to place many of the self-reported micropolitical strategies discussed previously into a broader micropolitical context. Our intent is to demonstrate that any micropolitical strategy can be used in an authentic or manipulative manner, depending on the larger context of the micropolitical environment of the school and school district.

As discussed in the Introduction, control within schools may be exercised through cultural, ideological and symbolic means. For instance, principals are increasingly rewarded for impression management because leadership is viewed as the effective and unobtrusive management of organizational meaning (Anderson, 1991; Firestone and Wilson, 1985; Smircich and Morgan, 1982). The shift from authoritarian approaches of leadership to more open and facilitative ones may not necessarily be a move away from control-oriented models towards true empowerment models. As technologies of control become more subtle and ideological, ostensibly more open and participatory management strategies must be carefully analysed.

This chapter examines the process of cultural or 'cognitive' politics in a suburban school and the extent to which ideological control is exercised when the principal is characterized by teachers as open and facilitative. This study, undertaken during the 1986–87 school year, describes a school with no formal shared governance structures at the building level, although teachers participated actively in district-wide curriculum committees. Through the display of representative interview and observational data, the study explores the ongoing negotiation of the definition of the school and internal authority relationships. It also illustrates the ways in which various forms of ideological control are used in an attempt to ensure teacher support of school district norms.

COGNITIVE POLITICS AND IDEOLOGICAL CONTROL

Finding the right combination of control and autonomy has long been a concern of those who work in organizations and those who study them. There have been many attempts to classify methods of organizational control (such as coercive control, charismatic control, bureaucratic control). Czarniawska-Joerges (1988) classifies control according to its target: control over a person (total control as in prisons or mental institutions), control over behaviour (behavioural control as in direct supervision, rewards and sanctions, rules and regulations) and control over a person's world view or perception of reality (ideological control as traditionally used in churches and political organizations). Although all forms of control exist to some extent in schools, in this chapter we explore the ways in which ideological control is exercised, not in highly ideological organizations like churches and political parties, but rather within the micropolitics of the school.

Schools, because they are loosely coupled organizations (i.e. various components tend to be 'weakly' connected), appear to be less susceptible to more direct modes of control. The data reported in this book demonstrate that the negative impact of authoritarian leadership on a school's micropolitical culture adds fuel to the argument against direct forms of organizational control. Recent attention to the management of 'organizational cultures' seems to indicate an increased awareness of the need for new forms of organizational control (i.e. tighter coupling) in schools (Firestone and Wilson, 1985).

Ideological control through meaning management is becoming a more explicit expectation of administrators in both the public and private sectors (Anderson, 1990). Moreover, increased reliance on ideological control is evidenced throughout American society. A case in point is the adept manipulation of myth and symbol of the Reagan administration. This new approach to leadership is perhaps best expressed by Smircich and Morgan:

Leadership is realized in the process whereby one or more individuals succeed in attempting to frame and define the reality of others. Indeed leadership situations may be conceived as those in which there exists an obligation or a perceived right on the part of certain individuals to define the reality of others.

(Smircich and Morgan, 1982, p. 258)

In schools the right to define the reality of others tends to belong – even in facilitative leadership models – to the principal, although, as we shall see, the definition of reality promoted by principals is seldom their own creation. In fact, in Chapter 7 we discuss the question of whose goals prevail in schools and present a democratic, empowering leadership model.

In this chapter we describe the district and school under analysis, followed by an account of three critical incidents that illustrate how ideological control is manifested in open-principal schools and a discussion of some theoretical implications.

THE STUDY

Context

The Affluent Suburb of Fairlawn Typical of many affluent American suburbs, Fairlawn is a highly educated community containing a large number of professionals, and sends 80 per cent of its high school graduates to college. Few residents of Fairlawn are members of minority groups, and some residents are even 'refugees' of mandated busing to desegregate schools in the neighbouring city.

To understand the cognitive politics of an individual school in Fairlawn, one must appreciate the influence of the district's emphasis on harmony and the avoidance of overt conflict and 'politics'. Thus, the following brief description of the place of principals, teachers and students in Fairlawn's formal district hierarchy sketches out the broader context.

Teachers in Fairlawn have few formal avenues of political power. Complaints must go 'through channels', which means that they tend to stop at the principal's office. District-wide teachers have the opportunity to serve on curriculum committees, and they have a professional association (the term 'union' is avoided) that provides them with a unified voice on some issues. Furthermore, because they work at the service-delivery level, teachers enjoy a great deal of discretionary decision-making power in their classrooms. A few teachers also have informal contacts at higher levels of the authority structure. By and large, teachers in Fairlawn are content. They are well paid by most standards and hard-working (lots of committee work after school). 'Burnout' is rare. If anything, Fairlawn teachers might find themselves bored or on a professional plateau. Open conflict and hostility between teachers and principals are also rare.

Notable for their absence in most micropolitical studies, students are at the bottom of Fairlawn's hierarchy and have no formal authority, except through student councils, which are essentially powerless entities. The source of their informal power is their potential recourse – seldom exercised – to not play by the school's rules. The smooth functioning of the school and its legitimacy are ultimately tied to the consent of its clients to the rules of the institution (Cusick, 1973).

Principals in Fairlawn are classic examples of middle management. They are not part of the central-office inner circle, nor are they part of the teachers' association. A major task of principals is to mediate conflict and legitimate various organizational stakeholders to each other. They mediate between parents and teachers, teachers and teachers, teachers and central office, teachers and students, and so on. In analysing the micropolitics of schools at the building level, it is important to remember that principals are as much middle management as they are building-level leaders. At least in Fairlawn, principals may technically be the teachers' immediate bosses, but they are, in their own way, as vulnerable as teachers.

Frank Bradley, Fairlawn's assistant superintendent for elementary education, describes the vulnerability of principals in Fairlawn.

Frank: I think the principals here have two kinds of pressures.
          One is keeping the parents happy and that's no easy task.
          I would say, however, that as great a challenge is that we
          basically expect in this district for principals to keep their
          staff happy and have a good climate. When there is a
          problem with staff it is expected to be solved and to be
          worked out in a positive way. If it isn't you really take a
          lot of criticism. A lot of people think, well suburbia, that's
          easy, but a teaching staff in this district basically has a lot
          of influence and power. Principals are really under the gun.
          If they do not satisfy staff it just comes out all over the
          place, and principals keep things in line because they know
          they have to do that. They feel a lot of pressure to put
          things out for staff – keep staff happy. Teachers know
          politically how to put the pressure on principals. Staffs can
          basically run principals right out of here.
Interviewer: Is it through the teachers' organization?
Frank: It is the teachers' organization but it is also our
          expectations. We firmly believe that we want climate and
          cooperation. It's our model and if the staff rebels against
          you, you are not doing it. You are not doing the job. I
          don't want you to misunderstand that we don't back our

> principals – we do. The principals understand that, they
> have been through it. Most of them were once teachers and
> they know. The ones that come from the outside are the
> ones that have the problems because they are coming from
> a different – they don't understand. It takes them a little
> while. We always say that basically you have to be
> 'Fairlawnized' to really work effectively.

The 'climate and cooperation' stressed at central office requires that principals successfully mediate the conflicting expectations of organizational stakeholders. In attempting to resolve conflicts, however, principals must be aware of organizational norms and policies whose legitimacy they are expected to uphold. If the school is a negotiated order, the principal must develop a keen sense of which norms and policies are negotiable and which ones are not. This knowledge of limits in part constitutes what Frank Bradley calls being 'Fairlawnized', and it is required if principals are to be entrusted with the management of organizational meaning.

As the above quote illustrates, teachers in a school have the collective power to get rid of a principal. Principals deal with this vulnerability in a number of ways, but the primary tactic is to build a political base – either among teachers, as was the case in Fairlawn, or among powerful community interest groups, as tends to be the case in the more overtly political urban school systems. However, if principals are vulnerable, so are teachers. Again, Frank Bradley:

> This community can come down on teachers pretty strongly, and
> this is a true measure of how a staff is going to feel about a
> principal. The principal that seems to make it here is one that
> will support that teacher and protect that teacher to the parents
> and to a certain extent cover up for them and try to help them in
> terms of the parents. But behind the scenes the principal has got
> to get on that teacher good. We try to keep the parents off the
> backs of the teachers but if there is a problem, the principals are
> expected to get it straightened out with that teacher. In most
> cases, unless it is a pretty weak teacher, in two or three years a
> principal learns how to deal with that kind of thing. There are
> some teachers that are weak, and you can't fool the parents
> about that.

Some principals, however, even reported being able to legitimate weak teachers to the community and central office by keeping disruptive children out of their classrooms and not assigning the children of aggressive parents to them.

In Fairlawn, micropolitics are played out in the context of this fundamental bargain between principals and teachers. Similar bargains are struck between teachers and students and provide a context for classroom micropolitics. Each time this fundamental bargain is betrayed, it increases everyone's sense of vulnerability. Why would principals want to 'cover' for weak teachers? Why would teachers and principals want to avoid student suspensions? One reason that firing teachers and suspending students is kept to a minimum in Fairlawn is that such acts tend to break down the rules of political exchange and throw off the delicate power balances among teachers, principals, central office and parents.

This may make for good organizational maintenance but, as Fraatz (1987) and McNeil (1986) have documented, the need to maintain existing organizational arrangements may take precedence over the need to address educational problems that these arrangements seem incapable of remedying. For this reason, the recent move to shared governance is a positive one, but for shared governance structures to work, we must better understand why these broad micropolitical bargains are struck in the first place. If they are struck to protect social and political interests that prefer the status quo not be challenged, then shared governance structures will also be coopted by those interests.

Fairlawn's Cognitive Politics The ways in which principals achieve 'climate and cooperation' in their schools vary, but they nearly always involve some form of cognitive politics. Meaning is managed symbolically, and the most effective form of symbolic communication is language. The promotion of a conflict-free vocabulary in the district and schools is pervasive, and through this medium the extent of one's 'Fairlawnization' is revealed.

For example, Frank Bradley is proud of what he calls Fairlawn's 'humanistic' philosophy and stresses the importance of selecting administrators and teachers who personify it. Staffs in Fairlawn are 'teams' or 'families'; arguments are 'conversations' or 'interactions'; problems are 'challenges' or 'growth experiences'. Optimism, hard work and harmonious relations are rewarded. Teachers and administrators openly use the vocabulary of psychological typing. People are 'expressives' or 'amiables'. (There are no 'driver' or 'analytical' types among Fairlawn principals.) Extensive and costly workshops and perceiver inventories are given to determine personnel leadership styles, and hiring of new personnel is also done partly on this basis.

Being 'Fairlawnized' requires, among other things, learning to use the language of harmony and consensus. The objective is to project the reality of a world relatively free of real conflict of interest. Whether projected within the district or the society at large, most principals and teachers are aware that such a reality is, at best, a half-truth, and at worst, an illusion. A major part of their job, however, is to maintain the legitimacy of this definition of Fairlawn's social reality and the language out of which it is constructed.

Morningside Elementary School Morningside Elementary is located a few blocks from Fairlawn's elegant main street. Its 458 students, 17 teachers and 16 support staff occupy sunny, bright classrooms whose walls are covered with children's artwork. Kathy Martin took over as principal of Morningside six years ago and is viewed by most people in the district as a rising star. Kathy's interactions with parents, teachers and even students take place across a conference table in her office where the trappings of authority are eschewed in favour of a more equal and intimate setting. The outer office is a warm and inviting place where parents and staff can mingle comfortably with secretaries and administrators. There are no counters for parents to wait behind, and Kathy keeps an open-door policy, scheduling her time so that 'interruptions' become an integral part of her workday.

During the year of this study, there were several contentious issues at Morningside Elementary. One involved a conflict between Kathy and the Morningside librarian over staffing needs. Another involved an increasing potential for conflict between teachers advocating literature-based, whole language approaches to reading instruction and those who preferred a basal approach. Finally, there was teacher resentment over a decision made by Kathy and other principals in the district to have teachers code their lesson plans to state competencies for the upcoming state evaluation. The following sections briefly describe these three critical incidents and illustrate some ways in which ideological control emerged as a recurrent theme.

Three Potential Conflicts

Upholding the Ideology of Containment and Averting Collective Action

Recently the district librarians, who had been working extremely long hours, got together and decided that if they did not have access to aides, they would all work only their required hours. Kathy acknowledged that Marsha, the Morningside librarian, was very good and frequently worked overtime. In fact, on a recent Friday night, Kathy and the librarian had both been working at the school past midnight. Nevertheless Kathy comments:

> The librarianship is a really important position. It's a person who touches every child and teacher in the building. That library needs to be a focal point of the school, and I have certain expectations for that job. I expect beyond the minimum from every staff member ... I had said to her yesterday, 'Marsha, we need to get it worked out for our building. If things are not going well, then we need to work it out. If what I've done to help isn't enough, let's talk it through'. But when we get that mentality – that district mentality – of we're not going to do this or that, then there's a certain block that goes straight up and down in me and I'm not going to be responsive and I doubt that the other principals would be either.

It is apparent that librarians in the district are attempting to develop an alternative power base. In a district that prides itself on 'talking things through' one-on-one and achieving consensus, such actions imply that real conflicts of interest might exist. Kathy knows that, beyond resolving this specific conflict, she is charged with re-establishing the legitimacy among staff of the norms of giving extra effort and time, of school loyalty, and of working out problems individually rather than collectively. To achieve this goal, Kathy expresses her sense of betrayal at the librarian's lack of solidarity. Employing a family metaphor, she implies that there is nothing wrong with networking with the other librarians in the district, as long as one doesn't forget where one's loyalties belong. When Kathy talks of getting things worked out for 'our' building, she is appealing to a sense of familial solidarity. When she speaks of talking it through individually rather than getting that 'district mentality', she is upholding an ideology of containment. In Fairlawn, problems are to be contained to the building level whenever possible; collective actions are anathema. Having effectively headed off a conflict with potential for ramifications beyond the building level, Kathy welcomes the prodigal librarian back into the family.

In Fairlawn, established norms are reinforced, policies implemented and hierarchical control maintained largely through the effective management of meaning. Fairlawnization is never taken for granted, it must be constantly won. The librarian and Kathy Martin were ultimately able to come to an understanding about the lack of the availability of aides, but the real threat that the incident represented was to the district norm of 'extra effort' and the school-level norm of building solidarity ('our building') over district solidarity ('that district mentality'). Understanding this, Kathy was careful to manage meaning in such a way as to re-establish the legitimacy of these norms.

Language Games and the Politics of Marginalization Another issue at Morningside with a potential for conflict involved a split among teachers concerning the use of a literature versus a basal-based reading programme. Kathy had staved off the crisis at her school, largely through hiring teachers who were not 'fanatical' about literature, but pro-literature teachers had mounted an impressive campaign in other schools. Moreover, two new pro-literature principals were behind-the-scenes actors, lending legitimacy to the use of literature at the building level. Both quietly put in large book orders for literature, brought in speakers to explain the literature-based philosophy, and 'stacked' the district reading committee with aggressive and articulate supporters of literature-based instruction. One of them explained how she uses hiring to tip the balance of power in her building:

> It really helps when literature-based is supported by the
> principal, that you hire those people that support that. For all
> of the people that I hired this summer, literature was a real
> concern. I asked questions like: 'What is the best way to teach
> reading? How would you feel if you didn't have any books?'

Meanwhile, Frank Bradley was stacking his own committees to make sure the outcome was not determined by the so-called literature 'fanatics'. According to Kathy, Frank told her, 'Kathy I want you to serve on that reading committee because I need some balance there.'

Although the above types of political strategies are well documented in the micropolitical literature, less well documented are the ways in which language is used as a tool in the management of meaning at the building and district levels. Pro-literature teachers promoted the concept of literature-based instruction. Realizing that the use of literature in some form was inevitable, pro-basal teachers and principals attempted to control the definition of the reading programme. Another Fairlawn principal illustrates how important language is in this process:

> I almost hesitate to be against literature-based. I'm not against it. I'm for it. But it does bother me a little bit, and I'm a little worried about it. It is another one of those things that comes down the road that has got some great things to offer children and the teachers. The reason I sometimes hesitate and say, let's go slow with it or be careful is because it makes me sound like an old stick-in-the-mud who's all for basal readers and basal workbooks, and I'm not. I'm concerned about literature – not so much the word 'literature', but the word 'based'. It bothers me because I'm not sure our teachers will be trained in developing their own reading programme. I think that many of them will not have the time or the expertise to do that, so I think we still need to purchase a prepared reading programme, give them that, and let them teach it to the children. Now 'literature-supplemented', I like.

Besides the clearly disempowering message that teachers need a curriculum that is structured for them, this narrative demonstrates an explicit concern for language and how it is used to shape the reality of the school's reading programme. In the battle over the definition of the reading programme, the pro-basal 'stick-in-the-muds' and the pro-literature 'fanatics' have been marginalized through labelling. If the labels can be made to stick, then the two extremes will be discredited, 'balance' can be achieved, open conflict averted, and 'climate and cooperation' sustained.

Spin control and the Mediation of Meaning Kathy's attempt to legitimate lesson-plan coding for the state evaluation exemplifies how meaning is often constructed for teachers in arenas in which they do not participate. Teachers were upset by the massive amount of extra work that coding lesson plans to state minimum competencies required and their lack of input into the decision. Kathy used a divide-and-conquer strategy by dealing with teachers by grade level rather than collectively on the coding issue. The goodwill Kathy had accrued with teachers and her appeals to school loyalty and competitiveness ('we really want to shine on this one') got her through some stiff resistance from the fifth grade teachers. However, when the report from the state department came back, there were few accolades for any of the elementary schools and Kathy did not want the teachers to know that their extra efforts were not reflected in the evaluations.

During a meeting the eight district principals and Frank Bradley discussed how or if the disappointing state evaluations should be shared with teachers. Comments among principals at the meeting provide a flavour of this discussion.

Principal 1:   What will teachers say after all the work we put them through?

Kathy: I don't want my staff to read it. I'm going to make it real positive. I'll tell them there's a copy in my office.

Bob: I think the teachers have a right to have copies of the report. We can't hide it from them.

Kathy: I'm not hiding it. I'm making it available, but I think it's really important how it's presented.

Frank Bradley: We can't have 15 different versions here.

Bob: Why does everyone have to do the same thing? Either hand out the report or make it available.
                 [Several more minutes of discussion]

Frank Bradley: Bob, you have to be careful how you handle this. We needn't feel that we need to apologize for the big push we did. Maybe we were in overkill looking back. [After a couple more minutes of discussion] OK. Here's what I hear us saying. [He summarizes each principal's position.] It will be each principal's decision if you want to give out the report. But stress that there's a copy available and that you don't want to use up the paper.

Bob had been opposed to the coding from the beginning. The underlying attitude towards teachers that he demonstrates in the meeting is consistent with the comments he made in an interview:

> Those teachers out there are professional people with a lot of blue collar responsibilities, such as you will be here at eight o'clock in the morning. You will stay on the job until 3:45. You will take those silly pictures and put the kid's name on the back of them so we can put them in ... you know? What has that got to do with being a professional person? Some day we're going to wake up and let them function as professional people.

Frank's admonition to Bob during the principals' meeting suggests that he cannot be trusted to present this report in a way that will not make teachers feel justified in their opposition to coding. He is being encouraged to buy into the distorted reality which the principals have constructed and wish to present as a united front. At stake here is the power over the definition of organizational events. If meaning is not effectively managed by these principals, the teachers may establish their own meanings as dominant and in so doing challenge the principals' right to make such decisions in the future. Pfeffer summarizes nicely how power can hide behind social constructions created for subordinates' consumption:

> Substantive organizational actions, by which we mean actual decisions and choices with observable, physical referents, are largely predicted from circumstances of power and dependence. The task of those who benefit from these decisions is to legitimate and justify them, *to render power less visible.*
>
> (Pfeffer, 1981a, p. 182)

THEORETICAL IMPLICATIONS

Although cognitive politics exist in all schools, ideological control is not necessarily the dominant form of control in every school. In contrast, more traditional forms of political control appeared to be dominant in a nearby inner-city school (a 30-minute drive from Fairlawn). There the principal went about systematically building a political base within the local community power structure. In this way he acquired sufficient autonomy to manage the micropolitics of the school with near impunity. The following quotes taken from interviews of the principal and selected teachers provide some flavour of the school's micropolitics:

Principal: I tell people exactly what I think, whether they're my superiors or not. I would not recommend that to people. That's a helluva risk. I take that risk probably more often than I should, but I'm comfortable taking that risk because of the power base I've developed.

Teacher A: When he came to this school he really came in gangbusters, and he turned a lot of people off. He turned us off. But the more you get to know him, the more you know that he just sort of spouts off. You let it roll off your back. You can't take it personally.

Teacher B: He forced a lot of teacher transfers.

Researcher: How does one do that? How does one force a transfer?

Teacher B: Put a lot of pressure on them. Make their lives miserable.

Teacher A: Bad evaluations. Say either leave or I'll make your life miserable for the next few months.

Teacher B: He can get teachers to transfer. He's good at getting rid of teachers.

Principal (referring to teachers): They come to me with their problems
and I have no problem with that. I can deal with their
problems and I can help them with some of their problems.
They'll get what they want and then they are going to owe
me, which is what I want.
I can't make the guy here before me [the former principal]
look bad because he's downtown [central office] now on
special assignment. That could very easily change and I
could be working for him, so I can't afford to make him
look bad.

Principal [discussing his new assistant principal]:
The tactic I'm going to use with him is I'm going to put my
foot in his butt, and he will die politically if that's what it
takes. He's going to be out of here one way or the other in
June. He's either going to get his own school, which is what
he was promised, or if he crosses me, I'll see that he doesn't
get his school.

As the above quotes indicate and as noted throughout this book, much of
what occurs in micropolitics can be explained by some version of exchange
theory. Exchange theories assume that people attempt to maximize the gains
and minimize the costs of social interaction in order to obtain desired outcomes.
Both Frank Bradley's comments and those of the urban principal quoted above
provide a practitioner perspective on how exchanges among teachers, principals
and parents occur in schools.

However, a critical theory lens is needed to understand how ideological control makes it less evident that an exchange is taking place, as well as who really
benefits from the exchange. This is especially true since, despite the management discourse of 'kids come first', children are seldom the direct beneficiaries
of most micropolitical exchanges. To the extent that language is used to construct an official reality that discounts real conflicts of interest as 'negativism',
'disloyalty', 'that district mentality', 'aggressiveness' or any other label that
results in the marginalization of dissenters, a critical perspective is needed. This
is consistent with Ball's finding that:

the control of school organizations ... is significantly concerned
with domination (the elimination or pre-emption of conflict).
Thus, domination is intended to achieve and maintain particular
definitions of the school over and against alternative, assertive
definitions. The process which links these two basic facets of
organizational life – conflict and domination – is micro-politics.

(Ball, 1987, p. 218)

Edelman elaborates on the importance of language in the micropolitics of domination:

> It is language about political events, not the events in any other
> sense, that people experience; even developments that are close
> by take their meaning from the language that depicts them.
> So political language is political reality; there is no other so
> far as the meaning of events to actors and spectators is
> concerned.
>
> (Edelman, 1988, p. 104)

A critical perspective may be even more helpful in analysing Fairlawn's cognitive politics within a broader social context. It may be that affluent suburban school systems project a definition of social reality in which their children are allocated to the best colleges and professional schools as a matter of course and that their student population consists of few poor and minority children. Real estate associations and parents concerned with property values help to define this reality as a non-political one in which there is no conflict of interest over the allocation of scarce resources.

Although the data in this study are not sufficient to support such a macro-level interpretation, it is important to recognize that schools are embedded in larger social contexts that inevitably influence micropolitics. Marcus and Fischer claim that the researcher has an obligation to go beyond the mere documentation of those outside forces and macrostructural elements that affect the local cultural unit under analysis:

> The 'outside forces' are an integral part of the construction and
> constitution of the 'inside', the cultural unit itself, and must be
> so registered, even at the most intimate levels of cultural
> process.
>
> (Marcus and Fischer, 1986, p. 77)

According to Marcus and Fischer, if relations of domination and inequality – whether of class, race or gender – are part of a society's social fabric, they will manifest themselves in subtle ways at micro-levels of analysis. Therefore, the critical ethnographer, although always taking care to be aware of the dangers of overdeterminism, views the highly contested cultural construction of meaning at the micro-level as a product, at least in part, of broader political and economic interests (Anderson, 1989).

IMPLICATIONS FOR TEACHER EMPOWERMENT AND THE PRINCIPALSHIP

Ideological control, most often referred to in the educational administration literature as 'the management of culture', is increasingly being used to tighten loose coupling in hierarchical organizations. It remains unclear whether the current rhetoric of managing the organizational culture, 'empowering' teachers and sharing decision-making means anything more than new management techniques for greater control and efficiency. Teachers are right to examine critically empowerment movements promoted from above; they need to be aware of the subtle forms that ideological control can take.

On the other hand, although cognitive politics can serve vested interests and the maintenance of the status quo, it can also be a means for progressive change in the interests of democracy, equity and teacher professionalism. In fact, the literature-based instruction 'movement' among some teachers in Fairlawn had as much to do with teachers having a voice in their professional decisions as it did with preference of teaching methods.

For this reason, the introduction of participatory governance structures is an important step in moving from normative-instrumental leadership to a type of facilitative leadership with the potential to create democratic workplaces. However, we cannot assume that these structures will result in more democratic workplaces without a thorough understanding of how power and control are currently exercised. That would be a naive assumption, and teachers are not naive. They know the feeling of being labelled and marginalized if they are too outspoken in 'democratic' forums. They know the feeling of being locked out of the centres of power where important information is shared. They have felt the risks of collective action even on a small scale. They know all the subtle and not so subtle ways that teachers are silenced. And ironically many of them end up using the same strategies on students and parents in the micropolitics of their classrooms and communities. As McNeil (1983) has illustrated, schools as they are currently run are more about control than they are about education. Unless these issues are addressed, facilitative leadership and shared governance structures will represent the latest in a series of efforts to avoid change through creating the impression of change.

Power gained at the expense of other organizational stakeholders is not empowerment. Empowerment occurs when the powerless begin to understand those broader political and economic interests that get played out at the school level and the ways in which those interests are sustained through a politics of cognition. Who wins control over definitions of 'empowerment', 'restructuring' and other terms that provide a frame for school problems will determine the outcome of cognitive politics. The effort to control cognition will be carried out in universities, academic journals, teachers' unions, state and federal legislatures and the media. But, perhaps most critically, it will be played out at the school building level among principals, teachers, parents and students.

In the following chapter we discuss in more detail the barriers to democratic, empowering leadership and provide some idea of what a democratic and empowered school might look like.

Chapter 7

Democratic, Empowering Leadership
Leadership as 'Power With'

> To lead is to be at the center of a group, rather than in front of
> others (Hartsock, 1981, p. 116)

The research on the micropolitics of schools discussed in this book suggests that
(a) the nature and exercise of power needs to be more central to theories of leadership and (b) formal leaders have a strong influence on the micropolitical culture
that develops in a given school. Understanding these issues of power and a
school's micropolitical culture is a prerequisite to establishing the kind of
democratic, empowering leadership advocated in this chapter.

Real-life examples of democratic, empowering leadership are difficult to
find. Although one example is presented at the end of this chapter, democratic,
empowering leadership is still more rhetoric than reality. In a sense, this is not
surprising. Participatory democracy can be threatening to the beneficiaries of
a social system, whether a small school district or a large country. Unfortunately, it is usually those beneficiaries who, throughout history have been in
a position to define 'democratic' behaviour and to promote definitions of
democracy that do not challenge the status quo (Rizvi, 1989).

The reform rhetoric of school restructuring is full of democratic terminology
such as 'participatory decision-making' and 'teacher empowerment', but its aim
has been limited to promoting organizational effectiveness and increasing
teachers' intrinsic motivation. The aim of a democratic, empowering approach
to leadership does not, according to Keith (in press):

> rest on a philosophy of humane management and its aim is not
> to improve teacher morale, decisions, and standardized test
> scores. Rather, it is premised on limiting and eventually
> eradicating power differentials and reconstructing the workplace
> as a just, democratic community. In its broadest sense, the
> concept of participation allows teachers, students, and
> community members to participate in an emancipatory
> discourse.

Keith further indicates that teacher empowerment, when understood
merely as greater professionalization, fails to address the ways in which

well-intentioned professionals have often worked together to control their clients, particularly when those clients are different with regard to race and social class. After all, professionalization is usually associated with authority *over* one's 'clients'. To empower teachers in isolation from parents, students and other school stakeholders is to risk empowering one constituency at the price of disempowering others (Delpit, 1993).

CAN WE CREATE AND SUSTAIN POWER-WITH APPROACHES TO LEADERSHIP IN A POWER-OVER WORLD?

Throughout this book we have discussed the limitations of authoritarian, adversarial and facilitative approaches to school leadership. Although we are comfortable in rejecting authoritarian leadership as both unethical and ineffective, adversarial and facilitative approaches to leadership are often highly effective and may be the best we can expect in most schools under current micro- and macropolitical conditions. In proposing that schools move in the direction of greater democracy and empowerment, our intention is not to denigrate effective adversarial or facilitative school principals who are struggling under extremely difficult and stressful working conditions. Our experience in the public school system makes us aware of the systemic constraints on educational practitioners.

Although it is difficult to find current examples of democratic, empowering leadership, some do exist, proving that this approach to leadership is not a utopian dream. Examples can be found among informal groups, academic departments, and others who find ways to create democratic communities within educational institutions. In the real world, achieving this kind of approach is always partial, always tentative, and must be constantly re-created as teachers, students, parents and administrators come and go. Moreover, because democracy is fundamentally process-oriented, each school must forge its own approach to democratic, empowering leadership. Although models can be suggestive and helpful, the specific issues that must be tackled will vary from school to school.

Futhermore, because schools are part of larger social systems and communities, they are limited by both policy and custom in what they can do. Many principals who consider themselves advocates for poor and minority children might convincingly argue that only through an adversarial, political approach can one force progressive reforms through the system. However, the cost to these leaders is often martyrdom. Many of the very best adversarial leaders with laudable transformative aims have, in fact, been fired by school boards and central offices. Perhaps the most famous was Dennis Litky, the Coalition of Essential Schools principal in New Hampshire, who was reinstated through a successful challenge in the courts (Wood, 1993). Carmen Guappone, featured in Chapter 1, was eventually fired by his school board; now in retirement, the spirited Mr Guappone managed to get himself elected to the school board and was successful in reinstating the fine arts programme that the school board had attempted to eliminate.

The lesson here may be that within the current constraints of power and custom, democratic, empowering leadership would result in even more martyrs. Empowered individuals who challenge entrenched interests are seldom rewarded by their institutions. Another possible conclusion is that adversarial versions of transformative leadership are insufficiently democratic and empowering. That is, once the strong adversarial leader is removed, there is often not a sufficient base of empowered teachers, parents and students to carry on the project. The principal's transformative vision might not have been *their* vision in the first place. The central dilemma of democratic, empowering leadership is perhaps best expressed by Hartsock, who draws on the experience of alternative feminist organizations:

> Creating political change requires that we set up organizations based on power defined as energy and strength, groups that are structured, not tied to the personality of a single individual, and whose structures do not permit the use of power to dominate others in the group. At the same time, our organizations must be effective in a society in which power is a means of making others do what they do not wish to do.
>
> (Hartsock, 1981, pp. 117–18)

The dilemma that Hartsock highlights is our need to create power-with organizations that can thrive within a power-over world. This situation may ultimately require some combination of adversarial, facilitative and democratic, empowering behaviours. For example, the power-with approaches that create democratic cultures at the school level are likely to be ineffectual in the school's interface with a traditional, district central office.

PUSHING BEYOND FACILITATIVE LEADERSHIP

Authoritarian and adversarial approaches to leadership are not typically promoted as effective styles of school leadership, at least among researchers and those who prepare educational administrators. Facilitative approaches to leadership, currently the most advocated approach, appear congruent with achieving site-based management and power sharing. In fact, at least on the surface, many of the leadership behaviours and personal characteristics comprising facilitative leadership are also those exhibited in democratic, empowering leadership.

The facilitative leadership behaviours described in Chapter 5, such as demonstrating trust, providing support and encouraging creativity and risk-taking, as well as personal characteristics like caring, honesty and friendliness, are also required by democratic, empowering leadership. But, unlike facilitative leadership, which draws on a human relations tradition with primary goals of teacher and student motivation and productivity, democratic, empowering leadership draws from a different tradition: democracy and social justice are the primary goals of its emancipatory, transformative tradition (Foster, 1986).

Drawing on this emancipatory tradition, Hampton *et al.* (1994) have summarized the attitudes that Paulo Freire argues are necessary to foster the kind of 'true dialogue' required for democratic, empowering leadership and societal change. These attitudes, taken from Freire's (1972) *Pedagogy of the Oppressed*, are the following:

1. Love: 'Dialogue ... cannot exist in the absence of a profound love for the world and for human beings.' (p. 78)

2. Humility: 'Dialogue ... is broken if the parties lack humility. How can I dialogue if I always project ignorance on others and never perceive my own?' (p. 78)

3. Faith: 'Dialogue ... requires an intense faith in people, faith in their power to make and re-make, to create and re-create, faith in their vocation to be more fully human.' (p. 79)

4. Trust: 'Dialogue becomes a horizontal relationship of which mutual trust between the dialoguers is the logical consequence.' (pp. 79–80)

5. Hope: 'Dialogue cannot be carried on in a climate of hopelessness. If the dialoguers expect nothing to come of their effort, their encounter will be empty, sterile, bureaucratic, and tedious.' (p. 80)

6. Critical thinking: 'Finally, true dialogue cannot exist unless the dialoguers engage in critical thinking. The important thing is the continuing transformation of reality on behalf of the continuing humanization of people.' (p. 81)

Twenty years ago, a suggestion that Freire's emancipatory discourse could form a basis for educational leadership would have been greeted with scepticism within the field of education. However, many of these same qualities have been recently advocated by mainstream researchers and practitioners in education who are affiliated with site-based, shared governance approaches to educational leadership, what we have been calling facilitative leadership. We argue in this section, however, that it makes a difference whether these characteristics serve transactional or transformative ends.

In arguing that facilitative leadership serves transactional ends, we mean that it fails to raise critical questions about the institutional and social status quo. Although this approach to leadership may, in contrast to adversarial approaches, create a more open, humane and participatory school culture, its limited concept of democracy and empowerment tends to leave existing power

relations intact. Nevertheless, we believe that democratic, empowering leadership approaches should draw from the political realism of adversarial leadership
and the open and participatory orientation of facilitative leadership.

In fact, there has already been impressive movement among 'open' principals from transactional to transformative approaches to leadership, as shown
in Chapter 5 in the descriptions of normative-instrumental and shared governance approaches. At the same time that democratic, empowering leadership
requires pushing the rhetoric of shared governance leadership to its logical,
democratic conclusion, such an approach also requires a fundamental rethinking
of what empowerment means.

Blase and Blase (1994) have discussed the importance of how principals provide support for teachers and facilitate the change process in shared governance
schools. Reitzug (1994) have also indicated the importance of support and
facilitation for what they call 'empowering leaders'. Drawing on these two
studies, Figure 7.1 compares how various leadership roles (i.e. support, facilitation and action) are used differently by facilitative and democratic, empowering
leaders.

In real life, those representing one leadership approach might demonstrate
leadership behaviours more typical of the other approach. For example,
facilitative leaders would occasionally address issues of equity and justice, and
democratic, empowering leaders would not necessarily ignore district-wide
restructuring policies. *The difference is whether reforms equally benefit all constituencies.* Not only are the processes of democratic, empowering leadership
less hierarchical, but the goals are more oriented to issues of social justice.

Figure 7.1 Leadership behaviours: facilitative versus democratic, empowering

	Support
Facilitative	Providing a supportive environment for teacher autonomy and professionalization
Democratic/ Empowering	Achieving a supportive environment for critique and voice (emancipatory discourse)

	Facilitation
Facilitative	Stimulating the adoption of reforms emphasizing 'mutual adaptation'
Democratic/ Empowering	Examining educational processes and outcomes that are unjust and inequitable

	Action/Possibility
Facilitative	Collaboratively guiding the implementation and institutionalization of reforms
Democratic/ Empowering	Promoting an ongoing spiral of dialogue and action aimed at creating just and equitable conditions for *all* students and teachers

Starratt (1991) calls this process 'building an ethical school' and argues that this requires an ethic of critique, justice and caring. According to Starrat, an ethic of *critique* involves, among other things, critiquing the school's own bureaucratic context and its technicist approaches to teaching and assessing learning. It also raises questions about the social arrangements of schools, such as, 'Who benefits by these arrangements? Which group dominates this social arrangement? Who defines the way things are structured here?' (Starratt, 1991, p. 189). As noted above, democratic, empowering leadership supports this kind of critique and strives to create an environment in which it can be done safely.

The ethic of critique uncovers and names unethical practices in schools and 'implies in its critique some ethical values such as equality, the common good, human and civil rights, democratic participation, and the like' (Starratt, 1991, p. 191). An ethic of *justice* moves the critique to action as unjust practices are confronted and responded to.

Finally, an ethic of *caring* returns us to Freire's (1972) notions of love, humility, faith and trust, previously discussed. According to Starratt, an ethic of caring:

> focuses on the demands of relationships, not from a contractual
> or legalistic standpoint, but from a standpoint of absolute regard
> ... Such an ethic does not demand relationships of intimacy;
> rather, it postulates a level of caring that honors the dignity of
> each person ... This ethic reaches beyond concerns with effi-
> ciency, which can easily lead to using human beings as merely
> the means to some larger purpose of productivity, such as an
> increase in the district's average scores on standardized tests or
> the lowering of per-pupil costs.
>
> (Starratt, 1991, p. 197)

The limitation of the facilitative power-through approach to leadership is precisely in its emphasis on using individuals and groups as means to achieving ends, ends that have largely been determined elsewhere.

BARRIERS TO DEMOCRATIC, EMPOWERING LEADERSHIP: ACHIEVING POLITICAL LITERACY

Clearly, a democratic, empowering approach to leadership resembles more recent forms of facilitative leadership in its commitment to sharing and, in some cases, transferring power. However, the recent track record of shared governance in education has not been good. Studies of site-based management have found that governance committees in which administrators, teachers and parents participate are typically coopted by district and building administrators.

Perhaps the most dramatic evidence is Malen and Ogawa's (1988) district-wide case study of site-based governance councils in Salt Lake City, Utah. These councils were given broad jurisdiction, formal policy-making authority, parity protection (e.g. equal voting power) and training provisions. Even under these highly favourable arrangements, Malen and Ogawa found that teachers and parents actually exerted little influence on significant issues in decision arenas. Unless we understand the subtle ways in which democracy may be subverted, shared governance leadership will prove to be one more ineffective solution for the very real crisis in which many of our schools and school districts find themselves.

For true democratic and empowering leadership to become a reality, the real challenge for educational practitioners may be not so much what they need to learn as what they need to *unlearn*. The latter may include how practitioners enact organizational roles, how 'school' is supposed to be done, and how they view the traditional role of parents and students. However, there is also much to be learned that is seldom taught in university courses or district staff development activities. Along these lines, we believe that one of the key tasks of educational leadership is the demystification of power relations in schools, so that principals and teachers can become more aware of how power is exercised in school settings.

The following sections offer a few 'basics' in political literacy by analysing the limitations of current models of shared governance and teacher empowerment. The move to true democratic, empowering approaches to leadership is grounded in demystifying the control-oriented and transactional nature of much of the current restructuring discourse.

Understanding the Relationship Between Schools and Their Broader Social Context

The move to shared governance and empowerment is reflected in the discourse of management ranging from business administration to educational leadership. This discourse, which reflects a strong management bias, fails to address some fundamental contradictions in management-led empowerment efforts. For example, the business administration literature seldom notes that at the same time that US workers are being 'empowered' in the workplace through participatory, site-based management, their unions are being systematically weakened, their salaries and benefits are being rolled back, their companies are being 'downsized' and their jobs are being moved overseas (Anderson and Dixon, 1993). This social disempowerment of workers, carried out under the banner of workplace empowerment, is like an Alice in Wonderland world in which language is turned on its head.

Likewise, as we exhort teachers to demand more control over decisions that affect their status as professionals, the United States is gearing up for a new national standardized achievement test. Such a test will drive a new national curriculum that teachers will feel obligated to follow. Decentralized decision-making at the local level within a context of increased control and centralization of decision-making at broader levels seems to be the order of the day. Why?

Weiler (1990) argues that in highly conflictual arenas such as educational policy, decentralization allows sources of conflict to be diffused throughout the system and provides additional layers of insulation between the state – or in the specific case of site-based management, the school district – and the rest of the system. Such a strategy is particularly helpful in the current era of cutbacks and downsizing. For example, one local school district recently allowed individual schools to decide how they wanted to cut back their budgets. Under the guise of local decision-making, the district administration was able to diffuse criticism for massive cutbacks. Thus, according to Weiler, the selective devolution of power can be an effective way to manage system conflict.

A second 'hidden' function of decentralization of power, according to Weiler (1990), is that in a time of crisis, the state (and its various governance units) gains legitimacy by appearing to be sensitive and responsive to democratic expression and local needs. However, Weiler brings into sharper focus the ongoing contradiction between decentralization and the need for state control:

> All real decentralization (in the sense of genuinely shared
> regulatory and allocative power among levels of governance) does
> imply a loss of control for the center. If it is true that
> decentralization also holds out the attractive prospect of
> compensatory legitimation at a time when legitimacy is in short
> supply, a major challenge for the modern state lies in reconciling
> these two conflicting objectives; retaining as much centralized
> control over the system as is possible without severe loss in
> legitimacy, while at least appearing to be committed to
> decentralization and thus reaping the benefits in legitimation to
> be derived from that appearance. The frequent wavering between
> centralized and decentralized modes of behavior – or, to be more
> exact, between decentralization rhetoric and centralization
> behavior – may well have to do with this difficult task of walking
> the fine line between the conflicting imperatives of control and
> legitimacy.
>
> (Weiler, 1990, p. 442)

If Weiler (1990) is correct, these two hidden functions – conflict management and legitimation – of shared governance at the district level may explain, in large part, why participatory decision-making remains superficial and restricted to what central authority structures allow. At the national level these ideas help to explain the apparent contradiction between the rhetoric of empowerment and the centralization of testing and evaluation.

For teachers, then, micropolitical literacy involves not only understanding the relationship between different levels of the education system, but also the ability to monitor which decisions are being shared with them and why. The point here is not to encourage teacher cynicism, which already runs high in many shared governance districts, but rather to aid teachers and principals in approaching these political arenas with a sense of realism.

Understanding the Difference Between Collaboration and Collusion

It might be helpful to think about the various approaches to leadership discussed in earlier chapters in the following way. Generally, authoritarian leadership tends to seek the *compliance* of subordinates. Adversarial and normative-instrumental approaches to leadership tend to seek the *cooperation* of subordinates. Shared governance approaches tend to seek *collaboration* among all school and community stakeholders.

When school-restructuring committees consist of administrators, teachers and parents, it is often assumed that some form of democratic, empowering activity is taking place. This is what facilitative approaches to leadership call collaboration, participatory decision-making or shared governance. Seldom, however, do we look closely at who the participants in the collaboration are. This is, in part, because the players (administrators, teachers, parents and occasionally students) associated with participatory decision-making are seen as one-dimensional. Here is where micropolitical literacy is crucial to understanding how what often appears to be collaboration may, in fact, be a form of *collusion*.

Too many current restructuring efforts are implemented as if such groups as teachers, parents and students are monolithic. However, social class, gender, race, ethnicity, ideology and teaching philosophy may very well cut across these groups. For example, in some districts African–American parents, students, teachers and administrators might form a more cohesive group than the school's teachers or the parent community. Given this, how representative is a school-restructuring committee that consists primarily of white, middle-class administrators, teachers and parents? If such apparently diverse groups have common interests, what appears to be collaboration can in reality become a form of collusion.

Across the country, members of school-restructuring committees, regardless of the conditions of their appointment, tend to share a similar conceptual framework. They have similar interests, perceptions and socioeconomic backgrounds. Unlike parents from lower socioeconomic classes, middle-class parents have greater access to the school environment and are related to schools by language and experience (Delpit, 1993). Teachers also share a middle-class economic and political base. These differences in background often leave poor parents and their children out of the shared governance process. As long as the arena for change does not involve a loss of power for administrators, teachers or middle-class parents, there is little conflict among the three groups within the shared governance structure.

Mere collaboration or participation does not guarantee an adequate say for diverse constituencies. Participation continues to be limited, not by overt administrative manipulation, but rather by a failure to understand the importance of such factors as social class, race and gender. This is one of the ways that power over others can operate through an apparent 'consensus' rather than through 'coercion'.

Understanding How Institutional Silencing Occurs

Assume that we achieve a form of shared governance in which there is true rather than contrived inclusion. That is, shared governance councils consist of a fair representation of poor and minority students, parents and members of the school community, and all micropolitical factions of the teaching staff. Malen and Ogawa (1988) have documented the ways in which norms of propriety and civility function to mute criticism. Not only is 'being nice' highly regarded in such forums, but few teachers will publically contradict even open, facilitative principals.

Another more subtle form of silencing occurs through professional socialization. Power in organizations is seldom exercised in overt, observable ways. Power is more commonly embedded in the work process itself and the organizational vocabulary through which the work is defined. As illustrated in the previous chapter, control is increasingly exercised through ideological means; administrators are expected to manage and mediate organizational meaning. The transfer of decision-making power from administrators to teachers is relatively safe if meaning has been managed effectively, since most organizational members have internalized the same norms. This does not mean that dominant meanings will not occasionally be contested. Rather, conflict is derailed early on by appealing to bureaucratic discourse, and dissent is silenced by defining it outside appropriate bureaucratic discourse. This is done through the common practice of labelling resistant subordinates as, for example, 'negative', 'not a team player', 'troublemaker' and 'emasculating'.

To the extent that institutional critique can be turned back onto the individual, institutional legitimacy is maintained. The individual is marginalized and pathologized through labelling in order to protect the legitimacy of the institution. A central role of educational administrators traditionally has been to maintain the legitimacy of their institution by managing the various forms of critique and resistance that take place within it.

Distinguishing Espoused Theories from Theories-in-Use

The distinction between espoused theory and theory-in-use is what in colloquial language might be called the difference between people's 'walk' and their 'talk'. Expressions like 'talk is cheap' capture the contradictions of those who espouse democratic leadership but exhibit authoritarian behaviours. Educational administrators need to acknowledge that they are partly to blame for the cynicism with which most teachers view school micropolitics. Too often, teachers have watched administrators at all levels espouse high ideals while caving in to political pressures and their own interests.

However, as Argyris *et al.* (1985) point out, the distinction between espoused theory and theory-in-use is not always intentional. Often people's image of themselves bears little resemblance to how others view them. Whether the gap between a practitioner's espoused theory and theory-in-use is intentional or simply the result of non-reflective practice, it constitutes a problem for the achievement of democratic, empowering leadership. In fact, we would argue that perhaps even more potentially harmful than authoritative leaders are a new breed of 'facilitative' leaders who use the language of democratic, empowering leadership, but behave in a similar way to authoritarian leaders.

Space does not permit any in-depth discussion of the complex processes of critical reflection required to move from contrived to authentic dialogue (what Schön (1983) calls Model I and Model II behaviour). However, several authors have elaborated on how to move individuals and groups into more authentic forms of self-reflection and interpersonal communication (Argyris *et al.*, 1985; Schön, 1983).

Understanding the Effects of Professional Socialization and Careerism

What kinds of people tend to enter leadership positions, and why do they aspire to leadership? How are teachers and administrators socialized into bureaucratic values as they move through their careers? How do some teachers and administrators effect a balance between educating as a career and educating as a calling? These questions are vital to understanding the nature of school leadership. An impressive amount of research describes professional socialization and the ways in which dominant values are inculcated in professionals as they move through their careers (Becker, 1980; Bullough *et al.*, 1984). Only through the kind of critical reflection described in the previous section can this taken-for-granted 'baggage' from professional socialization be examined.

Some argue that the movement of more women into administrative positions may counter the emphasis on hierarchical, closed forms of leadership. Ferguson suggests that those qualities that women might bring to make organizations more humane and democratic are 'socialized' out of them early on:

> Women entering organizations are usually required to put aside
> the person-oriented values of women's traditional role in order to
> embrace the organization and prove themselves 'one of the boys.'
> Career advice to upwardly mobile women directs them to retain
> the form of feminine interaction skills but to abandon the
> content.
>
> (Ferguson, 1984, p. 94)

Upward mobility in the organization raises the issue of 'careerism' in schools and school districts. While career advancement can be a positive motivator when kept in perspective, it too often results in flashy administrators who are better at impression management than creating truly democratic and empowered schools. Moreover, Huberman and Miles (1984) have found, when administrators or teachers create successful innovative programmes, that they are often rewarded with promotions, leaving the innovation in the hands of someone who may or may not be supportive.

BUILDING DEMOCRATIC, EMPOWERED SCHOOLS

> Active participatory citizenship is a process through which
> individuals create themselves with others through the shared
> processes of speaking, deliberating, and judging, ordering their
> collective lives through institutions they have designed and in a
> language they have made their own.
>
> (Ferguson, 1984, p. 174)

In spite of the cautions and constraints discussed in the previous section, there are proactive ways in which teachers, parents and administrators can go about building democratic, empowered schools. In fact, as we mentioned previously, there are real-life examples, if only partial and imperfect, of what democratically, empowered schools are like. Here are some places to start.

Begin at the Base

Real and meaningful change cannot be mandated from legislatures or 'delivered' by research and development think tanks. Rather, it must begin with the inclusion of all stakeholders at the school level. This does not mean that schools can operate outside the fiscal and political realities that state legislatures and school boards represent. These are, in fact, the people with whom practitioners need to cultivate a relationship in order to obtain the flexibility that democratic school restructuring will require.

However, restructuring schemes conceived without *real* (as opposed to *symbolic*) input from school practitioners and community members have little chance of succeeding. Educational 'experts' may have a great deal to offer; however, the notion of staff development needs to change from a model that glorifies high-priced consultants to one of local school practitioners and community members who bring their own expert knowledge to bear on their problems.

Furthermore, social relations cannot be changed in the school without changing social relations in the classroom. Teachers who do not model democracy and empowerment in their classrooms will not be able to do so outside the classroom. Schools that are professionally liberating places for teachers must also be liberating places for students.

Lastly, schools should reflect their communities, not the other way around. School professionals who view their communities as culturally deprived, noncaring and ignorant cannot create democratic, empowering schools. In dialogue with their communities, school professionals must learn how to create culturally appropriate environments for learning. Extensive research and numerous conceptual models are available for teachers and administrators to bring poor and minority parents and communities into the process of schooling (Cummins, 1986; Delpit, 1986, 1993; Moll and Greenberg, 1993).

Create Non-hierarchical Structures

Within hierarchical organization models, the principalship is 'middle' management. As Anderson (1990) has argued elsewhere, the school principal's location in the hierarchy means that principals mediate between hierarchical levels and among various constituencies. With this mediation role comes a legitimation function. Principals must legitimate central-office mandates to teachers and the school to the community. Principals who are not successful at this legitimation role usually find themselves in trouble. In other words, a major amount of the principal's energy goes into 'impression management', i.e. making sure that the school's various constituencies view the school positively.

In some schools, particularly those with large poor and minority populations, this involves obscuring the ways in which schools participate in reproducing social inequalities. Under such conditions, it is hard for principals and teachers to be honest and authentic about school problems for fear that such honesty will be used against the school. In an adversarial atmosphere, principals can hardly be blamed for covering up problems.

Although the principalship began as the notion of 'principal teacher', it has, through the influence of scientific management, increasingly distanced itself from concerns with and loyalty to teachers. In most districts principals no longer belong to the teachers' associations, although their contract negotiations are often tied to those of teachers. In recent years there has been an increasing recognition that principals have been too far removed from the concerns of teachers.

The elimination of the principalship will not drastically change this situation, but it might make central office and other constituencies more accountable to teachers and make communication more open and above board. The kind of principal collusion described in Chapter 6 is perhaps less likely, with teacher committees running the schools. Many examples of teacher-run schools currently exist, a point that leads to the next suggestion.

Explore Alternative Models

Unfortunately, researchers and reformers have a tendency to hold up educational models for emulation that do not look very different from what we already have. Most research on school principals, particularly research on effective schools, tends to confuse description with prescription. Qualitative research tends to describe 'best practices' of principals identified as good by their peers. These descriptions are then taught as models for new principals to emulate.

While these models are helpful in that they may represent the best of current practices, they also tend to limit new teachers' and principals' imagination to what currently exists. For example, these models tend to perpetuate an image of schools as hierarchical organizations. Administrative interns and assistant principals internalize the current hierarchical system as 'the way things are'. Even conservative reformers like Peters and Waterman (1982) argue that the current system represents a dysfunctional organizational model incapable of responding to the increased complexity of social life. In fact, it may be those oddball schools, some of which are working on the margins of respectability, where the truly innovative can be found.

CENTRAL PARK EAST: AN EXPERIMENT IN DEMOCRACY

The Central Park East experiment is an example of a democratic, empowering approach to leadership. Clearly not a school on the margins of respectability, Central Park East is remarkable for pushing democracy and empowerment so far within the constraints of New York City's infamous educational bureaucracy. In 1974, Anthony Alvarado, then the superintendent of district No. 4 in New York City, offered Debra Meier an opportunity to create an alternative elementary school in East Harlem. The result has been the establishment of several democratic, empowered schools at the elementary, middle and high school levels.

The Central Park East experience is, like all democratic, empowering experiments, particular to local conditions and therefore should not be taken as a blueprint for change in other settings. However, it has been chosen as an example of the potential of democratic, empowering leadership for several reasons:

1. It has stood the test of time. Unlike many highly touted but short-lived restructuring experiments that depend on charismatic, adversarial leadership, Central Park East has an empowered base community of teachers, parents and students who have internalized the values and goals that they constructed together.

2. Unlike many exemplary schools that serve a homogeneous, middle-class population, Central Park East serves a diverse population of mainly poor and minority students.

3. While other examples of democratic, empowered schools exist, Central Park East's experience is well documented, and teachers and administrators can gain access to information about it. See, for example, Faust (1993), Goldberg (1991), Lowe and Miner (1992), Meier (1987, 1992), Telsch (1987) and Wood (1993).

Many of the strategies that Meier (1987) discusses have to do with surviving within bureaucratic systems and creating democratic communities among teachers, parents, students and administrators. Meier admits that she had several advantages, among them the initial support of the superintendent and the ability to surround herself with dedicated and democratically minded teachers. She elaborates:

> We began very small and very carefully. First there was the question of 'we'. Creating a democratic community was both an operational and inspirational goal. While we were in part the products of what was called 'open' education, our roots went back to early progressive traditions, with their focus on the building of a democratic community, on education for full citizenship and for egalitarian ideals. We looked upon Dewey, perhaps more than Piaget, as our mentor.
>
> (Meier, 1987, p. 36)

Part of what it means to be an open, transformative leader is knowing what tradition you belong to and promoting those ideals while adhering to democratic principles in the process of promoting them. Meier describes her frustration prior to being offered this political workspace:

> After struggling for years to make my beliefs 'fit' into a system that was organized on quite different principles, after spending considerable energy looking for cracks, operating in the margins, 'compromising' at every turn, the prospect that the district bureaucracy would organize itself to support alternative ideas and practices was irresistible.
>
> (Meier, 1987, p. 36)

Her Deweyian influence led Meier to understand that democracy had to be pervasive throughout the school and be modelled by teachers. Furthermore, her exposure to more contemporary critical perspectives on the hidden curriculum of schooling helped her to understand that students can only learn about democracy by living it. Meier elaborates on her vision in this way:

> We saw schools as models of the possibilities of democratic life. Although classroom life could certainly be made more democratic than traditional schools allowed, we saw it as equally important that the school life of *adults* be made more democratic. It seemed unlikely that we could foster democratic values in our classrooms unless the adults in the school also had significant rights over their workplace.
>
> (Meier, 1987, p. 37)

In democratically empowered schools, leaders work to make sure that both the *process* and the *content* of democracy are present. At Central Park East Secondary School, which Debra Meier helped establish in 1985, the process of democracy is apparent among administrators, faculty and students. This community is characterized by collaboration, mutual responsibility, intimacy and caring.

This kind of power-with culture represents the *form* of democratic leadership, which is achieved by many facilitative leaders and staffs in their schools. However, the *content* of democracy, which has to do with issues of equity, is too often missing in these schools. What sets Central Park East apart is the commitment among the staff to challenge practices that serve to stratify groups unfairly within the school and the larger society. A concern with the development of community is combined with a critical posture towards equity issues. This approach is exemplified in Central Park East's elimination of tracking practices and in its curriculum, which places issues of power and equity at the centre rather than the periphery.

At Central Park East, the curriculum is guided by a series of 'essential questions'. In all their work, students use the essential questions as a framework to integrate the material. Wood describes how essential questions relating to the role of power throughout history are used in a humanities block:

> When they ... begin their study of world cultures they will not be treated to the usual fare of twenty countries in fifty-two weeks featuring food and tourism. Rather, they will explore the literature, history, and culture of a few areas through the following questions: What is the relationship between culture and world view? How is political power achieved and maintained? What is 'civilized' and what is 'barbaric'? Who writes history, for whom, and why? How are cultures affected by imperialism? What happens when people of different cultures come in contact with one another?
>
> (Wood, 1993, p. 181)

These essential questions, derived from a concern with how power has operated throughout history and in their own lives, make the concept of democracy come alive, rescuing it from the realm of platitudes that students dutifully study for tests. Tracking has also been eliminated at Central Park East. There are no tracks labelled college prep or vocational, regular or special education.

This synergism between running a school democratically and making democracy central to curriculum and instruction is what characterizes a democratically empowered school. As discussed in Chapter 5, leaders who empower followers to become leaders themselves must be willing not merely to share power but to transfer power. This means that teachers must trust students and that principals must trust teachers. Meier elaborates on this point and shows how the form and content of democracy in schools are related:

> Faculties need maximum freedom over their own budget,
> curriculum, staffing, examination and assessment procedures.
> Only the most parsimonious general rules should be
> imposed – rules that prevent racial segregation, creaming off
> 'easy-to-teach' students, political, religious, or racial bias, and
> assume basic safety standards. Fancy proposals are irrelevant
> without changes in where and how power is legitimately
> exercised.

> (Wood, 1993, p. 244)

The Central Park East experiment has had its ups and downs. Teachers still struggle with finding time to do the kind of collaborative planning necessary for democracy to work. This has been partly resolved by holding planning meetings while students are doing community service required for graduation.

Leadership and decision-making have evolved over the years. By the end of the second year, Debra Meier had made some critical decisions regarding the organization and structure of Central Park East. One of these involved her leaving the classroom to become a somewhat more traditional principal. Although the issue of who makes decisions and how has never been entirely resolved, the staff continues to play a central role in all decisions, big and small. Nothing is 'undiscussable', though they have learned not to discuss everything (Meier, 1987).

Dissenting voices also exist. One former teacher at Central Park East Secondary School (CPESS) felt that the programme was too philosophically driven and that the curriculum was too disconnected from the lives of 'at-risk' students (Faust, 1993). He states:

> While CPESS may have motivated them to stay in school, these
> students needed something other than a loosely structured and
> in reality undemanding course of study that placed a premium
> on political awareness and 'personal growth' at the expense of
> more immediate and practical concerns.

> (Faust, 1993, p. 338)

Clearly, the construction of democratically empowered schools is a constant struggle in which all voices must be heard and all practices must be rethought on a continuous basis. Institutions that silence the voices of teachers and students are deprived of the input they need to be effective. Only in an open environment can school micropolitics change from a culture of resistance to a positive force for change.

CONCLUSION

We contend that most existing constructions of leadership and schooling are dysfunctional for teachers, students and their communities. A micropolitical perspective illustrates the complex ways in which people's interactions are distorted in authoritarian and hierarchical organizations. In this sense, we align ourselves with a long tradition of critique of bureaucratic institutions. Ferguson (1984) makes a similar case in her critique of bureaucracy from a feminist perspective. Her description of bureaucracy and its fit with most educational systems gives us some idea of the challenges we face as we attempt to create democratically empowered institutions. Furguson (1984) outlines the Weberian approach to modern bureaucracy which promotes a rational and scientific perspective to organizational management with its emphasis on control and standardization. Ferguson further contends that:

> Modern bureaucracies are sufficiently large so as to prohibit
> face-to-face relations among most of their members. They aim
> at arranging individuals and tasks so as to secure continuity
> and stability and to remove ambiguity in relations among
> participants, but are nonetheless usually beset by a variety of
> internal conflicts. *In fact, bureaucracies are political arenas in*
> *which struggles for power, status, personal values, and/or*
> *survival are endemic.'*
>
> (Ferguson, 1984, p. 7)

The recognition in recent years that schools are, in fact, political arenas in which principals, teachers, students and parents 'struggle for power, status, personal values, and/or survival' (Ferguson, 1984) has important and previously ignored implications for school restructuring. As long as we continue to perpetuate stratified educational institutions based on bureaucratic principals, we will continue to create dominant and subordinate groups. People in subordinate positions develop coping strategies. The role of the subordinate in social relations is a learned role, and throughout history subordinated groups have learned to survive, often through guile. These same characteristics are apparent in descriptions of teachers and students in previous chapters.

Leaders described as open can ameliorate the experience of subordination. However, only by radically reconstructing our institutions around democratic principles can we replace the domination/subordination dynamic with one of critical democratic community.

Unlike most prescriptive models of leadership, democratic, empowering leadership is grounded in an understanding of micropolitical forces. The biggest obstacle to its implementation will be those macro- and micro-level forces whose interests are threatened by it. However, as the century draws to a close, it should be obvious, more than at any other time in our history, that macro-level democracy can never be achieved without the democratization of our social institutions. Schools, those social institutions in which our young are socialized, are clearly the most logical and justifiable places to begin to model democracy.

Appendix

The Research Method and Procedures

Data collection and analysis procedures for all of the studies discussed in Chapters 1 to 5 were based on a symbolic interactionist perspective. This perspective recognizes that although structural factors influence action, the interpretation and meaning that people assign account for action. In other words, people's capacity for reflexivity is more compelling than structural factors. The individual is viewed as a social product who is influenced by others but who also maintains distance from others and is able to initiate individual action (Blumer, 1969; Mead, 1934). In contrast to some qualitative research orientations, symbolic interactionism stresses the structure of individual consciousness and perceptions (Blumer, 1969; Tesch, 1988).

CHAPTER 1: RESEARCH PROCEDURES

The study described in Chapter 1 was designed to focus on the general question: what do teachers mean when they refer to politics in schools? Using qualitative research guidelines, the Teacher Work-Life Inventory (TWLI) was constructed to collect detailed descriptive data reflecting the teachers' perceptions of politics in schools. According to Allport (1942), a questionnaire can be a useful personal document in qualitative inquiry that focuses on subjective perceptions. A personal document is "any self revealing record that intentionally or unintentionally yields information regarding the structure, dynamics and functioning of the author's life" (Allport, 1942, p. xii). A questionnaire is considered a personal document when the research participant controls the response content of the document.

The TWLI, an open-ended instrument, was developed to gather data regarding the perceptions of teachers on politics in schools. The goal was to encourage free expression of personal meanings about the topic under investigation. The first version of the TWLI was inspected by a committee of four teachers and four professors. Subsequently, it was pilot-tested with 47 graduate students in education enrolled in course work at a major state university. The suggestions of the committee and student group were used to inform the design of the final version of the questionnaire.

On the TWLI (which consisted of two legal-size pages), teachers were asked to present detailed descriptions of their perspectives on politics in schools. The actual instructions were as follows:

(a) Identify *one* aspect of what politics means to you.

(b) Describe fully what the political factor that you identified above means. Please give an example to illustrate what the political factor means to you.

(c) In your view, why do people do what you described above.

(d) Explain how (if at all) the political factor you identified affects you as a teacher. Please give at least one example for each: a) your performance/involvement in the classroom, b) your performance/involvement in the school.

(e) Describe your typical feelings associated with the political factor.

In exploratory research in which the focus is on generating substantive categories and data-based statements, data are gathered to maximize variation among the respondents (Bogdan and Taylor, 1975; Glaser, 1978; Glaser and Strauss, 1967). However, given the open-ended format of the TWLI, the time necessary for completion (about 30 minutes), and the sensitivity of the research topic to practitioners, a mailout survey approach was not used. Instead, six professors of education administered the TWLI between 1987 and 1988 to public school teachers enrolled in courses in five on- and off-campus centres located in one southeastern state. This procedure allowed access to full-time teachers from a variety of schools and regions. Participation in this research project was voluntary; teachers were not requested to include their names on the questionnaire.

Data from the 902 teachers who completed the TWLI were coded specifically according to guidelines for comparative analysis (Glaser, 1978; Glaser and Strauss, 1967). This technique requires a comparison of each element found in the data to elements already coded in terms of emergent categories and subcategories. Of the total sample, 281 teachers specifically focused on school principals. Close analysis of meanings inherent in these data indicated that most of the teachers ($n = 276$) described tactics used by principals that could be categorized in terms of *control* (internally oriented tactics used to manipulate teachers) or *protection* (externally oriented tactics employed with superintendents, school board members, parents/community members, and to some extent with teachers, to reduce vulnerability). These data are the focus of Chapter 1.

Data from this subsample of teachers who focused on the control and protection strategies of principals were further analysed in terms of the specific tactics to which teachers referred. For example, tactics identified with the control strategy included the manipulation of sanctions and rewards. Subsequently,

149

each tactic was analysed within the framework of each questionnaire item appearing on the TWLI. In essence, data relevant to reasons, effects on teacher involvement/performance in the classroom and in the school and feelings were coded into subcategories and themes. Display charts summarizing each dimension of each tactic were created (Miles and Huberman, 1984). These charts allowed easy numerical analysis as well as comparative analysis of tactics and their respective dimensions (e.g. reasons, effects on the classroom and so on).

Each questionnaire was analysed for only *one* political tactic: i.e. the tactic identified and described by teachers in response to question (a) (see p. 149). Therefore, the number of tactics coded is equal to the number of teachers ($n = 276$) who chose to describe school principals and their control/protective political behaviour. However, since many teachers often discussed more than one reason, effect on involvement, or feeling for each tactic they described, the total frequency of each of these categories is greater than 276. Therefore, f refers to the frequency of responses associated with a particular category.

The total database was also inspected to determine if certain types of responses were linked to particular demographic characteristics, such as gender of the teacher or type of school. No discernible patterns were evident.

Although the researcher analysed the questionnaire data alone, two professors and three doctoral students were consulted when questions arose. In addition, two doctoral students examined the descriptive summary charts constructed by the researcher to achieve consistency in coding the raw data. Again, questions were discussed.

Consistent with the principles for inductive analysis, each of the descriptive categories, themes and conceptual ideas to be discussed was derived from data appearing on the TWLI. Due to space limitations, only brief excerpts from the raw data are presented to illustrate some ideas.

CHAPTERS 2 AND 3: RESEARCH PROCEDURES

Chapter 2 focuses on teachers' everyday political relationships with students and parents; Chapter 3 deals with political relationships among teachers themselves. Data discussed in these chapters were derived from a three-year case study (1983–86) of socialization outcomes in teachers. Following a tradition initiated by Waller (1932), this comprehensive project addressed the question, what does teaching do to teachers?

Collection of data occurred in three one-year phases. The sample included between 75 and 80 (the number of teachers varied over the years) teachers in a biracial high school located in the southeastern United States. The mean number of teaching years was 11. The school included one principal, two assistant principals, three counsellors and about 1500 students.

Data were analysed according to criteria for grounded theory inquiry. Beginning with open-ended questions rather than hypotheses, data were produced and analysed simultaneously through an inductive process designed to produce categories, themes and substantive theory related to the research topic (Glaser, 1978; Glaser and Strauss, 1967).

During the first phase of the project (1983–84), experienced teachers were asked to identify and discuss professional and personal-life factors that they believed contributed to changes in their perspectives on work. Analyses of observational, interview and questionnaire data suggested that teachers became significantly more political as a result of their work experience. Data gathered during the second phase of the project (1984–85), which investigated teachers' relationship with school principals, yielded additional findings associated with the political theme.

Consequently, in accord with theoretical sampling procedures, a third phase of the project (1985–86) was planned specifically to collect detailed data relevant to the political theme that had emerged earlier (Bogdan and Taylor, 1975; Erickson, 1986; Glaser, 1978; Glaser and Strauss, 1967). To increase variation in the research site, teachers inspected an initial list of 30 interview participants and suggested others who, they believed, held perspectives not adequately represented. Forty full-time schoolteachers were included in the final stage of the research project.

In-depth interviews (unstructured and structured) were used to generate open-ended data regarding meanings associated with the political theme. Three interviews were conducted with each research participant. General research questions focused on (a) differences between teachers' beginning and current work perspectives, (b) factors that contributed to political changes in teachers over their careers, and (c) meanings attributed to the political dimensions of interaction with school principals, students, parents and other faculty. Non-directive questioning techniques were used to explore, in depth, ideas the teachers produced.

Informal interviews and observations of other teachers in the school were used throughout the duration of the research project. Field notes were constructed, coded and incorporated into the database. Although a major portion of the data analysed for this report consisted of interview transcriptions, observational data were particularly helpful in the verification of emergent categories (Denzin, 1978; Erickson, 1986). Data produced in the final phase of the project were transcribed and combined with pertinent data from previous phases. Constant comparative analysis, i.e. open coding procedures and line-by-line analysis, was used to identify emergent patterns in the data (Glaser, 1978; Glaser and Strauss, 1967).

In all, about 550 hours were spent collecting data in the research setting between 1983 and 1986. The longevity of the project appeared to be useful in developing rapport with the teacher participants; this rapport increased the likelihood of generating valid data (Bogdan and Taylor, 1975; Erickson, 1986). Teachers were required to give detailed examples for all statements reported, as another means of increasing the validity of the database. Moreover, data were evaluated for consistency within and between interviews, and ambiguities were pursued with interviewees. In addition, major hypotheses and conclusions were corroborated by a combination of at least two types of data (interview, observation and questionnaire).

Eleven teachers critiqued the descriptions of the raw data discussed in the Results section of this chapter (Guba, 1981). Their suggestions, which focused on clarification and illustration of ideas, were incorporated into the final manuscript. Finally, a panel of four experts (two professors, two doctoral students) was consulted when questions arose regarding coding and interpretation of the data (Bogdan and Taylor, 1975; Denzin, 1978, Erickson, 1986; Glaser, 1978; Glaser and Strauss, 1967).

CHAPTER 4: RESEARCH PROCEDURES

The study described in Chapter 4 focused on the question, what strategies do teachers use to influence and protect themselves from school principals? The Inventory of Teacher Influence Strategies (ITIS), an open-ended instrument, was created to solicit subjective data from teachers in a way that would encourage free expression (Allport, 1942).

Two versions of the ITIS was administered to samples of public school teachers. After the first administration, the instrument was refined according to theoretical sampling criteria discussed by Glaser and Strauss (1967) and Glaser (1978) with the assistance of a committee of experts, three professors, and four teachers.

The first ITIS simply asked teachers to describe and illustrate the strategies they used frequently to influence or protect themselves from school principals. Although a number of definitions of the term *strategy* appear in organizational and micropolitical literature, all are similar in suggesting that strategies are "lines of action" (Lofland, 1976, p. 42) based on human intention and goal-directed behaviour. In micropolitical studies it is assumed that individuals and groups in organizations use overt and covert strategies to influence others and to protect themselves from others (Bacharach and Lawler, 1980; Ball, 1987; Blase, 1991; Henderson, 1981; Kipnis *et al.*, 1980; Pfeffer, 1981b).

Study participants were 74 full-time teachers who were taking graduate education courses in a variety of programmes at a major university in the southeastern United States. Content analysis of the data generated revealed that several general categories – the workstyles of principals as well as teachers' reasons/purposes for using various strategies and the feelings they associated with strategy use – should be investigated further.

The questions on the second (final) ITIS were developed to reflect the general categories that emerged from the initial procedures. The micropolitical literature confirms the theoretical importance of each idea reflected on the questionnaire, e.g. reasons/purposes for the use of strategies.

It should be mentioned that several theoretical ideas – e.g. the relevance of broad exchange and reciprocation processes – emerged from analysing the data produced by the first version of the ITIS. Despite this fact, greater item specificity would have prematurely controlled the direction of data collection and undermined the inductive nature of the research (Glaser, 1978; Glaser and Strauss, 1967). Consequently, questions were phrased on the second ITIS in general terms, providing refinement by including three 7-point scales designed to measure teachers' perceptions of (a) their principals' openness, (b) the effectiveness of these principals, and (c) the effectiveness of the political strategies that the teachers used with principals.

Specifically, on the ITIS teachers were asked to describe in detail their principals' style of working with them and to rate their principals in terms of closeness–openness and ineffectivenes–effectiveness. In addition, two legal-size pages were provided for teachers to describe two strategies they used most frequently to influence/protect themselves from their school principals. On each page, teachers were directed to (a) describe and illustrate a strategy, (b) discuss why the strategy was used, (c) describe their purposes in using the strategy, and (d) identify their feelings associated with the strategy. Finally, teachers were asked to rate the effectiveness of each strategy that they described (7-point scale) and to explain its effectiveness.

The ITIS was administered to 770 full-time teachers taking graduate courses in education at two major universities in the southeastern and northwestern United States. Approximately 40 minutes was required to complete each questionnaire. Twelve professors of education administered the questionnaire over a one-year period (1987–88). At the southeastern university, data collection occurred at seven sites, on and off campus. This general approach allowed access to teachers from a variety of schools and school districts. Participation was voluntary; participants' names were not required.

Of the 770 teachers who completed the ITIS adequately, 404 identified their principals as "open" and "effective". The mean principal openness and effectiveness scores were 6.2 and 6.2 respectively on 7-point scales. The 404 respondents discussed and illustrated 625 examples of strategies. A total of 366 teachers discussed specifically the political strategies they employed with closed and ineffective school principals. The mean principal openness and effectiveness scores were 3.0 and 3.2 respectively on 7-point scales. Some 558 examples of strategies were coded.

Data gathered on the ITIS were coded with a comparative method of analysis (Glaser, 1978; Glaser and Strauss, 1967). All data regarding teachers' perceptions of the political strategies they had used with school principals went into emergent categories or created new categories.

Data were then clustered for each of the strategies, and additional analyses were conducted. The available data were summarized for each questionnaire item that appeared on the ITIS (e.g. working styles of principals, purposes identified with each strategy, feelings and so on), and descriptive display matrices were constructed to identify the specific dimensions of each strategy and to permit comparisons between and among strategies. Also, theoretical displays were used to identify more abstract codes; for example, the salience of exchange processes across categories became especially apparent as a result of this procedure (Miles and Huberman, 1984). Data were scrutinized within individual questionnaires and across questionnaires for consistency (Denzin, 1978; Guba, 1981); then case study data were used focusing on the same topic for further comparisons. Questions were discussed with two professors and three teachers (Guba, 1981). Two independent analysts reviewed all of the descriptive and theoretical displays.

Consistent with guidelines for grounded theory research, all descriptive and theoretical statements presented in Chapter 4 were drawn directly from the ITIS. Included also are frequencies of descriptive categories that allowed for numerical analysis and excerpts from questionnaire answers as illustrations.

CHAPTER 5: RESEARCH PROCEDURES

The first study reported in Chapter 5 employed open-ended questions and focused on the broad question, what are teachers' perceptions of the strategies that school principals use to influence them? An open-ended questionnaire, the Inventory of Strategies Used by Principals to Influence Teachers (ISUPIT), was designed to elicit personal meanings regarding the research topic. To develop the first version of the questionnaire, the researcher consulted with a committee of three professors and five teachers. This instrument was piloted with 39 graduate students in education at a major state university. Suggestions made by the committee and students were considered in the construction of the final form of the instrument.

The ISUPIT consists of three legal-size pages. On the first page, teachers are asked to provide basic background information and to rate their principals with regard to three aspects of leadership – closeness–openness, ineffectiveness–effectiveness and authoritarian–participatory – on three 7-point scales. On the two subsequent pages, teachers are asked to provide detailed descriptions of *two* strategies used by their school principals. The specific items listed on page 2 and repeated on page 3 are as follows:

(a) Describe and give a detailed example of a strategy or tactic (overt or covert; formal or informal; positive or negative) that your principal uses frequently to influence what you *do* or *think* in the school or in the classroom.

(b) Describe and give an example of the *effects* (impact) that the strategy has on your thinking and behavior (if any).

(c) Describe and illustrate what you believe to be your principal's *goals/purposes* in using the strategy identified above.

(d) How *effective* is the strategy in getting you to think and do what the principal intended [7-point scale]? Please explain why.

(e) What feelings (if any) do you have about your principal's use of this strategy?

Fourteen professors of education administered the ISUPIT between 1989 and 1990 to full-time public school teachers who were taking courses in five on- and off-campus centres located in one southeastern, one northeastern and one northwestern state. Involvement in this study was voluntary; teachers were instructed not to write their names on the research instrument.

Of the more than 1200 respondents who completed the ISUPIT, 836 identified their principals as open, effective and participatory on the 7-point scales provided (means were 5.7, 5.9 and 5.2, respectively). This chapter emphasizes that portion of the data, with a focus on the strategies themselves, because of the theoretical and practical significance of research on effective principals. (Blase and Roberts (1994) examine fully the specific affective, cognitive and behavioural impacts of these strategies on teachers.)

Data from the subsample of 836 teachers were coded according to principles for comparative analysis (Glaser, 1978; Glaser and Strauss, 1967). This procedure consists of a comparison of each new element encountered in the data to those coded previously in terms of emergent categories and subcategories. Analysis of each open-ended questionnaire page produced 1323 examples of strategies. These were analysed into eight major strategies, each consisting of several practices (i.e. actions designed to implement strategies). For example, support is a major *strategy* used by principals to influence teachers. Some specific *practices* associated with support include giving advice, reducing interferences with time, providing financial/material resources, and training.

Each strategy was further analysed within the context of the questionnaire items on the ISUPIT. Specifically, data related to principals' goals as well as data describing affective, cognitive and behavioural impacts of strategies were analysed. Display matrices were constructed to synthesize these data for each of the strategies coded (Miles and Huberman, 1984). These matrices also facilitated numerical analyses of the data.

Descriptive matrices were also employed to identify conceptual and theoretical codes grounded in the data (Miles and Huberman, 1984). For example, such matrices permitted comparisons across strategies and were especially helpful in identifying and refining analyses of general emergent ideas (e.g. the control orientation and the empowerment orientation). This approach also facilitated comparisons of the study data with the relevant literature (Glaser, 1978; Glaser and Strauss, 1967).

Respondents were instructed to discuss one strategy on each of the two questionnaire pages available for description. (Some respondents, however, described only one strategy.) Each completed page was analysed for only *one* strategy, the strategy identified in item "a" on each questionnaire page. (This point is important, since respondents often alluded to other strategies in their descriptions of a particular strategy.) The number of examples of strategies coded is equal to the number of pages completed, with the exception of 17 pages coded for miscellaneous strategies, which are not discussed in this chapter. In all, 836 teachers described 1323 (*f*) examples of strategies used by principals with whom they worked and who they believed were open and effective. Throughout this chapter, the *f* refers to the frequency of responses associated with a given strategy.

The researcher spent approximately 800 hours analysing the questionnaire data. In addition, three professors and two doctoral students were consulted when questions arose. As a final check of the researcher's analysis, three doctoral students were trained to examine samples of the study data. This procedure produced an interrater reliability score of 0.97.

Consistent with the principles for inductive analysis, each of the descriptive categories and conceptual ideas to be discussed was derived from data appearing on the ISUPIT.

The second study reported in Chapter 5 used open-ended questions and investigated the broad question, what are teachers' perceptions of the characteristics of school principals that influence their sense of empowerment? Typically, micropolitical studies have focused on the influence 'strategies' used by individuals and groups to achieve their goals in organizational settings. However, such approaches are somewhat limited because they emphasize only 'lines of action' (Lofland, 1976, p. 42) that are considered intentional and goal directed. Theoretically, 'any action, consciously or unconsciously motivated, may have political significance in a given situation' (Blase, 1991, p. 11), depending upon people's perceptions (Bachrach and Baratz, 1962; French and Raven, 1959; Galbraith, 1983; Goffman, 1972; Hall, 1972; Hardy, 1987; Kreisberg, 1973; Lukes, 1974). Therefore, it was decided to examine broadly and inclusively the 'characteristics' of principals that teachers perceived to have political influence significance *vis-à-vis* their empowerment.

No *a priori* definitions of leadership characteristics or teacher empowerment were used to direct data collection. Instead, perceptual data were collected and analysed inductively to generate descriptive categories, themes and conceptual and theoretical ideas related to both leadership characteristics and teachers' experience of empowerment (Bogdan and Biklen, 1982; Bogdan and Taylor, 1975; Glaser, 1978; Glaser and Strauss, 1967).

The Inventory of Principals' Characteristics that Contribute to Teacher Empowerment (IPCCTE), an open-ended questionnaire, was constructed to collect personal meanings on the study topic. An initial version of the questionnaire was developed in consultation with professors and a group of six teachers. This instrument was pilot-tested with 27 full-time teachers who were graduate students at a major university in the southwestern United States. Suggestions made by both groups were used to design the final form of the instrument.

In addition to a cover page that introduces the research topic, the IPCCTE consists of three legal-size pages for completion. On the first of these pages, teachers are asked to give background information and rate their principal with regard to her/his overall contribution to their sense of empowerment on a scale of 1 to 7. On the second page, the following question appeared: "Of all the things in the school that may/could contribute to your sense of empowerment, how much do characteristics of your principal (e.g. behavior, attitudes, values, goals, etc.) contribute?" On the two following pages (pages 3 and 4), teachers are asked to provide detailed descriptions of *two* characteristics (one on each page) of their principals (e.g. attitude, behaviour, values, etc.) that influence their empowerment and meanings they identified with empowerment. Each of the following items is listed on page 3 and repeated on page 4:

(1) Describe one *characteristic* (attitude, value, behavior, etc.) of your principal that contributes to your sense of empowerment. Please illustrate this characteristic by describing real-life examples of it below.

(2) Please explain *why* this characteristic makes you feel empowered. Again, give real examples to illustrate why.

(3) To show what *you* mean by being empowered as it relates to this characteristic of your principal, please describe and give examples of *your* feelings, thoughts, and behaviors. We want to know what feelings, thoughts, and behavior result.

The IPCCTE was administered to a total of 285 teachers in a select group of 11 schools (i.e. 5 elementary, 3 middle, 3 high), all of which had been members of the League of Professional Schools in Georgia since its inception in 1990 (Glickman, 1993; Glickman and Allen, 1992). One teacher in each of these schools administered the questionnaire to teachers during a meeting, collected completed questionnaires, and mailed them directly to a university address. School principals were not present during these meetings. Given the open-ended nature of the IPCCTE, about 35 minutes was required for its completion.

As charter members of the League of Professional Schools, these 11 schools each began implementing *shared governance* structures and *action research* protocols during the autumn of 1990. The League's purpose is to establish representative, democratic decision-making structures to promote teacher involvement in school-wide instructional and curricular decisions. Governance structures often deal with topics such as staff development, educational materials, programme innovation, classroom management, scheduling, budgeting, hiring and textbook adoption. Action research involves school staff members in collecting, analysing and interpreting data to assess the effects of shared decision-making on students, teachers, administrators and parents and to improve decision-making processes and outcomes.

The League of Professional Schools does not prescribe specifically how member schools are to realize their commitment to shared governance. Each school is encouraged to create policies and procedures that fit its unique situation. Membership in the League provides (a) opportunities to network with other schools at periodic meetings involving teams from all League Schools; (b) a biannual network exchange newsletter; (c) access to an information-retrieval system to honour requests for information relevant to instructional initiatives; (d) planning, evaluation, research and instrumentation services via telephone; and (e) a yearly, on-site visit by either a League staff member, university associate or League practitioner.

Schools interested in League membership send a team (typically, three teachers and the principal) to a two-day orientation and planning workshop in which the central premises of the league – shared governance and action research – are described in the context of instructional and curricular issues. Based on this information, staff members of a school vote (by secret ballot) on becoming League members. An 80 per cent favourable vote is required before schools are eligible to join the League. Using similar voting procedures, each school decides either annually or semiannually whether it wants to continue membership in the League. Further, each school releases a minimum of six persons to attend four days of League conferences each year. Currently, 52 schools in Georgia are members of the League of Professional Schools.

Data from the study respondents were coded according to principles for inductive research and comparative analysis (Glaser, 1978; Glaser and Strauss, 1967). Each questionnaire page generated one example of principals' influence characteristics. In total, 367 examples of influence characteristics were coded. These characteristics were further analysed into seven major facilitative strategies (i.e. intentional goal-oriented actions designed specifically to empower teachers) and one category of personal characteristics (e.g. honesty) that contributed to empowerment.

Study participants were asked to discuss *one* leadership characteristic on each of the two questionnaire pages available for description. (However, some participants used only one page and described one characteristic.) Each completed questionnaire page was coded for only one major characteristic. The number of examples of influence characteristics derived from the data equals the number of usable pages completed. In total, 285 (n) teachers discussed 367 (f) examples of principal characteristics that directly contributed to their empowerment.

Two researchers analysed the entire data set. Professors, doctoral students and teachers were consulted on a regular basis when questions arose. To check the researchers' analysis, three coders were trained to inspect segments of the research data. This procedure produced an interrater reliability score of 0.96.

Consistent with guidelines for inductive-grounded analyses, all of the descriptive, conceptual and theoretical ideas discussed in the second part of Chapter 5 were gleaned directly from data produced by the IPCCTE.

CHAPTER 6: THE RESEARCH METHOD AND PROCEDURES

Critical theory and ethnographic methods were employed in the case study of Fairlawn reported in Chapter 6. Critical ethnography seeks to provide accounts of social reality sensitive to the dialectical relationship between the social structural constraints on human actors and the relative autonomy of human agency (Anderson, 1989). Critical political and communications theory also informed the study (Deetz, 1985; Edelman, 1988).

The goal of the study was to obtain as many perceptions as possible of selected critical events. The intent was to understand better the decision-making process that administrators engage in and how meaning is negotiated and managed at both the school and school-district level.

Ethnographic data for the study were collected at two schools – one in an affluent, suburban district, the other in a poor, urban district. The data reported in this chapter are drawn largely from the suburban case study, since a dominant control mode in that district was ideological. Data for the study consisted primarily of interview transcripts, observation field notes and school documents. Over an entire school year, 66 interviews were conducted, 28 meetings were attended, and over 30 school documents analysed.

Although many of the study's original questions sought a better understanding of how administrators legitimate the social orders within which they work and the forms of control that sustain them, the specific themes of cognitive politics and ideological control emerged during the study.

References and Further Reading

Allport, G. (1942) *The Use of Personal Documents in Psychological Science*. New York: Social Science Research Council.

Alutto, J. A. and Belasco, J. A. (1972) A typology for participation in organizational decision making. *Administrative Science Quarterly*, 17, 117–25.

Anderson, G. L. (1989) Critical ethnography in education: origins, current status, and new directions. *Review of Educational Research*, 59(3), 142–68.

Anderson, G. L. (1990) Toward a critical constructivist approach to school administration: invisibility, legitimation, and the study of non-events. *Educational Administration Quarterly*, 26(1), 38–59.

Anderson, G. L. (1991) Cognitive politics of principals and teachers: ideological control in an elementary school. In J. Blase (ed.) *The Politics of Life in Schools: Power, Conflict, and Cooperation*, pp. 120–30. Newbury Park, CA: Sage.

Anderson, G. L. and Dixon, A. (1993) Paradigm shifts and site-based management in the United States: toward a paradigm of social empowerment. In J. Smyth (ed.) *A Socially Critical View of the Self-managing School*, pp. 49–61. London: Falmer Press.

Apple, M. W. (1986) *Teachers and Texts*. New York: Routledge & Kegan Paul.

Argyris, C., Putnam, R. and McLain-Smith, D. (1985) *Action Science*. San Francisco: Jossey-Bass.

Bacharach, S. B. and Lawler, E. J. (1980) *Power and Politics in Organizations: The Social Psychology of Conflict, Coalitions, and Bargaining*. San Francisco: Jossey-Bass.

Bachrach, P. and Baratz, M. S. (1962) Two faces of power. *American Political Science Review*, 56(4), 947–52.

Ball, S. J. (1987) *The Micro-politics of the School: Towards a Theory of School Organization*. London: Methuen.

Barnard, C. I. (1948) *The Functions of the Executive*. Cambridge, MA: Harvard University Press.

Barth, R. S. (1988) School: a community of leaders. In A. Lieberman (ed.) *Building a Professional Culture in Schools*, pp. 129–47. New York: Teachers College Press.

Barth, R. S. (1990) *Improving Schools from Within: Teachers, Parents, and Principals Can Make a Difference*. San Francisco: Jossey-Bass.

Bates, A. P. and Babchuk, N. (1961) The primary group: a reappraisal. *Sociological Quarterly*, 2, 181–92.

Bates, R. J. (1986) "The culture of administration, the process of schooling and the politics of culture". Paper presented at the annual meeting of the American Educational Research Association, San Francisco.

Beale, H. K. (1936) *Are American Teachers Free? An Analysis of Restraints Upon the Freedom of Teaching in American Schools*. New York: Scribner.

Becker, H. (1980) *Role and Career Problems of the Chicago Public School Teacher*. New York: Arno Press.

Bennis, W. and Nanus, B. (1985) *Leaders: The Strategies for Taking Charge*. New York: Harper & Row.

Biklen, S. D. (1988) "Teachers in conflict: a case study". Paper presented at the annual meeting of the American Educational Research Association, New Orleans, LA.

Blase, J. (1984) School principals and teacher stress: a qualitative analysis. *National Forum of Educational Administration and Supervision*, 1(32), 35–43.

Blase, J. (1986) A qualitative analysis of sources of teacher stress: consequences for performance. *American Educational Research Journal*, 23(1), 13–40.

Blase, J. (1987a) Dimensions of ineffective school leadership: the teacher's perspective. *Journal of Educational Administration*, 25(2), 193–213.

Blase, J. (1987b) Dimensions of effective school leadership: the teacher's perspective. *American Educational Research Journal*, 24(4), 598–610.

Blase, J. (1987c) Political interactions among teachers: sociocultural contexts in the schools. *Urban Education*, 22(3) , 286–309.

Blase, J. (1988a) The politics of favoritism: a qualitative analysis of the teachers' perspective. *Educational Administration Quarterly*, 24(2), 152–77.

Blase, J. (1988b) Dimensions of effective school leadership: the teacher's perspective. *American Educational Research Journal*, 24(4), 589–610.

Blase, J. (1988c) The teachers' political orientation vis-à-vis the principal: the micropolitics of the school. In J. Hannaway and R. Crowson (eds) *The Politics of Reforming School Administration*, pp. 113–26. New York: The Falmer Press.

Blase, J. (1989) The micropolitics of the school: the everyday political orientation of teachers toward open school principals. *Educational Administration Quarterly*, 24(4), 377–407.

Blase, J. (1990) Some negative effects of principals' control-oriented and protective political behavior. *American Educational Research Journal*, 27(4), 727–53.

Blase, J. (1991) *The Politics of Life in Schools: Power, Conflict, and Cooperation*. Newbury Park, CA: Sage.

Blase, J. (1993) The micropolitics of effective school-based leadership: teachers' perspectives. *Educational Administration Quarterly*, 29(2), 142–63.

Blase, J. and Blase, J. (1994) *Empowering Teachers: What Successful School Principals do*. Newbury Park, CA: Corwin.

Blase, J. and Roberts, J. (1994) The micropolitics of teacher work involvement: effective principals' impacts on teachers. *Alberta Journal of Educational Research*, xl(1), 67.

Bloome, D. and Willett, J. (1991) Toward a micropolitics of classroom interaction. In J. Blase (ed.) *The Politics of Life in Schools: Power, Conflict, and Cooperation*, pp. 207–36. Newbury Park, CA: Sage.

Blumberg, A. and Greenfield, W. (1986) *The Effective Principal: Perspectives on School Leadership*, 2nd edn. Boston: Allyn & Bacon.

Blumer, H. (1969) *Symbolic Interactionism*. Englewood Cliffs, NJ: Prentice Hall.

Bogdan, R. and Biklen, S. (1982) *Qualitative Research for Education: An Introduction to Theory and Methods*. Boston: Allyn and Bacon.

Bogdan, R. and Taylor, S. (1975) *Introduction to Qualitative Research Methods: A Phenomenological Approach to the Social Sciences*. New York: Harper & Row.

Bolman, L. G. and Deal, T. E. (1984) *Modern Approaches to Understanding and Managing Organizations*. San Francisco: Jossey-Bass.

Bredeson, P. V. (1989) Redefining leadership and the roles of school principals: responses to changes in the professional worklife of teachers. *High School Journal*, 23, 9–20.

Bridges, E. M. (1970) Administrative man: origin or pawn in decision making? *Educational Administration Quarterly*, 6(1), 7–24.

Brieschke, P. A. (1983) A case study of teacher role enactment in an urban elementary school. *Educational Administration Quarterly*, 19(4), 59–83.

Bullough, R. V., Githin, A. D. and Goldstein, S. L. (1984) Ideology, teacher role, and resistance. *Teachers College Record*, 86, 339–58.

Burlingame, M. (1988) Review of *The Micro-politics of the School: Towards a Theory of School Organization. Journal of Curriculum Studies*, 20, 281–3.

Burns, J. (1978) *Leadership*. New York: Harper & Row.

Burns, T. (1961) Micropolitics: mechanisms of institutional change. *Administration Science Quarterly*, 6, 257–81.

Carnegie Commission for the Advancement of Teaching (1988) *Report Card on School Reform: The Teachers Speak*. Princeton, NJ: Carnegie Commission for the Advancement of Teaching.

Carnegie Forum on Education, Task Force on Teaching as a Profession (1986) *A Nation Prepared: Teachers for the 21st Century*. New York: Carnegie Forum on Education and the Economy.

Chubb, J. E. and Moe, T. M. (1986) No school is an island: politics, markets, and education. *Brookings Review*, 4(4), 21–8.

Clift, R., Johnson, M., Holland, P. and Veal, M. L. (1992) Developing the potential for collaborative school leadership. *American Educational Research Journal*, 29, 877–908.

Comstock, D. E. (1982) Power in organizations: toward a critical theory. *Pacific Sociological Review*, 25(2), 139–62.

Connell, R. W. (1985) *Teachers' Work*. Sydney: George Allen & Unwin.

Cook, K. (1988) Principals with interest. *Savvy*, April, 63–6.

Corbett, H. D. (1991) Community influence on school micropolitics: a case example. In J. Blase (ed.) *The Politics of Life in Schools: Power, Conflict, and Cooperation*, pp. 73–95. Newbury Park, CA: Sage.

Cormier, W. H. and Cormier, L. S. (1979) *Interviewing Strategies for Helpers: A Guide to Assessment, Treatment and Evaluation*. Monterey, CA: Brooks-Cole.

Crandall, D. P., Eiseman, J. W. and Seashore, L. K. (1986) Strategic planning issues that bear on the success of school improvement efforts. *Educational Administration Quarterly*, 22(3), 21–53.

Cummins, J. (1986) Empowering minority students: A framework for intervention. *Harvard Educational Review*, 56, 58–72.

Cusick, P. (1973) *Inside High School: The Student's World*. New York: Holt, Rinehart & Winston.

Cusick, P. A. (1983) *The Egalitarian Ideal and the American High School: Studies of Three Schools*. London: Longman.

Cyert, R. M. and March, J. G. (1963) *A Behavioral Theory of the Firm*. Englewood Cliffs, NJ: Prentice Hall.

Czarniawska-Joerges, B. (1988) *Ideological Control in Nonideological Organizations*. New York: Praeger.

Dahl, R. A. (1957) The concept of power. *Behavioral Science*, 2, 201–18.

Dahl, R. (1961) *Who Governs?: Democracy and Power in an American City*, New Haven: Yale University Press.

Deal, T. and Kennedy, A. (1984) *Corporate Cultures: The Rites and Rituals of Corporate Life*. Reading, MA: Addison-Wesley.

Deetz, S. (1985) Critical-cultural research: new sensibilities and old realities. *Journal of Management*, 11(2), 121–36.

Delpit, L. (1986) Skills and other dilemmas of a progressive black educator. *Harvard Educational Review*, 56(4), 379–85.

Delpit, L. (1993) The silenced dialogue: power and pedagogy in educating other people's children. In L. Weiss and M. Fine (eds) *Beyond Silenced Voices: Class, Race, and Gender in United States Schools*, pp. 119–39. Albany: SUNY Press.

Denzin, N. K. (1978) The logic of naturalistic enquiry. In N. K. Denzin (ed.) *Sociological*

Methods: A Source Book, pp. 245–76. New York: McGraw-Hill.

Donmoyer, R. (1983) The principal as prime mover. *Daedalus: Journal of the American Academy of Arts and Sciences*, 112(3) 81–94.

Dreeben, R. (1968) *On What is Learned in School*. Reading, MA: Addison-Wesley.

Dreeben, R. (1970) *The Nature of Teaching*. Glenview, IL: Scott Foresman.

Dunlap, D. M. and Goldman, P. (1991) Rethinking power in schools. *Educational Administration Ouarterly*, 27, 5–29.

Edelman, M. (1988) *Constructing the Political Spectacle*. Chicago: The University of Chicago Press.

Erickson, F. (1986) Qualitative research on teaching. In M. C. Wittrock (ed.) *Handbook of Research on Teaching*, 3rd edn, pp. 1–192. New York: Macmillan.

Erickson, K. (1976) *Everything in its path: Destruction of Community in Buffalo Creek Flood*. New York: Simon & Schuster.

Etheridge, C. P. and Hall, M. L. (1991) "The nature, role, and effect of competition, cooperation, and comprehension in multiple site implementation of SBDM". Paper presented at the annual meeting of the American Educational Research Association, Chicago.

Etzioni, A. (1961) *A Comparative Analysis of Complex Organizations*. Glencoe, IL: Free Press.

Etzioni, A. (1975) *A Comparative Analysis of Complex Organizations*, revised edn. New York: MacMillan, Free Press.

Faust, M. A. (1993) 'It's not a perfect world': Defining success and failure at Central Park East Secondary School. In R. Donmoyer and R. Kos (eds.) *At-risk Students: Portraits, Policies, Programs and Practices*, pp. 323–42. Albany: SUNY Press.

Fayol, H. (1949) *General and Industrial Management*, trans. Constance Starrs, London: Sir Isaac Pitman.

Ferguson, K. (1984) *The Feminist Case Against Bureaucracy*. Philadelphia: Temple University Press.

Firestone, W. A. and Wilson, B. L. (1985) Using bureaucratic and cultural linkages to improve instruction: the principal's contribution. *Educational Administration Quarterly*, 21(2), 7–30.

Foster, W. (1986) *Paradigms and Promises: New Approaches to Educational Administration*. Buffalo, NY: Prometheus.

Foucault, M. (1977) *Power/knowledge*. New York: Pantheon Books.

Fraatz, J. M. B. (1987) *The Politics of Reading: Power, Opportunity, and Prospects for Change in America's Public Schools*. New York: Teachers College Press.

Freire, P. (1972) *Pedagogy of the Oppressed*. New York: Seabury Press.

French, J. P. R. and Raven, B. (1959) The bases of social power. In D. Cartwright (ed.) *Studies in Social Power*, pp. 150–67. Ann Arbor: University of Michigan Press.

Fuchs, E. (1967) *Teachers Talk: Views from Inside City Schools*. New York: Anchor Books.

Fullan, M. (1992) *The New Meaning of Educational Change*. New York: Teachers College Press.

Galbraith, J. K. (1983) *The Anatomy of Power*. Boston: Houghton Mifflin.

Getzels, J. W. and Guba, E. G. (1957) Social behavior and the administrative process. *School Review*, 65(4), 423–41.

Gilman, G. (1962) An inquiry into the nature and use of authority. In M. Haire (ed.) *Organization Theory and Industrial Practice* pp. 105–42. New York: John Wiley and Sons.

Gitlin, A. (1983) School structure and teachers' work. In M. Apple and L. Weis (eds) *Ideology and Practice in Schooling*, pp. 193–212. Philadelphia: Temple University Press.

Glaser, B. G. (1978) *Theoretical Sensitivity: Advances in the Methodology of Grounded Theory*. Mill Valley, CA: The Sociology Press.

Glaser, B. G. and Strauss, A. L. (1967) *The Discovery of Grounded Theory: Strategies for Qualitative Research*. Chicago: Aldine.

Glickman, C. D. (1993) *Renewing America's Schools: A Guide for School-based Action*. San Francisco: Jossey-Bass.

Glickman, C. D. and Allen, L. (eds) (1992) *The League of Professional Schools: Lessons from the Field*, Vols 1 and 2. Athens: University of Georgia, Program for School Improvement.

Goffman, E. (1959) *The Presentation of Self in Everyday Life*. New York: Anchor.

Goffman, E. (1972) *Strategic Interaction: An Analysis of Doubt and Calculation in Face-to-face, Day-to-day Dealings with One Another*. New York: Ballantine Books.

Goldberg, M. F. (1991) Portrait of Deborah Meier. *Educational Leadership*, 48(4), 26–8.

Goldner, F. H. and Ritti, R. R. (1977) The production of cynical knowledge in organizations. *American Sociological Review*, 42(4), 539–51.

Gouldner, A. (1966) The norm of reciprocity: a preliminary statement. In B. J. Biddle and E. J. Thomas (eds) *Role Theory Concepts and Research*, pp. 134–44. New York: John Wiley.

Green, J. (ed.) (1986) *What's Next?: More Leverage for Teachers*. Denver: Education Commission of the States.

Greenfield, T. (1984) Leaders and schools: willfulness and nonnatural order in organizations. In T. Sergiovanni and J. Corbally (eds) *Leadership and Organizational Culture: New Perspectives on Administrative Theory and Practice*, pp. 142–69. Urbana: University of Illinois Press.

Greenfield, W. D. (1986) "Moral imagination, interpersonal competence, and the work of school administrators". Paper presented at the annual meeting of the American Educational Research Association, San Francisco.

Greenfield, W. D. (1991) The micropolitics of leadership in an urban elementary school. In J. Blase (ed) *The Politics of Life in Schools: Power, Conflict, and Cooperation*, pp. 161–84. Newbury Park, CA: Sage.

Gronn, P. (1986) Politics, power and the management of schools. In E. Hoyle (ed) *The World Yearbook of Education 1986: The Management of Schools*, pp. 45–54. London: Kogan Page.

Guba, E. (1981) Criteria for assessing the trustworthiness of naturalistic inquiries. *Educational Communication and Technology Journal*, 29(2), 75–91.

Hall, P. M. (1972) A symbolic interactionist analysis of politics. *Sociological Inquiry*, 42(3–4), 35–75.

Hampton, W. L., Holman, D. and Vanatta, J. (1994) Tying Paulo Freire's concepts to restructuring. *Journal of School Leadership*, 4(1), 112–16.

Hannay, L. M. and Stevens, K. W. (1984) "The indirect leadership role of a principal". Paper presented at the annual meeting of the American Educational Research Association, New Orleans.

Hanson, E. M. (1981) Organizational control in educational systems: a case study of governance in schools. In S. M. Bacharach (ed) *Organizational Behavior in Schools and School Districts*, pp. 245–76. New York: Praeger.

Hanson, M. (1976) Beyond the bureaucratic model: a study of power and autonomy in educational decisionmaking. *Interchange*, 7(1), 27–38.

Hardy, C. (1987) The contribution of political science to organizational behavior. In J. W. Lorsch (ed) *Handbook of Organizational Behavior*, pp. 96–108). Englewood Cliffs, NJ: Prentice Hall.

Hargreaves, A. (1979) Strategies, decisions, and control: interaction in a middle school classroom. In J. Eggleston (ed) *Teacher Decision-making in the Classroom*, pp. 137–9. Boston: Routledge & Kegan Paul.

Hargreaves, A. (1990) Teachers' work and the politics of time and space. *Qualitative Studies in Education*, 3(4), 303–20.

Hargreaves, A. (1991) Contrived collegiality: the micropolitics of teacher collaboration. In J. Blase (ed) *The Politics of Life in Schools: Power, Conflict, and Cooperation*, pp. 46–72. Newbury Park, CA: Sage.

Hargreaves, A. and Dawe, R. (1990) Paths of professional development: contrived collegiality, collaborative culture and the case of peer coaching. *Teaching and Teacher Education*, 6(3), 227–41.

Hartsock, N. (1981) Staying alive. In C. Bunch *et al.* (eds) *Building Feminist Theory: Essays from Quest*, pp. 41–63. New York: Longman.

Henderson, A. H. (1981) *Social Power: Social Psychological Models and Theories*. New York: Praeger.

High, R. and Achilles, C. M. (1986) An analysis of influence-gaining behaviors of principals in schools of varying levels of instructional effectiveness. *Educational Administration Quarterly*, 22(1), 111–19.

Holmes Group (1986) *Tomorrow's Teachers: A Report of the Holmes Group*. East Lansing, MI: Holmes Group.

Hoy, W. K. and Brown, B. L. (1986) "Leadership of principals, personal characteristics of teachers, and the professional zone of acceptance of elementary teachers". Paper presented at the annual meeting of the American Educational Research Association, San Francisco.

Hoy, W. K. and Brown, B. L. (1988) Leadership behavior of principals and the zone of acceptance of elementary teachers. *Journal of Educational Administration*, 26(1), 22–38.

Hoyle, E. (1969) *The Role of the Teacher*. London: Routledge & Kegan Paul.

Hoyle, E. (1986) *The Politics of School Management*. London: Hodder and Stoughton.

Huberman, M. and Miles, M. (1984) *Innovation Up Close: A Field Study in 12 School Settings*. Andover, MA: The Network Inc.

Hunter, C. (1979) Control in the comprehensive system. In J. Eggleston (ed) *Teacher Decision-making in the Classroom: A Collection of Papers*, pp. 118–33. London: Routledge & Kegan Paul.

Hunter, C. (1980) The politics of participation – with specific reference to teacher–pupil relationships. In P. Woods (ed) *Teacher Strategies: Explorations in the Sociology of the School*, pp. 213–36. London: Croom Helm.

Iannaccone, L. (1975) *Education Policy Systems: A Study Guide for Educational Administrators*. Fort Lauderdale, FL: Nova University.

Isherwood, G. B. (1973) The principal and his authority: an empirical study. *High School Journal*, 56, 291–303.

Jackson, P. (1968) *Life in Classrooms*. New York: Holt, Rinehart & Winston.

Johnson, N. A. (1984) The role of the Australian principal in staff development. Unpublished master's thesis, University of New England, Armidale, New South Wales.

Johnston, G. S. and Venable, B. P. (1986) A study of teacher loyalty to the principal: rule administration and hierarchical influence of the principal. *Educational Administration Quarterly*, 22(4), 4–27.

Jones, E. (1964) *Ingratiation: A Social Psychological Analysis*. New York: Appleton-Century-Crofts.

Kasten, K. L., Short, P. M. and Jarmin, H. (1989) Self-managing groups and the professional lives of teachers. *The Urban Review*, 21(2), 63–80.

Katz, D. and Kahn, R. L. (1978) *The Social Psychology of Organizations*. New York: John Wiley & Sons.

Keith, N. (in press) A critical perspective on teacher participation in urban schools. *Educational Administration Quarterly*.

Kipnis, D. (1976) *The Powerholders*. Chicago: University of Chicago Press.

Kipnis, D., Schmidt, S. and Wilkinson, I. (1980) Intraorganizational influence tactics: exploration in getting one's way. *Journal of Applied Psychology*, 65(4), 440–52.

Kirby, P. C. and Colbert, R. (1992) "Principals who empower teachers". Paper presented at the annual meeting of the American Educational Research Association, San Francisco.

Kirp, D. (1989) Education: the movie. *Mother Jones*, October, 35–45.

Kline-Kracht, P. and Wong, K. (1991) When district authority intrudes upon the local school. In J. Blase (ed.) *The Politics of Life in Schools: Power, Conflict, and Cooperation*, pp. 96–119. Newbury Park, CA: Sage.

Kriesberg, L. (1973) *The Sociology of Social Conflicts*. Englewood Cliffs, NJ: Prentice Hall.

Leithwood, K. and Jantzi, D. (1990) "Transformational leadership: How principals can help reform school cultures". Paper presented at the annual meeting of the American Educational Research Association, Boston.

Lieberman, A. and Miller, L. (1984) *Teachers, Their World and Their Work*. Alexandria, VA: Association for Supervision and Curriculum Development.

Lightfoot, S. L. (1983) The lives of teachers. In L. S. Shulman and G. Sykes (eds) *Handbook of Teaching and Policy*, pp. 241–60. New York: Longman.

Lindle, J. C. (1991) "The usefulness of the micropolitical framework for evaluating clinical experiences". Paper presented at the annual meeting of the American Educational Research Association, Chicago.

Lipham, J. M. (1981) *Effective Principal, Effective School*. Reston, VA: National Association of Secondary School Principals.

Little, J. W. (1982) Norms of collegiality and experimentation: workplace conditions of school success. *American Educational Research Journal*, 19(3), 325–40.

Lofland, J. (1976) *Doing Social Life: A Qualitative Study of Human Interaction in Natural Settings*. New York: John Wiley and Sons.

Lortie, D. C. (1963) The balance of control and autonomy. In A. Etzioni (ed.) *The Semi-professions and Their Organization*, pp. 1–53. New York: Free Press.

Lortie, D. C. (1975) *Schoolteacher: A Sociological Study*. Chicago: University of Chicago Press.

Lowe, R. and Miner, B. (eds) (1992) *False Choices: Why School Vouchers Threaten Our Children's Future*. Milwaukee: Rethinking Schools.

Lukes, S. (1974) *Power: A Radical View*. London: Macmillan Press.

Maeroff, G. I. (1988) *The Empowerment of Teachers: Overcoming the Crisis of Confidence*. New York: Teachers College Press.

Malen, B. and Ogawa, R. T. (1988) Professional-patron influence on site-based governance councils: a confounding case study. *Educational Evaluation and Policy Analysis*, 10(4), 251–70.

Mangham, I. (1979) *The Politics of Organizational Change*. Westport, CT: Greenwood Press.

Marcus, G. and Fischer, M. (1986) *Anthropology as Cultural Critique: An Experimental Moment in the Human Sciences*. Chicago: University of Chicago Press.

Marshall, C. (1991) "Expansion of socialization theory: micropolitics, gender and race". Paper presented at the Annual Meeting of the American Educational Research Association, Chicago.

Marshall, C. and Mitchell, B. (1991) The assumptive worlds of fledgling administrators. *Education and Urban Society*, 23(4), 396–415.

Martin, N. H. and Sims, J. H. (1956) Thinking ahead. *Harvard Business Review*, 34, 26–140.

Martin, O. L. (1990) "Instructional leadership behaviors that empower teacher effectiveness". Paper presented at the annual meeting of the Mid-South Educational Research Association, New Orleans.

Maxcy, S. J. (1991) *Educational Leadership: A Critical Pragmatic Perspective*. New York: Bergin & Garvey.

Mayes, B. T. and Allen, R. W. (1977) Toward a definition of organizational politics. *Academy of Management Review*, 2, 672–8.

McNeil, L. (1983) Defensive teaching and classroom control. In M. Apple and Luis Weis (eds) *Ideology and Practice in Schooling*, pp. 114–42. Philadelphia: Temple University Press.

McNeil, L. (1986) *Contradictions of Control: School Structure and School Knowledge*. New York: Routledge & Kegan Paul.

McPherson, G. H. (1972) *Small Town Teachers*. Cambridge, MA: Harvard University Press.

Mead, G. H. (1934) *Mind, Self and Society* Chicago: University of Chicago Press.

Meier, D. (1987) Success in East Harlem. *American Educator*, 11(3), 34–9.

Meier, D. (1992) Reinventing teaching. *Teachers College Record*, 93(4), 595–609.

Melenyzer, B. J. (1990) "Teacher empowerment: the discourse, meanings and social actions of teachers". Paper presented at the National Council of States on Inservice Education, Orlando.

Meyer, J. W. and Rowan, B. (1978) The structure of educational organizations. In J. W. Meyer and W. R. Scott (eds) *Environments and Organizations; Ritual and Rationality*, pp. 71–97. San Francisco, CA: Jossey-Bass.

Michener, H. and Suchner, R. (1972) The tactical use of social power. In J. Tedeschi (ed.) *Social Influence Processes*, pp. 239–86. Chicago: Aldine.

Miles, M. B. and Huberman, A. M. (1984) *Qualitative Data Analysis: A Sourcebook of New Methods*. Beverly Hills, CA: Sage.

Miles, R. H. (1980) *Macro Organizational Behavior*. Santa Monica, CA: Goodyear.

Moll, L. and Greenberg, J. (1993) Creating zones of possibilities: Combining social contexts for instruction. In L. Moll (ed.) *Vygotsky and Education*. Cambridge: Cambridge University Press.

Morgan, G. (1986) *Images of Organizations*. Beverly Hills, CA: Sage.

Naegle, K. D. (1956) Clergymen, teachers, and psychiatrists. *Canadian Journal of Economics and Political Science*, 22 46–62.

Nias, J. (1989) *Primary Teachers Talking: A Study of Teaching as Work*. London: Routledge.

Noblit, G., Berry, B. and Dempsey, V. (1991) Political responses to reform: a comparative case study. *Education and Urban Society*, 23(4), 379–95.

Parsons, T. (1951) *The Social System*. Chicago: Free Press.

Peters, T. and Waterman, R. (1982) *In Search of Excellence*. New York: Warner Books.

Pettigrew, A. (1973) *The Politics of Organizational Decision-making*. London: Tavistock.

Pfeffer, J. (1981a) Management as symbolic action: the creation and maintenance of organizational paradigms. *Research in Organizational Behavior*, 3, 1–52.

Pfeffer, J. (1981b) *Power in Organizations*. Marshfield, MA: Pitman.

Pollard, A. (1985) *The Social World of the Primary School*. London: Holt, Rinehart & Winston.

Rappaport, J. (1984) Studies in empowerment: introduction to the issue. In J. Rappaport and R. Mess (eds) *Studies in Empowerment: Steps Toward Understanding and Action*, pp. 101–24. New York: Haworth Press.

Reitzug, U. C. (1994) A case study of empowering principal behavior. *American Educational Research Journal*, 31(2), 283–307.

Rizvi, F. (1989) In defense of organizational democracy. In J. Smyth (ed.) *Critical Perspectives on Educational Leadership*, pp. 205–34. London: Falmer Press.

Rosenholtz, S. J. and Simpson, C. (1990) Workplace conditions and the rise and fall of teachers' commitment. *Sociology of Education*, 63(4), 241–57.

Sarason, S. B. (1982) *The Culture of the School and the Problem of Change*, 2nd edn. Boston: Allyn & Bacon.

Schempp, P. G., Sparkes, A. E. and Templin, T. J. (1993) The micropolitics of teacher induction. *American Educational Research Journal*, 30(3), 447–72.

Schlechty, P. C. (1990) *Schools for the Twenty-first Century: Leadership Imperatives for Educational Reform*. San Francisco: Jossey-Bass.

Schön, D. A. (1983) *The Reflective Practitioner: How Professionals Think in Action*. New York: Basic Books.

Schwartz, T. (1990) Making the grade: principal Lottie Taylor's extraordinary success in Harlem. *New York*, June, 37–47.

Sikes, J., Measor, L. and Woods, P. (1985) *Teacher careers: Crises and Continuities*. London: Falmer Press.

Smircich, L. and Morgan, G. (1982) Leadership: the management of meaning. *Journal of Applied Behavioral Science*, 18(3), 257–273.

Smith, J. K. and Blase, J. (1991) From empiricism to hermeneutics: leadership as a practical and moral activity. *Journal of Educational Administration*, 29(1), 6–21.

Smylie, M. A. and Brownlee-Conyers, J. (1990) "Teacher leaders and their principals: exploring new working relationships from a micropolitical perspective". Paper presented at the annual meeting of the American Educational Research Association, Boston.

Sparks, A. C. (1988) The micropolitics of innovation in the physical education curriculum. In J. Evans (ed.) *Teacher, Teaching and Control in Physical Education*, pp. 157–177). Lewes, England: Falmer Press.

Sparks, A. C. (1990) Power, domination and resistance in the process of teacher-initiated innovation. *Research Papers in Education*, 5(2), 153–178.

Starratt, R. (1991) Building an ethical school: a theory for practice in educational leadership. *Educational Administration Quarterly*, 27(2), 185–202.

Strauss, G. (1962) Tactics of lateral relationship: the purchasing agent. *Administrative Science Quarterly*, 7(2), 161–86.

Surrey, J. L. (1991) Relationship and empowerment. In J. V. Jordan, A. G. Kaplan, J. Baker Miller, I. P. Stiver and J. L. Surrey (eds) *Women's Growth in Connection: Writings from the Stone Center*, pp. 162–80. New York: The Guilford Press.

Taylor, F. W. (1947) *Scientific Management*. New York: Harper.

Tedeschi, J. (1972) *Social Influence Processes*. Chicago: Aldine.

Teltsch, K. (1987) An East Harlem learning citadel where openness rules. *New York Times*, 16 June, Section 2:8.

Tesch, R. (1988) "The contribution of a qualitative method: phenomenological research". Paper presented at the annual meeting of the American Educational Research Association, New Orleans.

Townsend, R. G. (1990) Toward a broader micropolitics of schools. *Curriculum Inquiry*, 20(2), 205–24.

Treslan, D. L. and Ryan, J. J. (1986) Perceptions of principals' influence bases. *Canadian Administrator*, 26(2), 1–7.

Veenan, S. (1984) Perceived problems of beginning teachers. *Review of Educational Research*, 54(2), 143–78.

Waller, W. (1932) *The Sociology of Teaching*. New York: John Wiley and Sons.

Wamsley, G. L. and Zald, M. N. (1973) *The Political Economy of Public Organizations: A Critique and Approach to the Study of Public Organizations*. Lexington, MA: Lexington Books.

Weatherley, R. and Lipsky, M. (1977) Street-level bureaucrats and institutional innovation: implementing special education reform. *Harvard Educational Review*, 47(2), 171–97.

Weber, M. (1947) *The Theory of Social and Economic Organization*. New York: Free Press.

Weiler, H. (1990) Comparative perspectives on educational decentralization: an exercise in contradiction? *Educational Evaluation and Policy Analysis*, 12(4), 433–48.

Willower, D. J., Eidell, T. L. and Hoy, W. K. (1967) *The School and Pupil Control Ideology* (Monograph No. 24). University Park, PA: Pennsylvania State University.

Wilson, B. (1962) The teacher's role – a sociological analysis. *British Journal of Sociology*, 13, 15–32.

Winter, D. G. (1973) *The Power Motive*. New York: The Free Press.

Wood, G. H. (1993) *Schools That Work: America's Most Innovative Public Education Programs*. New York: Penguin Books.

Woods, P. (1990) *Teacher Skills and Strategies*. London: Falmer Press.

Wynne, E. A. (1987) "Schools as morally governed institutions". Paper presented at the annual meeting of the American Educational Research Association, Washington, DC.

Zaleznik, A. (1970) Power and politics in organizational life. *Harvard Business Review*, 48(3), 47–60.

Zeichner, K. M. and Tabachnick, B. R. (1984) "Social strategies and institutional control in the socialization of beginning teachers". Paper presented at the annual meeting of the American Educational Research Association, New Orleans.

Name Index

Subject Index